WAGER

Other Mariner's Library Fiction Classics

Voyage: A Novel of 1896

SAM LLEWELLYN
The Shadow in the Sands

RICHARD WOODMAN
The Darkening Sea
Endangered Species
The Flying Squadron: A Nathaniel Drinkwater Novel
A Private Revenge: A Nathaniel Drinkwater Novel
Under False Colours: A Nathaniel Drinkwater Novel

WAGER

Richard Woodman

S

SHERIDAN HOUSE

First U.S. edition published 1999
by Sheridan House Inc.
145 Palisade Street
Dobbs Ferry, New York 10522

Copyright © 1990 by Richard Woodman

First published in Great Britain 1990
by John Murray (Publishers) Ltd

Library of Congress Cataloging-in-Publication Data

Woodman, Richard, 1944-
    Wager / Richard Woodman.
        p.   cm.
    ISBN 1-57409-080-1 (alk. paper)
        I. Title.
PR6073.O618W66   1999
823'.914—dc21   98-49568
                                                    CIP

Printed in the United States of America

ISBN 1-57409-080-1

For Abigail
with love

1

HANNAH Kemball leaned on the teak rail that ran round the poop of the tea-clipper *Erl King* and stared across the muddy waters of the Whangpo River at the skyline of Shanghai. Unconsciously her fingers caressed the bare wood, in gentle imitation of the daily cleaning it received from the apprentices who, under the eye of Chief Mate Enright, scoured it with a mixture of sand and sea-water rubbed with sail canvas.

The river fascinated her, for its endless succession of changing scenes possessed an eternal quality. The curious batwing sails of the big junks moved upstream with a patience that seemed, in its infinity of effort, an embodiment of China as something too vast to be comprehended. Amid their slow majesty lesser sampans bobbed under sail or oar, the latter sculled tirelessly into the implacable current. Many of these, Hannah noticed, were handled by women, black-clad, pear-shaped figures with babies secured to their backs. Several seemed permanently stationed under the overhanging counter-stern of the *Erl King*, the women looking up expectantly as, with one arm twisting the long *yuloh* over the sampan's stern, they held the other outstretched in the universal supplication of the beggar.

Galley scraps, coins or wooden dunnage – almost anything could be turned into the necessities of life by these thrifty and industrious people with their ingenious talent for improvisation. Hannah shook her head; she had already tossed a few pence at one such woman, but her virtuous act was immediately confronted by another's need as an endless succession of broad, flat faces sought her compassion.

There was nothing left on the deck of the ship since Mr Enright had put a stop to the apprentices throwing planks of

1

dunnage into the river. She shook her head again, exasperated by the persistence of one particular woman.

'No,' she called, 'nothing . . . no-thing,' adding in imitation of the ship's crew, 'no have got.'

Still the woman looked up, her broad feet splayed upon the deck of the cockleshell craft, her shapeless black *samfoo* pyjamas high-buttoned at the neck and fluttering loosely about her body as it swayed to the rocking of the sampan. Her brown right arm swung in a ceaseless expenditure of energy as it twisted the long *yuloh*, holding the boat motionless against the current. Her left hand remained extended, palm open. Behind her russet face and tightly drawn-back hair, Hannah could see the bobbing head of her baby.

'Please Missee . . . for baby . . .'

Hannah looked about her. On the far side of the poop, beyond the mizen mast, Mr Munro's back showed he was busy. The men on deck were milling around the galley door with their mess-kids anticipating dinner. She could act unobserved, for she was prompted by a sudden surge of pity for the unfortunate woman below her, and her eye had fallen upon the white hemp line, neatly coiled in its varnished box beside the wheel.

She slipped aft, hesitating momentarily, aware that she was about to act imprudently, for the log-line was an important item of the clipper's equipment. She swept the thought aside. A spare log and line lay in a box in her father's cabin and the pathetic situation of the coolie woman touched her. She bent and picked up the end of the line, waving its brass impeller at the woman. The coolie woman nodded vigorously and began to scull closer. Hannah bent and picked up an armful of coils, throwing them over the side as fast as she was able. Then, with a pretended innocence, she resumed her place at the starboard rail. Below her the woman scooped at the soupy water, gathering in the tangle of white rope. She had forsaken the *yuloh* which trailed on its lashing, and the sampan drifted slowly downstream. On her frantically moving back the tiny head of her baby seemed to nod a wild and abandoned farewell.

'You shouldn't have done that, Miss Kemball. It'll cause a deal of trouble.'

She turned, flushing with guilt, and looked into the face

2

of Mr Munro. His bronze eyes accused her from beneath the peak of his cap.

'It's barratry,' Munro added, 'the fraudulent practice of a mariner to the prejudice of the ship's owner.'

'Then it doesn't apply to me,' she replied quickly, 'I'm no mariner, Mr Munro. Besides, I've done it now.'

'Aye, but 'tis others who'll be blamed, Miss.'

Hannah bit her bottom lip with annoyance and Munro seized his opportunity.

'I know you're the Master's daughter, Miss Kemball, but here in port things are not quite what they were at sea.'

'How so, Mr Munro?'

'Och, it is difficult to explain, but your father will accuse one of the crew of selling the log-line . . . an apprentice possibly, and then he'll turn out all their sea-chests until he discovers someone that's got a wee bit more money than the Captain thinks he should have, and then . . .' Munro shrugged his shoulders.

'And then?' Hannah prompted.

'Well, you've see it once this voyage, Miss Kemball – a beating.'

'Oh.' She had not thought of that and she remembered the incident only too well. The indignity of it had profoundly disturbed her and, although she had subsequently learned that her father rarely beat his men, the sight of him in his shirt-sleeves, thrashing the bared back of a grown man with a rope's end, had deeply shocked her. Captain Kemball had, of course, offered her no explanation of the man's offence, but this lack of information did nothing to lessen the impression the incident had made on her.

'I don't want that to happen,' she said, hanging her head and angry at her own lack of forethought.

'No.'

She threw her head up at the note of condescension in his voice. 'I will admit to my father that I did it, Mr Munro.'

'That's handsome of you, but I doubt that it'll serve.'

'Why not?' she snapped.

'Because', Munro began cautiously, 'I doubt that your father will be back aboard for a day or so and when he does return he'll expect the log to be ready to hand.'

'He told me nothing about going away,' she said, slightly shocked and bewildered to be left alone.

'It is his custom, Miss Kemball, to be, er, away from the ship for a couple of days in Shanghai.'

'What for?' she persisted.

Munro shifted awkwardly. 'Well, to attend to his business interests, that sort of thing.'

'I knew that. But he said nothing about staying overnight. Where will he sleep?'

'Oh, at the club, Miss, I expect.'

'I'm sure he'll be back tonight,' Hannah said firmly.

'Perhaps you're right, Miss Kemball,' said Munro with a perceptible air of relief that the subject was closed.

'Anyway,' she said coolly, 'there is a spare log in my father's cabin. It would be imprudent not to carry another.'

'Of course we have a spare, but by using it we reach the state of affairs you deplore. With half the world still to traverse, Miss Kemball, it is *your* action that has been imprudent.'

Hannah looked hard at the Second Mate. At twenty-three or four he was a year or so her senior, but she was accustomed to think of them more or less of an age. Now she heard in his voice that superiority of sex and experience that she suffered usually from the obnoxious Enright. At first, in her ignorance of nautical matters, she had accepted it; now it was becoming increasingly irritating. Coming from Mr Munro it seemed almost impertinent. But she did not wish to show her annoyance, so she smiled at the Second Mate.

'I'm sure you would not have denied that poor woman some charity, Mr Munro. Compared to her we are princes aboard *Erl King*.'

'China is full of such deserving cases, Miss Kemball, you cannot give away the ship.'

'No,' and Hannah smiled now with genuine amusement, 'but you could have sent a boat after that sampan.'

'Aye,' replied Munro, now himself caught off-guard and attracted by the forbidden curves of the wide, smiling mouth. Not for the first time he was powerfully affected by her beauty. Had the shadow of Captain Kemball not been as real as that of the hat's brim, he would have stooped and kissed her.

'Then you are a little sympathetic to my plight, Mr Munro?'

4

'Of course, Miss Kemball,' he said, and mumbling excuses he turned forward as the bell struck noon.

Still smiling, Hannah turned back to the endless panorama of the river as the four double strokes of eight bells rang out over the water. It was answered by the bells of eight other clippers that rode to their moorings in the Garden Reach. A movement caught her eye and she looked down. Another coolie woman sculled her tiny sampan one-handed in the shadow of *Erl King*'s counter while the other reached out.

It was nearly six months since the day that Hannah had buried her mother, and it was the first in all that time that she had been separated from her father. Prior to that, for the entire twenty-one years of her life, she had grown up in the circumscribed world of a quietly respectable London suburb, dominated, though not unpleasantly so, by her fiercely possessive mother. Her father's appearances in that now distant lifestyle had been brief punctuations of a blandly featureless existence.

Captain John Kemball, Master of the full-rigged ship *Erl King*, was never at home long enough to become anything other than exciting in the eyes of his daughter. Outwardly a model of High Victorian rectitude, with piercing blue eyes, prodigious whiskers and an upright carriage, he seemed a demi-god who stepped periodically down from the Olympian heights of his beautiful ship, to grace the claustrophobic Islington drawing-room and stuff its dark corners with a succession of oriental artefacts.

The ponderous Chinese furniture in ebony, teak and sandal-wood; the rose-wood carvings of the sea-goddess Kwanyin; the woodcutters, elephants, tigers and intricately cunning ivory puzzles remained after his departures to remind Hannah of the reality of his fabulous life. Over the fireplace hung Captain Kemball's portrait, a formal thing done by a Chinese artist at Foochow, from which the captain, glass in hand, stared perpetually down upon his wife and daughter, his eyes boring through them so that his spirit seemed omnipresent. If one turned for relief from their stern gaze, one was confronted with the same artist's rendition of the ship, the *Erl King*, the means by which all this stifling luxury was made possible.

In the gloomy room, the clipper's pyramid of white sails

seemed to glow with a faint luminosity of their own. Shown off Saddle Island, the coast of China was a misty blue, the sea a whirl of grey-green waves capped with white horses. This exotic atmosphere was intensified by the high-peaked sails of a distant junk. Amid this landscape the *Erl King* raced along, a testament to Western superiority, her sleek black hull with its single ribband of gold leaf and vivid figurehead cutting through the sea with a delicate white feather at her forefoot. Hannah could stare at this picture for hours, in marked contrast to her mother, whose glances were always brief and contained a curious, yet identifiable, quality of pain.

Mrs Kemball, Hannah's mother, saw her husband once a year for a period of about two months. After a fortnight at home, Captain Kemball's interest in domestic matters waned. His heart was already returning to the West India Dock, judging the wind and wondering what the rascally Enright was doing with his ship. Captain Kemball's conversation would drift away from the familial towards the reminiscent. Hannah had observed with a burgeoning shrewdness that this line of conversation pierced her mother's calm, inducing that twist of the mouth with which she regarded the painting of the *Erl King*. By such means Hannah learned early that the *Erl King*, more than the absences themselves, estranged her parents.

This estrangement was not an obvious thing, for emotion was well tamped down in such a successful and confident a household as that of Captain and Mrs Kemball; but as Hannah grew up her awareness of its existence grew with her. As she underwent the disturbing experiences of female adolescence, Hannah began to understand the reasons for her mother's half-concealed bitterness as a vague, clouded resentment against her father. And with the perception of instinct, she accepted her mother's fiercely possessive love without complaint. As a consequence she held herself aloof from the clumsy advances of the sons of her mother's few friends, sensing in them the threat of similar enslavement. This was not a deliberately conscious act, for she was confused by the extravagant demands of her own body and this bewilderment was made worse by a trivial, half-understood incident that occurred when she was fifteen.

It was towards the end of one of her father's leave periods and he had given notice that he intended visiting the ship at her berth in the West India Dock that afternoon. Piqued, her mother had decided to call upon a friend, and while taking tea the two women had agreed upon an exchange of books. Dutifully in attendance upon her mother, Hannah had volunteered to return home and collect the books, glad to escape the boredom of other people's gossip. Entering the house she had gone directly to her parents' bedroom where one of the books lay. Hearing steps upon the stair she had called out to the maid. The footsteps stopped and there was no reply. With a beating heart Hannah had run out on to the landing. Her father had been descending the attic stairs. He was in his shirt-sleeves, a newly lit cigar in his mouth, and the sight of his daughter had drained the colour from his face. Neither father nor daughter said a word, and the silence was only broken by a light-hearted burst of singing from the maid's bedroom above.

The silly noise launched her father into a long-winded and overloud explanation of his inability to go to the docks owing to a water pipe that had leaked in the roof space. Hannah, innocent to the point of ignorance, was aware that she had discovered a fragment of betrayal. This knowledge was intuitive, based on her father's obvious guilt, her own natural shrewdness, the stuffy air in the house and the illicitly happy tone of the maid's voice.

It was from this day that her father slipped from his foothold on Olympus and it was from this day, too, that Hannah inherited from her father a hardness of purpose that was due both to his genes and his example. Her sympathy for her mother's plight increased and her rejection of a conventional life, in which she would be led inevitably towards a suitable marriage, was complete. There had already been hints at a marriage advantageous to her father's interests, but that half-comprehended incident raised the spirit of mutiny in Hannah Kemball.

It seemed that fate would assist in her purpose, for not long afterwards her mother became ill and Hannah's life as a nurse appeared preordained. During the long period of her mother's illness Hannah came finally to adulthood in the discovery that her father had feet of very mortal clay. In bouts of intimacy and delirium, her mother revealed sufficient details of her married life to lower her daughter's opinion of Captain

Kemball, and to reinforce her growing prejudice against men in general.

As a young man Jack Kemball had been a tall, dashing and proud suitor who paid court with an ardour that persuaded its object of his sincerity. Perhaps he was in part a victim of his own situation, a lusty young officer of the Merchant Marine with ambitions beyond his means and few opportunities to mix with women of his own age and social standing. But for Hannah's mother, marriage without love was unthinkable and since the attentions and compliments of John Kemball were the manifestations of love, she was carried off a bride in the teeth of more staid, but less exciting competition. For a while happiness had seemed to wrap a cocoon of permanence around the young bride, a sensation that made its eventual loss far worse.

It would not be true to say that John Kemball did not love his wife. She was attractive in flesh and feature and her lack of worldliness was soon corrected by a man whose sexuality had received its training among the skilled and artful practitioners of the East. He was not unkind, nor ungentle, nor, according to his lights, undutiful. But to say *he* had married in the purple haze of romantic love would have been inaccurate. Unbeknown to his lovely wife, the marriage had carried with it a dowry which to John Kemball was of far greater importance than the person of his wife.

Kemball's new father-in-law was also his employer, a shipowner with a keen eye for a coming man; he had noted Kemball's abilities and such had been his confidence that he had put the aspiring Kemball in the Chief Mate's berth in his new tea-clipper, the *Erl King*. On the homeward run of her maiden voyage the *Erl King's* Master had been taken ill and Kemball, seizing his opportunity, had driven the clipper faster than the wind itself. Her owner, delighted at the profits of the voyage and aware that he had that unusual combination of man and ship that occurred rarely, confirmed John Kemball in his post as Captain. He also admitted the striking young Master Mariner to his house and the society of his daughter. Upon the resulting marriage he made, too, a handsome settlement; twenty-one of the statutory sixty-four shares in the *Erl King* were delivered to her new commander on his wedding day as promised.

Since the voyage following the honeymoon, the flame of Captain Kemball's passion had dimmed, never to regain its incandescence. There had been brief rekindlings: two tiny coffins and Hannah had been the results, but for Mrs Kemball the successive blows of enforced solitude, the grief of two deaths and the deeply felt rejection by her vigorous husband, slowly undermined her health. Only a fierce and possessive joy at the safe arrival of Hannah had compensated her for her disappointments in life. She smothered the child in a protective, claustrophobic intimacy in the gloomy house in Islington provided by the commercial energies of Captain John Kemball. For Kemball fifteen further shares in the *Erl King* were wrung out of a grandfather; five for each grandchild, not returnable if they predeceased their own father.

'Ye drive a hard bargain, Captain,' his father-in-law had said, never addressing his daughter's husband by any other name. But Kemball had seen the gleam of admiration in the old skinflint's eyes: John Kemball would protect the fortune of the shipowner, for a woman, particularly the dreaming and sickly creature his daughter had become, was incapable of such a thing. Thus did the old man approve of his son-in-law.

Captain Kemball had arrived home with the season's tea in time for his wife's funeral. His sense of timing was as dramatic in this as in all else he did. Long separation and bereavement failed to unite father and daughter, for more than a coffin lay between them as they paid their last dutiful respects to the body before it left the house.

Later, as she stood by the graveside, dry-eyed but overwhelmed by a sense of almost suffocating sadness at the unhappiness of the world, Hannah felt no apprehension for the future. She had given it no consideration. Things, she supposed, would stay as they were and she was slowly filled with the realisation of her own autonomy, drawing from it an enormous comfort. As she turned away from the grave she had almost forgotten her father, until she felt his gloved hand upon her arm.

'Hannah . . . my dear . . .'

She turned and saw for an instant a look of weakness in his face, but it was swiftly suppressed, the unmanly emotion cleared with the dryness in his throat.

'You must come with me now,' he commanded.

'With you, father?' she asked, uncomprehending.

'On the ship, my dear.'

'To . . . to China?' she asked incredulously.

He was marching her away, her hand tucked beneath his arm as he nodded politely to the handful of mourning friends who had attended the funeral.

'Of course,' he said, putting on his tall, black hat, and handing her into the carriage. 'Where else?'

The simple finality of this conversation lurched Hannah's life round its most acute corner; at a stroke the preordained shrivelling of prolonged spinsterhood was gone. Her imagination was confronted with a dimly perceived vista of days that conformed to the impression given by the painting over the sideboard. Her confusion subsided as she realised the sudden truth, that her autonomy was not to be circumscribed by domestic horizons. Instead, she was to be allowed into the hitherto remote fastness of the male world, a world from which her long-suffering mother had been excluded. In the carriage she stared at her father, wondering if he knew what he had just done. His eyes already seemed fixed on distant horizons and a disloyal excitement stirred within her, a feeling that was mitigated by a tiny presentiment of revenge, gone as quickly as it came, which might have been the last visitation of her mother's soul.

For Captain Kemball, riding away from his wife's last resting place, the death introduced complications into his life. Insofar as he considered his daughter, his mind was occupied by less suspect matters than the metaphysical. He had recovered from his momentary lapse by the graveside and was again the inflexible man of business. His wife had left a will, and her estate contained a number of shares in the *Erl King* that she had inherited from her own father. In a sad gesture of mild protest Mrs Kemball had made special provision to leave these to Hannah and it was the Captain's intention to protect his daughter's investment, not to mention his own, particularly from the interference of suitors and the like. There *were* other considerations of a more immediately paternal nature, but these were not paramount in Captain Kemball's constantly calculating mind. Excepting those of his daughter which he had already considered, *de facto*, his own, Kemball had some ten shares in the ship still to acquire.

In a moment of sudden misfortune some years earlier, having lost a topmast, spars and sails, and suffered other severe damage in a typhoon, Captain Kemball had been hurriedly compelled to raise a substantial sum of money in China in order not to miss the homeward freight which that year reached nearly six pounds per ton. To do this he had had no choice but to sell ten shares to Lenqua, comprador to the shipping company and a Chinese merchant of enviable acumen and noted honesty. It was a situation the Captain intended to rectify during his forthcoming voyage and with such thoughts John Kemball interred any sense of grief he might otherwise have felt on the day of his wife's burial.

In the weeks that followed, Hannah's memory of her mother faded together with any sense of the reality of the existence of the house in Islington. Instead, Hannah's world was a succession of new views, a kaleidoscope of impressions and sensations that left her no time for contemplative thought. Indeed, after the stultifying routines of the sick-bed, the mechanics and techniques of seamanship that she daily observed stimulated a most unfeminine interest and unlocked an unseemly but frustrated desire to acquire knowledge. The turgid stability of an airless house had been replaced by a moving and beautiful environment which was subject to the four winds of heaven and the onslaught of mighty seas. Her world now had about it an air of Old Testament proportions that delighted and stimulated her, effectively severing her from her past and leading to the rediscovery of her father.

She observed him in his own milieu now. His ceaseless energy, his obvious ability, his dependability and even his rough consideration for his crew, gradually revealed to her a side of him that she had not imagined. There was still that inscrutable impassivity that masked all his dealings, especially with her, but she saw his outlets for his emotions given furious and intense rein as he fought his ship through a gale. For nine days he clawed every inch to windward that the sleek and wilful thing was capable of, and so the beating of the seaman who had drawn his knife on Enright was all the more shocking to her. But later, after she had also witnessed him in a rage, furious

11

over some piece of stupidity on the part of the Third Mate, and she had felt the onslaught of his anger with almost as much force as the unfortunate young officer, she began to make excuses for him. She began to see the burden of the responsibility he bore and how it was *his* will alone that made the *Erl King* pass like a bird of passage across the vast ocean.

There was also a gradual unwinding on the Captain's part as he began to explain the workings of his ship to her. When she had overcome her greenhorn sea-sickness and the *Erl King* was racing southwards through the north-east trade winds, all her sails set and a great white bone in her teeth, he had more leisure to instruct her. She began to sit in on the navigation lessons Mr Munro gave to the apprentices, and her quick and neglected intellect was less and less confused by her emotional responses to her situation, and increasingly absorbed by its technical complexities.

At first Captain Kemball had been clumsily patronising, revealing that he considered Hannah, at twenty-one, little more than a child. But she had had her twenty-second birthday as the ship reeled off the knots twelve degrees north of the equator. The news had got about the ship, provoking a touching little celebration when both watches had come aft to present her with their good wishes and the hope that she would bring them luck and good fortune, particularly on the homeward voyage with their valuable cargo of tea.

She had been moved by this common act of kindness, never knowing that her presence on board had mellowed that hard-hearted skinflint they called 'The Old Man'. They sailed with her father because they knew him for a fine seaman, one of the best in the China trade, known as 'Cracker Jack' from his habit of 'cracking on' sail. And while his detractors might turn a pun and call him 'Jack Crackers' for his foolhardiness, there was envy in their sophistry. Captain Kemball had won a tea-race outright and had consistently commanded one of the first half-dozen ships home with the season's tea. He and his ship were thus much sought after by men eager to profit from the higher wages paid in the fastest ships, despite the fact that Captain Kemball was also known for his meanness, his harshness and his toughness as a task-master.

So Hannah's presence had already brought the *Erl King*'s

hands a measure of luck, softening the abuses of Enright, the Chief Mate, known traditionally as '*The* Mate', so that even he did not seem the slave-driving bastard of previous voyages. Since she had made her father's face to smile upon them from his lordly promenade of the break of the poop, and since she had coaxed a measure of respite from the Captain's satrap, Hannah was already regarded as a good omen among the majority of the men forward. To be sure there were a few dissenting voices, but women on shipboard were not at the time universally thought of as birds of ill-omen.

'She might have been his *wife*, my boys,' one forecastle philosopher pointed out as the watch belayed a lee brace waist-deep in water while *Erl King* dipped her starboard rail and lifted her long jib-boom to the southern sky, 'and then where'd we have been?'

And relieved, struggling out of the water, they spat to leeward and looked aft to where Hannah stood by the mizen mast, staring to windward as she and her father watched a northward-bound ship pass them. Her heavy dress was pressed against her body by the wind, revealing the soft curves to the men.

'By God, I could . . .'

'Shut your mouth! The officers'll be way ahead o' you.'

'Ah, rubbish. A woman like that needs a *real* man, not a walkin' beanpole wiv a brass hat!'

'You dirty old sod! She's young enough to be yer daughter . . .'

'Aye, she'd not touch an old pillgarlick like you . . .'

'I can still fiddle . . .'

'Over the Old Man's dead body!'

'Aye, Gopher, you do your spending in Shanghai.' A chorus of laughs greeted this remark and the men turned away, dispersing.

'There ain't any tits like that in Shanghai,' said Gopher wistfully.

Captain Kemball was well aware of the omnipresent threat to his daughter's virtue but, like the risk of drowning, it was something a careful mariner could avoid. He knew she was safe from the men; they would lust in blind onanism, but the officers, living cheek-by-jowl with his daughter, might let passion

13

overcome their good sense. So, like the prudent and calculating man he was, Captain Kemball let it be discreetly known what could be expected if the bounds of a strict propriety were once overstepped. Captain Kemball had no objection to his men whoring, whether with the lovely little Chinese flower-girls or the raddled drabs of the Ratcliffe Highway. A man needed a woman, any woman, from time to time as he well knew himself; but the proprieties had to be observed. A Briton should be a gentleman to women of his own class, no matter were he high or low born. Such a moral code went far beyond the protection of a father, and Kemball considered his officers knew his views upon the matter. Besides, they were beholden to him for their livelihoods and future prospects; even the dissolute Enright could be expected to understand that. Aboard the *Erl King*, John Kemball was Master under God alone.

Against a long-standing prejudice and to his delight, Captain Kemball discovered that Hannah had a keen and inquiring mind. Hitherto he had not found a woman capable of comprehending anything about a ship beyond a giggling bafflement at expressions of nautical jargon. This the Captain had found irritating, if not vaguely insulting, for such terms were the most eloquent technical descriptions possible. In some measure, therefore, Hannah's interest compensated John Kemball for the son he had wished she was. On the long outward passage to the South China Sea Captain Kemball imparted to his daughter a great deal of the accumulated wisdom of a lifetime's voyaging.

'You see, Hannah,' her father had said, 'you need to *know* a ship, to feel her respond as an individual, for they are all different, even two from the same plans. Take the *Erl King*; she is a thoroughbred among ships, not a draught horse like a Blackwaller, or an Onker barque . . .'

Hannah had only the sketchiest notion of what a Blackwaller was, and none at all of an Onker barque, but it was clear from her father's dismissive tone that in the hierarchy of marine affairs they were not to be compared with *Erl King*.

'Take a squall,' said Captain Kemball, leaning forward in his chair and pulling the unlit cigar stub from his mouth. 'What would you tell the Board of Trade examiner if, like one of our 'prentice boys, you were taking your Second Mate's examination?'

14

Hannah raised her shoulders in the faintest of shrugs.

'Why to run off before it, to square yards and run down wind until it moderated. And if you answered differently the examiner would toss you out as unfit to stand a watch aboard a sailing vessel.' Kemball paused for effect. 'But you'd be wrong! By heaven, don't you bear up in the *Erl King*, for she's a clipper, with long lower masts and a main yard seventy-eight feet in length, and if you put your helm up and turn the ship away from the wind before you get it aft it'll hit the beam and lay you right over! It'll drive your lee rail under so the men can't start the lee braces! And you'll drive so hard and fast that when you come to let fly the tops'l halliards the ship's at such an angle that the yards won't come down!'

Hannah knew enough to visualise this dreadful event, investing it with the added confusion of night in her mind's eye.

'No, by George, you luff her like a yacht. Edge her a point into the wind, keep her sails a-shaking until the squall's past . . . she'll have enough way on her to stay under the command of the rudder, then as the wind eases, up helm a trifle and on your way, not an inch lost to leeward!'

Kemball relit his cigar, filling the saloon with the sudden blue smoke and rich aroma of the Filipino cheroot and adding the caveat that most eloquently testified to the fineness of judgement necessary to his profession.

'But not too much! Come right up into the wind and get yourself caught aback and the squall'll likely take the sticks clean out of her!'

'The sticks?' Hannah queried uncertainly.

'Masts, yards, sails, rigging . . . the whole caboodle round your ears . . .' Cracker Jack grinned with a lupine glee, as though risking such a thing gave him the keenest pleasure.

And Hannah listened to these didactic little lectures with a retentive sharpness as, day after day, she saw before her eyes the savage beauty of the sea, the birds, flying fishes, the whales and the dolphins, and felt the excitement as the *Erl King* trembled like a living thing at her father's commands.

Like her father, Hannah came to love the ship. Unlike the seamen whose toil drove the clipper, she could regard the *Erl King* with the eye of an aesthete, having, in the manner of ancient kings, first fallen in love with the portrait. It was outside

15

her understanding to know that John Kemball, for all his shrewd business head, drove and handled her with the sensitivity of an aesthete too. And it was easy to see how the *Erl King* had become a legend in the China trade for, as Hannah learned, at first tentatively and then with growing confidence as she took a trick at the wheel in fine weather, she could ghost in the lightest of airs, yet claw to windward in a gale. There were many such smart ships on the run; their men would fight in the stews of Shanghai and Foochow over their respective merits, but the combination of fine ship and fine Master was rarer. A vessel's performance could alter for the worse with a change in command, even if her new Master had previously been her Mate and copied his predecessor in all things. It was strange, but the evidence was incontrovertible.

As the *Erl King* swept north-eastwards, obliquely crossing the Indian Ocean towards the Sunda Strait, her white sails stretching aloft to the majesty of the tropic heavens, John Kemball sat on deck in the evenings after dinner and smoked a cigar in his daughter's company. In the beautiful quiet of the night he revealed not merely more of his fund of professional knowledge, but also something of his soul. It was a measure of the affection and regard he felt for his daughter and of his pleasure in discovering she had not inherited the physiological weaknesses of her mother. As if reflecting this he spoke for the first time of his youth, and Hannah learned how the *Erl King* had acquired the advantage of reputation and the magic of anecdote.

'My rivals', Captain Kemball said, smiling, 'claim that I married this ship.' He chuckled into the soft, intimate darkness, seemingly unaware of the ironic truth or of the prick of conscience the remark gave Hannah. She was glad of the night to cover her expression. 'They say I spent all my money on her . . . You know *that* isn't true . . .'

He paused and Hannah wondered if he expected agreement but she remained silent, conjuring up images of the stuffed luxury of the dismal villa in Islington. But when Kemball resumed speaking it was clear that he felt no remorse, no doubt about his conduct, for he was embarking upon the full flood of reminiscence.

'How they all laughed when she first came out and anchored

16

at Foochow! Cocky Jack Kemball of the *Queen Mab*, a ship noted for the lavishness of her decorations, now Mate of a brand new clipper that was as bald and black as an undertaker's assistant! I can see 'em now, laughing into their rice wine and cracking melon seeds and spitting like country Chinese. But I vowed that every one of those Masters and Mates would eat his hat before six seasons were done!

'You know, Hannah, your grandfather was as shrewd a ship-owner as ever paid a premium at Lloyds. I worked for him as a young man and he put me on the poop of the *Queen Mab* as Mate when I was your age. We got home one voyage and I heard he was building a new ship. She was being designed by a brilliant young man who'd just come back from Donald MacKay's yard in New England. No expense was to be spared in her building, every trick the young fellow had learned from the Yankees plus a few of his own were to go into her. She was to be the most elegant, the fastest, most weatherly, strongest, lightest, loveliest ship that ever slid into the murky waters of the River Clyde, destined for the flying-fish trade of the China Seas . . .'

Hannah watched her father's face suddenly illuminated in the glow of the cigar as he drew on it. The brief, diabolical apparition was gone as he spoke again, lost in a haze of faint smoke that the light breeze coiled lazily away to leeward.

'I'd caught your father's eye as Mate of the *'Mab*. I had bulled her like a yacht; not a rope yarn was ever out of place on her deck and it took two men twelve hours to polish her brass-work in harbour. That included her mast-trucks, those buttons on the very tops of the mastheads. Aye,' he sighed, 'she was the very apple of my eye . . . until I heard your grandfather was building the *Erl King*.

'I saw a drawing of her lines first, then a half model of her hull which her designer showed me.' Kemball paused, as if contemplating some secretly intimate moment of his past. 'I knew at once that she would be a flyer. You could tell it from her dead-rise and the sweetness of her long entrance, and there wasn't that finicky sleekness in her run that made her flashily easy to back up astern, but prone to pooping in a heavy following sea. I had to have some part in her and told the young fellow so. He was an odd cove. When you spoke to him he'd stare abstractedly over your shoulder, as though he was looking at something in the distance, beyond you . . .

'Your grandfather had given him a free hand, which puzzled me at first, for ship-owners are by nature conservative, tight-fisted and not much given to generous gestures, particularly to young and inexperienced naval architects.

'But the old curmudgeon was cunning. The young fellow did what the old reprobate knew he would; he designed his masterpiece.

'So they laid her down, set up her new-fangled iron frames, planked and decked her, then knocked out the shores and sent her sliding down the ways with a clanking and a sparking of drag chains so that she hardly caused a ripple on the far bank of the Clyde, which raised three hearty cheers from the shipwrights.'

With practised ease Captain Kemball flicked the glowing butt of his cigar stub over the side in a graceful arc.

'They had little to cheer about a week later. As they fitted her out and the payment for launching the hull fell due, the cost was declared excessive. Party to the plot, the Chairman of the builders prevaricated over fittings and embellishments and the work ground to a halt. I remember the row; your grandfather sitting impassive between the designer and the Chairman of the board of the building company. He knew what had happened, he'd engineered the whole thing, bribed the foreman shipwright to ensure that, as far as the hull was concerned, the specification was followed down to the last copper roving. As for the folderols, they earned no freightage and he cared not tuppence!'

Captain Kemball drew another cigar from the case he kept in the breast pocket of his white drill jacket. Expertly he lit it amid Hannah's expressed outrage. 'What about the poor designer? Did he know he'd been fooled?'

'I don't know. I only know he never designed another sailing vessel but went off and contented himself with designing kettles for steamers.'

'But that's terrible, father . . .'

'Not so very terrible, my dear. After all, unlike a seaman, a ship designer doesn't go to sea and so risks little beyond his reputation.'

'I still think it was a dreadful thing to do deliberately.'

'Don't let sentiment ever interfere with business, Hannah,' Kemball said sharply. 'Young Matthew McAllister got his fee and created his masterpiece in essence. 'Twas but his pride that was damaged and most of us can stand that without ill effect.'

'Is that why you said the ship arrived at Foochow as black and as bald as an undertaker's assistant?'

'Just so. She was as unlike the *Queen Mab* as . . . as . . .' He had been about to say 'a nun to a whore' and cast desperately about for a figure of speech that was suitable.

'A baptist to a bishop?'

Kemball laughed. 'Exactly so, exactly so,' pleased with Hannah's quick-wittedness. 'She had no polished brass and her critics pointed at the miserable, penny-pinching and ugly lump of scroll-work on her bow in place of a figurehead. She looked more like a hard-run Down-easter flying the Stars and Stripes than a proper-fashion British merchant ship.

'Even while they laughed at her Skipper and myself, they felt it was a damned poor show. The fools claimed they had lost face in front of the heathen Chinese, believing that our lack of ornament somehow indicated weakness. They said the Chinese could laugh with impunity at the red-faced *fan kwei* whom they had thought rich and powerful but now saw could be as poor as themselves. Ridiculous! I tell you, Hannah, for our bald-headed appearance we were shunned by the British community, sent to Coventry for the puritan lines of our ship, and even when the Old Man went to note protest after we had had a bit of a blow, the Vice-Consul told him we had let the side down!'

Kemball laughed at the recollection, drawing at his new cigar. This time his face was no longer diabolical, but roseate with the genial expansiveness of a Santa Claus.

'Like all Britons, they were fools in their idleness, pre-occupied by their senseless prejudices, obsessed by the appearance they presented in the eyes of the natives. Not one of those self-appointed experts apparently noticed the beauty of the ship's sheer, nor the width of her sail plan. Neither did they take much notice of the claims of her shamefaced crew that they had logged fifteen knots for three days in a gale with nothing set above the topsails! Nor had the damned fools listened when we mentioned that we had never ceased to hear a chuckle of water

19

under the bow, nor lost steerage in a calm, for you see, Hannah, usually a ship is either good and weatherly in a blow and sluggish in a calm, or wet and a man-killer in heavy weather, but a witch in light airs. In the *Erl King'*, and here Kemball leaned down and sentimentally patted the deck, 'we truly possess a masterpiece, for, as I knew when I first saw her lines on paper and ran my hand over the shape of her half model, the *Erl King* excels in both.'

Again the glow of the drawn cigar illuminated his face and Hannah felt a sudden, powerful tug of kinship with this man, her father. He was no longer Olympian, but flawed and cruel, yet, for the instant his face showed in the darkness, she thought him a hero.

'No one believed the sailors' tales, of course,' he went on. 'The poor simpletons had to make up some yarn to save their wounded pride. As for the idling officers of the *Erl King*, we were so shunned by our colleagues on the other ships in the Min River that we kept ourselves to ourselves, refused to take part in the annual boat regatta and laid a few discreet bets with our tongues in our cheeks!'

He chuckled again; good-natured self-conceit flowed out of him so that Hannah was compelled to smile into the darkness. She already knew the end of the story, for the evidence was all about her.

'They called abuse after me when I visited the club or the comprador. "There goes Jack Crackers, Mate of a mongrel bitch . . ." They sat on the veranda and called me a fool and a dupe to be hazed out of the *Queen Mab* by an old tight-wad . . . such, I fear, Hannah, was the reputation of your grandfather. But I refused to be intimidated and Lenqua, the comprador, believed me. You see I knew the ship, I was her Chief Mate and I knew what she was capable of . . . we got damned good freight rates thanks to Lenqua . . . d'you know who the real *Erl King* was, Hannah?'

'Oh, yes, I've known since I was a child. You told me yourself.'

'I had forgotten.'

'He was king of the elves and he lured little children to their deaths. I always thought him a terrible figure to name a ship after.'

20

'Sometimes,' Kemball said in a low voice so that he should not be overheard by Mr Munro or the man at the wheel, 'there are other gods to propitiate beyond the one known to the Anglican synod.'

'Father!'

Somehow the mild blasphemy had none of the power it might have possessed in Islington. Staring into the darkness Hannah found it possible to imagine that no such place as Islington existed, that there was only this infinite sky with its innumerable stars.

Kemball chuckled, and Hannah was reminded again of dark powers.

'Who gave the ship her name, Father?'

'Mmm? Oh, I believe it was your mother . . .'

And Hannah experienced again that prickling of conscience, as though in all this trickery and triumph, her mother's shade fell over her to remind her of the cost of things. But her father passed over this reference to his late wife.

'Well, my dear, we showed 'em. I made 'em eat their words if not their confounded hats. We were the second ship home, but we made the fastest time, ninety-five days from the Outer Bar to the dock. The Old Man took a tumble in a line-squall off Tanjong Datu. I took her home and came out next voyage as Master!'

Hannah remembered that conversation now, as she turned from her contemplation of the Whangpo River, recalled to the immediate present by the sensation that she was being watched. At first she dismissed the thought as a silly product of the vague unease she felt at her father's absence.

She cast her eyes round the anchorage and caught the flash of sunlight on a brass telescope borne on the poop of an adjacent ship, a low black clipper that might, with one or two differences of detail, have been the *Erl King*'s sister. From her vantage point on the other vessel's port quarter she could see her name across her counter: *Seawitch, London.*

Behind the telescope she caught a brief glimpse of a figure in grey, watched him walk forward and descend the varnished teak accommodation ladder that hung from a stubby davit at the break of the *Seawitch*'s poop. He stepped lightly into a

21

bobbing gig and she watched as it was smartly swung away from the clipper's side, blue-bladed oars flashing in the sun. As it passed the *Erl King*, heading for the foreigner's landing-place on the Bund, the bearded occupant looked up at her and raised a tall, grey hat. Flushing at this unexpected courtesy, Hannah turned away, embarrassed at not knowing how to respond to this courtesy.

'Dandified Dick, the bastard,' she overheard a seaman milling in the waist say in an over-loud stage whisper.

Feeling slightly ridiculous, she sat on the raised portion of the poop. She recalled again the long talks with her father and his confidences. Today, the *Erl King* was not as bald and black as an undertaker's assistant. Today she reflected a degree of affection Hannah wished her errant father had lavished a little nearer home. And yet she could not fail to admire the splendour of his creation, for the *Erl King* as she now was, was Kemball's masterpiece too. It was the Captain that had breathed real life into the spars and hull of Matthew McAllister's masterpiece.

Leaning back on her hands Hannah stared upwards at the masts and spars and the miles of rigging that criss-crossed her vision but no longer quite so bewildered her. She tried to imagine the appearance of the ship on that first maiden voyage and found it impossible, for the ship's portrait had long ago seized her mind and the reality made an even stronger impression upon her. Today Hannah had been leaning on a teak rail that was finished at the poop ladders with gleaming brass dogs. The poop bell was suspended in a belfry formed from two diving dolphins, likewise buffed to a high gloss by the daily ministrations of the apprentices. Under the long jib-boom the Erl King himself strained forward, black-booted and silver spurred, his scarlet cloak swept from his shoulders; his handsome, crowned head curled a red lip and his magic sword pointed the way ahead. Carved side boards greeted the visitor at the top of the accommodation ladder, and the bulkhead panels under the break of the poop were painted to represent the Erl King's enchanted forest. The masts and spars sparkled with fresh varnish and white paint, and above her main skysail yard a crown of gilt encircled her truck, one hundred and fifty feet above the deck. Chinese craftsmen had finished her to a perfection even her distinguished designer would have wondered at, for John Kemball had made of the *Erl King* a sea-mistress of consummate loveliness in less than the boasted six seasons.

This was the ship that Hannah had come to know in the months since her mother's death. She was learning all aspects of the clipper's life, not simply her father's version of the crafty way she had been built, nor just the rigging of her spanker or the moment to set her skysails; not only the things that told you on the poop when the royals should come off her, or when to close reef the topgallants; not just the things of her fabric, but something of the muscle and blood that made of her inanimate beauty a truly living thing, the loveliest tool that man had ever created.

In conspiratorial whispers and wicked, sidelong glances that her father had affected after his confession of the *Erl King*'s origins, he spoke of Enright, the Chief Mate. A disgraced Master-Mariner who had wrecked his river steamer in the Yangtze Gorges with huge loss of life, Enright had a reputation for competence ruined by 'bad living', by which euphemism Kemball meant Chinese whores and *samsu*, the potent rice spirit so freely available, though he was careful not to be too specific in deference to Hannah. Kemball had found Enright in the gutter, and put him back on the exposed poop of an ocean-going clipper where the four winds of heaven dried him out. Enright was a soured man, kept in check by Kemball's powerful personality and his own obligations to the Captain who had given him that rare thing, a second chance. But Kemball recognised the fact that Enright was a man who knew ships when he was sober and would enforce discipline without a thought if the occasion demanded it.

'When I go, Hannah, and the ship is all yours as she surely one day will be, dismiss Enright or he'll wreck her,' her father had advised in one of those intimate moments they had lately enjoyed, adding, 'in harness he's tractable, but spare the curb and he'll bolt.'

Since the unlooked-for confidence, which seemed to the reflecting Hannah to mark a degree of acceptance of herself by her strange and complex father, she had always seen Enright against that cautionary qualification. He was a big, dark-browed man, his once handsome features slack, pocked and lent a fanatic quality by piercingly light blue eyes that belied their own weakness. A reputation for legendary sexual prowess still clung to him, surviving the wreck of his career with the persistence of truth, and even Hannah, in her innocence, was not unaware of his brooding and sinister attraction.

Age and dissipation had taken their toll of Enright, and his looks, though still potent, were no longer irresistible. Besides, he was displaced in Hannah's regard by his junior, Mr Munro the Second Mate. A pleasant-mannered Scot, Munro had shown an attentive interest that Hannah had responded to with a cool distance that lingered from the habit of her Islington experience. Munro had employed an equally remote courtesy which, to a more experienced woman, would have signalled both his continued esteem and his hurt.

'A showy young fellow,' her father had said, though without malice and referring more to Munro's self-confidence than to any exhibitionism in his character. Indeed, Hannah inferred from her father's tone that there was perhaps something of himself in the younger man. As time passed Hannah felt an imperceptible and scarcely acknowledged desire to earn Munro's good opinion. At first she considered this to be no more than the manifestation of a genuine interest in his tuition concerning the nautical mysteries; but later she privately acknowledged that the attraction was of a deeper nature. For his own part Munro sought gently to topple Hannah from her pinnacle of privilege as the Captain's daughter. The incident with the log-line earlier that forenoon was no more than the latest, and most triumphant, of his skirmishes.

Apart from the boy apprentices and Osman the Steward, the only other man of the *Erl King*'s company with whom she came into daily domestic contact was Mr Talham. Undeniably the best looking of the ship's officers, there was, Hannah sensed, something odd about him, as though the fact that he possessed such remarkable features with corn-gold hair, threatened her own assumed monopoly of beauty. Somehow James Talham posed a quite different threat to Enright. The effect his presence had upon Hannah was to make her, for the first time in her life, take pains about her appearance.

But many of these thoughts and emotions lay locked deep inside her, barely understood by herself, disturbing her occasionally, but more often than not amusing her as not impinging upon her real self. For between Hannah and the officers of the *Erl King* ran the protecting bulwark of her father, and even when she found herself, as now, alone on the ship, separated from him by his mysterious affairs, she felt perfectly safe.

All in all, she reflected as she watched a big Swatow junk tack faultlessly under the *Erl King*'s counter, the last months had been a remarkable succession of experiences and she had scarcely mourned the passing of her mother. Then even this pang of conscience was interrupted by the dinner gong announcing that the meal was served in the saloon.

Hannah realised that she was ravenously hungry.

2

IN THE absence of her father and in deference to her sex, Miss Kemball was allowed to preside over dinner in the panelled saloon of the *Erl King*. The officers' accommodation below the poop radiated from this central room which had been completed in walnut and bird's-eye maple and acquired a rosy glow by oil lamp and a homely warmth by day. Of course the symmetry of its appointments was disturbed by the heel of the ship at sea, when lamps and the suspended condiment tray remained stubbornly vertical and the table, chairs and buttoned settee lurched out of the comforting horizontal. But now, as the ship rode quietly on an even keel at her moorings, it might also have been a well-furnished dining-room in England. Above the saloon table the opened skylight admitted air and sunshine in the form of eight brilliant lozenges that made the tablecloth and silver cutlery sparkle. The Steward Osman moved deferentially behind the high-backed chairs that had been cast loose from their deck beckets, collecting the soup plates and placing clean, warmed dishes in front of each person before bringing in the kedgeree.

Later, Enright was saying, he would have the awning rigged, but the rain earlier that morning had washed the air clean and only now was the stench of the city reasserting itself. He went on to give Talham a list of tasks for the afternoon when he had the deck-watch while, at the far end of the table, the four apprentices remained silent in case Enright included them.

'Well, Mr Enright,' said Munro, 'I'm clear of duty this afternoon, and I mind to take Miss Kemball to see the sights of Shanghai if she'd care to accept my invitation. I'm sure the Captain would not object.'

Neither did Hannah and she said so.

'What if the Old Man wants his gig while you are away?' growled Enright. 'The boys are too light to pull the cutter.'

Hannah saw the light of affront kindle in the eyes of the apprentices. She knew they were as fit as fiddles, capable of pulling *two* cutters, if the need arose. But they were too wise to protest and kept silent while Enright aired his pique.

'The Captain'll not be back this side of midnight,' said Munro, and Hannah saw the ghost of a leer exchanged between the men. She did not know the meaning of it, but experienced a vague, ill-defined sensation of unease. This mention of the Captain's prolonged absence seemed suddenly to remove Enright's half-hearted objections.

'Very well,' he relented.

'I'm obliged to you both,' she smiled shyly, uncertain of her position with her father absent. 'And to you,' she smiled at the four apprentices, who grinned back, delighted that Miss Kemball's excursion would purchase them an afternoon's liberty for the trivial price of half an hour's hard pulling.

The gig was as smart as the *Erl King*, and her apprentices (whose parents had paid a premium of seventy-five pounds to have their sons trained by Cracker Jack) wore their brass-bound reefer jackets and white duck trousers to man the tiddley boat's oars, sending her dancing across the turgid waters of the Whangpo. Hannah was aware that the river was unworthy of the varnished gig. The Whangpo consisted of suspended mud, refuse, sewage, debris and unspeakable muck as it flowed through the misnamed Garden Reach, to wind its languid way between levéed banks north where, at Woosung, it joined its mighty brother, the Yangtze Kiang. But the elegant gig was an intruder as, with Mr Munro's hand on the ash tiller, it dodged swiftly round the sampans, passed decorously upwind of the stink of a night-soil boat and slipped arrogantly across the bow of a sea-going junk carrying the wind and current downstream.

'You know,' said Munro conversationally, 'the Chinese sent junks like her as far as south-west Africa four or five hundred years ago. They failed to double the Cape of Good Hope and the Emperor decided there was nothing worth discovering beyond the seas. He considered China the centre of the world . . . It's something that has affected the Chinese perspective ever since . . . Imagine if they had gone on, everything would have been different.'

'You mean they might have been in the Thames, loading . . . loading what, Mr Munro?'

'Perhaps', said Munro lightly, 'they'd have found woad a rare and acceptable commodity.'

Hannah laughed softly, staring up at the junk as it surged past. The high-sterned craft seemed untidily exotic after the disciplined order of the *Erl King*; her three curiously high-peaked lug-sails ribbed with bamboo battens, multi-patched and fluttering with tears as an advertisement of that frugality that characterised the impoverished Chinese.

They drew alongside the steps of the Bund and Hannah felt Munro's strong arm briefly encircle her waist to prevent her slipping on the viscous green slime and to guide her through the press of vendors, idlers and beggars who hung about the landing-place in the hope of business or alms from the hairy ones, the red barbarian invaders of the Celestial Empire. Hannah stared about her with unconcealed curiosity; the blue and ethereal landscape that had formed the background of the portrait of the *Erl King* was breached at last and she walked head and shoulders above the Celestial crowd, a foreign devil herself.

'I'm afraid they think you are ugly,' Munro said with an impish grin as Hannah drew back from the russet faces that stared at her, jabbering and laughing and pointing. 'Your dress is considered extravagant, your nose too long, your mouth indecently wide and, I regret to inform you, Miss Kemball, your complexion excessively blotchy. As for your overall dimensions, they are elephantine!'

The boyish twinkle in his eyes, the total impropriety of his remarks and their inherent ridiculousness, however near the truth, made Hannah laugh back.

'Thank you, kind sir,' she said, infected by the same careless joy, adding, 'I hope you are not of the same opinion?'

She regretted the words as soon as they were spoken, thinking that their shared mood of levity was no more than a symptom of their mutual release from the constraints of the ship, then as quickly realising she had been lured into the unfamiliar territory of half-sincere coquetry. But she could not deny the feeling of exquisite pleasure that brought the blood rushing to her face as Munro stopped, compelling her to retreat a step and face his look of sincere longing.

'You offend me,' he said in the low tone of sudden irrepressible desire. 'You offend me by even suggesting I would consider such an assumption.'

'Mr Munro, I . . .' She cast down her eyes so that her long, dark lashes lay on her cheeks. Munro too flushed and then their eyes met and she was looking at him, smiling dazzlingly at his own discomfiture while around them a grinning, chattering, pointing crowd of Chinese had gathered, tugging at Hannah's wide skirt.

The trivial but significant little incident conferred upon them a new intimacy, rending the artificial barriers imposed by the conventions of shipboard life, and they became two young people on an excursion, taking a rich delight in themselves and their surroundings.

'They say', said Munro, resuming his walk, 'that your father married the *Erl King*, Miss Kemball. I can only add that the union was a fortunate one in bringing you amongst us. Your beauty surpasses that of your father's ship.'

It was all lies of course, but she laughed easily.

For the next hour Munro introduced her to the myriad sights and overpowering smells that were the essence of Shanghai. They wandered happily beneath the banners of curious script that hung from the decaying stucco walls of tenements bedizened with washing; along alleys jammed with the shops and stalls that sold country produce and the tawdry products of back-room enterprise. Hannah saw vegetables whose names she did not know, weird and obscene looking things in jars whose names Munro demurred to reveal, though the coils of pickled snake and antique eggs were obvious. There were baskets and trinkets, carvings in ivory, jade, soap-stone, rose-wood and ebony; figures and animals made for the foreign sailors who strolled like aliens among the dark pigtails of the Celestials. Hannah stared at the paper umbrellas and the squealing piglets encased in rush baskets from which their legs and trotters protruded, flailing indignantly; stalls which bore live coals over which sizzled wide iron bowls throwing off the smell of cooking, the savoury sharpness of dishes which,

30

Hannah feared, would be identified with evident relish by the knowledgeable Munro as squid, or birds' nests, fried locusts or any of the thousand and one horrors that this strange, smiling, industrious and noisy people ate.

In common with all those thronging the street they were forced to draw aside as a mandarin passed. A bearer preceded his palanquin with a scroll announcing his titles and degree. Pigtails bobbed respectfully as he went by and Hannah watched with fascinated revulsion as his four wives shuffled past on their tiny bound feet.

'*They* are considered pretty,' Munro said, 'though had they been truly beautiful they would not have been able to walk at all.' Hannah stared after the priceless silk of their gowns, and their flat, identical faces. Somehow the ludicrous foreignness of it all made Munro's recent declaration all the more exciting. In a moment of unprecedented impulse she caught his arm and their eyes met.

'But the peasant women are more attractive than those, those dolls,' she said, coming to the support of ordinary womanhood.

He laughed. 'D'you think so? They leave their girl-children to die as often as not, or sell them, binding their feet tightly to get a good price . . .' He broke off.

'*Sell* them?' Hannah said, outraged. 'What as?'

'Och, er . . .' Munro blushed, 'slaves, servants, that sort of thing.'

'Why mutilate their feet if they're going to fetch and carry?'

'I don't know,' he replied awkwardly, and Hannah sensed an evasion.

A rickshaw rolled past them, the haulier as thin as a bundle of sticks, a pale cotton vest and drawers covering his pitiful emaciation, a straw hat shading his ancient face. In the rickshaw lolled another doll. She was sheathed in silk, her mouth a painted rosebud, her eyes dark with secret knowledge. Her bound feet peeped from beneath the skirts of her brocaded robe and she fluttered a fan artfully before her face. Hannah felt the thrill of wickedness at her passing, noting how the eyes of the men in the narrow street followed the painted woman. It was a forbidden thing that Hannah saw, such as was only whispered about in the respectable streets of Islington. Hannah had biblical knowledge of scarlet women and knew instinctively

31

that this was one. As if sensing her astuteness, or perhaps because, in the circumstances, he had not liked his earlier evasion, Munro said, 'I expect *she* was sold as a girl . . .'

'Into licentiousness,' said Hannah, 'yes, I understand.'

Munro looked down at her astonished. He was about to say something when the moment of intimacy was blasted by a roaring voice.

'Mr Munro! What the hell are you doing with my daughter?'

They had come to an intersection of streets. On the opposite corner the dilapidated buildings had given way to the covered veranda of a tavern. At each end a languidly moving cotton banner bore its name in Chinese characters. They both turned like guilty children called to account. In the company of several other bearded Europeans, some in the uniform of shipmasters, some in civilian clothes, they were confronted by an irate and fulminating Captain Kemball.

Munro swore audibly and, handing Hannah across the street, made his explanations. But Kemball swept him aside and drew Hannah up to introduce her to his brother commanders. He was proud of her, as proud of her as he was of his handsome clipper, and Hannah was too busy acknowledging who was who and who commanded what to notice at first that they were drunk.

''Faith but she's a winsome girl,' exclaimed O'Halloran of the *Actaeon*, his eyes resting on Hannah's bosom. 'She puts me in mind o' my first ship, a little barque whose mains'l had a bunt . . .'

'Oh, to hell with your barque, Patrick. Here, Hannah, I want you to meet an old antagonist of mine, a man who jeered at me in Foochow all those years ago, though he was no more than Third Mate at the time: Captain Richard Richards of the *Seawitch*.'

She was tugged round to face a man some ten or twelve years younger than her father, thinner, but with the same heavy beard, his whiskers unmarked by grey and with eyes that were black as coal. He rose to greet her, his face lugubrious with its beard and dark eyes, his manner reserved, observant, yet studiously courteous. Alone among the group, he seemed sober. He wore a suit of dove grey with soft leather gloves of the same colour which he did not remove as he took her hand. His cravat was of lavender silk, secured by a pearl-mounted pin, and he held a cane with an elaborate jade head. He bowed over her hand as she recognised him as the watcher of the morning, the man who had had himself rowed ashore at noon and to whom one of *Erl King*'s crew had referred as 'Dandy Dick'.

'It is an honour to make your acquaintance, Miss Kemball. I had the pleasure of meeting your mother on one occasion. Please accept my sincere condolences.'

His voice was softly Welsh, beautifully modulated, and his quiet speech held only the merest suggestion of its powerful possibilities, for he could out-bellow a full gale and have his orders understood on the uppermost yards of his ship.

'Thank you,' murmured Hannah awkwardly, unused to the attention she was receiving and guiltily aware for the second time that day that she had scarcely mourned her mother. In her preoccupied self-consciousness she did not recognise the barb aimed unerringly at her father.

'Now Richards,' interrupted Kemball as the Welshman relinquished her hand and sat again, the cane between his knees, 'you and I will have a wager on the homeward run, eh? Come, what d'you say?'

The other Masters took up the cry with the enthusiasm of schoolboys at a game of football. 'A wager! Come Chang, you idle devil, where's the book?'

Hands were clapped imperiously and a shuffling Celestial arrived, nodding obsequiously and smiling with the exhausted enthusiasm of the perpetual inferior. He bore the ledger in which the clipper captains annually inscribed their bets. He placed the book on the table with some reverence, and eager hands opened it at the appropriate page. A hush fell on the company and expectant faces turned towards Richards.

'This may be the last toime, my boys, if those French divils dig their damnation ditch through Egypt!' cautioned O'Halloran.

'Rubbish, Paddy . . . they haven't a hope in hell of doing any such thing . . .'

'The Red Sea's six feet lower than the Med . . . the bloody water'll run out . . .'

'Oi heard they had near completed the work, so Oi did . . .'

'Look, as long as they drink tea in London, there'll be tea-races.'

Hannah was over her initial bewilderment. She was beginning to realise her father and his cronies were drunk. She cast about for Munro. He was standing awkwardly in the background, humiliated in the presence of his seniors, embarrassed at their churlishness and furious that his afternoon with Hannah which had promised so well, had been terminated so suddenly. He made a reassuring half-smile that only communicated his unhappiness and regret. Hannah felt a surge of pity for him and anger for her father as she too realised what she had lost.

Only recently had she come to understand the degree to which her lonely and embittered mother had sheltered her from reality, the extent to which she herself had fallen in with that withdrawal. This afternoon, for the first time in her life she had tasted the delights of youthful freedom, of untrammelled exuberance, catching a glimpse of a garish, dangerous world, a world to which she had a right to belong, and the knowledge thrilled her. To have her domineering father terminate her first adventure seemed a cruelty not to be endured, particularly as it clearly inflicted pain on poor Mr Munro. But she felt trapped, unsure of what to do, so she sought an exit from her predicament.

Captain Kemball was carried away with drunken enthusiasm, bragging in front of his daughter as the clipper captains fell to arguing the respective merits of their ships and the likelihood of the French piercing the isthmus of Suez. No one had thought to offer her a seat until she felt a slight pressure in her calves and turned to find the Chinaman named Chang standing with a chair. She smiled her thanks and sat down. A little bowl of green tea arrived and, slightly mollified by Chang's courtesy, she sipped its delicate flavour as she watched and listened.

'Come on then. Make an entry in the book. O'Halloran must witness it.'

'Get the divil to witness it, Jack me boy, for 'tis Patrick who'll be betting once he hears the terms. Let Willis or Moore do it.'

But Willis wanted to bet too and Moore objected to the

whole Godless business on grounds of strict morality and contented himself with ordering more *samsu*. Kemball looked round and caught sight of his Second Mate.

'Ah, Mr Munro! Come here and make yourself useful, damn it . . .'

Reluctantly Munro came forward and they made a place for him at the table with the ledger in front of him. Again they turned to Richards.

'Come then . . . what is the stake?'

'I have not yet agreed to take the bet, gentlemen.'

Hannah watched those unusual coal-black eyes as they moved from one to another of his colleagues. From time to time they settled on her and she felt their gaze with a disturbing mixture of guilt and compliance.

At first she had thought Richards's stare no more than the seaman's long-sighted glance, like that of her father; a severe-seeming sham that was no more than a physiological distortion. Then she realised that Captain Richards's eyes were those of a hawk, with an acuity that saw beyond flesh. She realised with an unaccountable bumping of her heart that he was a man who expressed himself with his eyes as other men did with the inflections of their voices, gestures and posturings. She found she could not meet those eyes, feeling more shamefully naked before this stranger than before Enright's knowing leers.

Looking up with a shock she saw they were all following the Welshman's eyes and looking at her in a sudden, intense quiet.

'Very well,' he said, 'what is the wager to be then, Captain Kemball?'

His tone was solemnly formal, as though he was conscious of a need to terminate the schoolboy atmosphere and dignify the proceedings with all due pomp. It drew attention to the fact that a race between the clippers would run a course of some fifteen thousand miles, hazard nearly a hundred lives and two valuable ships. 'I presume this is a matter between the two of us? Between the *Seawitch* and the *Erl King*?'

Kemball nodded. 'Aye, Richards, between the two of us: to try which is the faster ship and the better Master . . .'

Richards nodded his approval, his eyes now fastened on Kemball.

'And upon my success,' went on Kemball, 'I'll wager my hat and a hundred guineas!'

'More, for shame!' bellowed O'Halloran, ''Tis not enough. Ah, you put me in mind o' the widow-woman o' Skibereen who was so mean that she . . .'

But O'Halloran's reminiscence was lost in shouts of agreement. The hat was customary, the hundred guineas a fair stake, but it was too miserly to make the match memorable. They all knew there was that long-ago derision still ringing in Jack Kemball's proud ears and that he had always hated Richards, a younger man with abilities to match his own.

O'Halloran cocked a shrewd eye at Hannah. 'Come now, Jack me boy, 'tis certain sure you are now that the *Erl King's* all your own. You can venture a trifle more on such a bet. 'Tis loike to be a remarkable occasion, so it is, and you'd not be wanting to go down in history as an old skinflint, would you now?'

Kemball was shocked, despite the inaccuracy of O'Halloran's statement, and gulped the refreshed dish of *samsu* that Chang thoughtfully provided. To a man of his disposition a hundred guineas was downright generous and, whilst he had no intention of losing, he was too prudent a mariner, even in his cups, not to recognise that he might carry away gear, or suffer other misfortunes with which the impartial gods mocked all skilful endeavour.

'Well, damn it, man,' he said to Richards, ignoring O'Halloran, 'd'you take it?' He thrust out his hand aggressively. Richards's remained clasped over the jade head of his cane. 'You're feared of the *Seawitch* being outsailed,' taunted the affronted Kemball, lowering his paw.

'Don't tempt providence, Jack,' warned Moore superstitiously.

'I fear nothing but the consequences of my own sins,' said Richards at last, and the power of his bass voice subdued them. They swallowed more *samsu* as Chang circled the table. Richards cast a black and reflective glance at Hannah again. 'Kemball,' he said slowly, 'set aside for a moment *what* you will stake. Let us see what you propose for the passage.'

A sigh of anti-climax went round the others. They wanted the wager entered up so they might make their own, but Kemball, sensing imminent victory, narrowed his eyes in calculation.

36

'We shall both be loading in Foochow within the month . . .'

'I'm not waiting until you are loaded . . .'

'Very well,' agreed Kemball, for of all things concerning his ship, loading was the only one in which he tolerated a degree of slow care. 'Shall we say the match is on from the moment both ships *begin* to load?'

'You mean we wait for each other?' asked Richards, frowning.

'That would be fair,' Willis slurred.

'Ah, but you others must not load before us.' Kemball swung round on Willis, Moore and O'Halloran to be greeted by loud protests.

''Tis a wager, not a damned monopoly!'

'I'll not stand for that!'

'It's that or nothing,' said Richards. 'Let us agree that the first two junks down the Min go to *Seawitch* and *Erl King*. We will already have loaded our ballast, so once we've begun, you others may do as you please. Well, gentlemen?'

There was eventual grumbling agreement between the captains.

'All roight, all roight, we agree, but you note our protest at your confounded chicanery. Now, Jack, you divil, what about the stake? You must give us a stake that's worth all this co-operation.'

Willis and Moore chorused assent at O'Halloran's concession.

'Aye, come on, the stake!'

'Well, Richards? My hat and a hundred guineas?'

'First,' said Richards slowly, again dignifying the proceedings with a maddening deliberation, 'the terms of the win. I propose the first ship to land tea in bulk . . .'

'You'll not be that close,' laughed Willis, 'not after fifteen thousand miles.'

'Aye. Be a miracle if you make the same day, never mind the same tide,' O'Halloran added. 'Come on, Dandy, stop prevaricating and agree the stake. Jack's offered you his terms: his hat and a hundred. D'you take it?'

'No.'

'Why the bloody hell not? Are you going to sit here and argue whether to take the Gaspar or the Karimata Strait? For God's sake you can stop and take tea with the Dutchmen at Anjer for all Oi care . . .' O'Halloran slapped the table, making the *samsu* dishes jump, then flung himself resentfully back in his chair, exasperated.

'Why won't you take the stake?' asked Willis with some difficulty.

'It is not a fair bet.'

'That depends upon what *you* wager, Richards, damn you,' snapped Kemball, rapidly losing his patience as the rice spirit fumed in his brain.

'No. It is not fair because it lacks piquancy.'

'Piquancy?' roared Kemball.

'Nothing of yourself, Kemball. The loss of your hat and a hundred guineas would scarcely touch you.'

'I protest the honour of my ship . . .'

'Damn your ship, Kemball. I know her worth. This is between *you* and *me*! We both know it.'

Kemball frowned, suspicious of Richards's metaphysics, and slowly becoming confused by the *samsu*. Chang diligently refilled the dishes O'Halloran had spilled.

'Stake something you'd really miss, Kemball,' said Richards, leaning forward and adding a physical dimension to his words, 'something I'll *relish* if I win, for the loss it's caused you. Eh?' Richards cast loose the last monosyllable with an upward jerk of his head, the disembowelling rip of the antlered stag. The mood of anti-climax had been succeeded by an almost reverent silence.

Hannah was filled with a chilling apprehension. This was another glimpse into a world of reality so different from the ordered formality that she had come to expect from men of her father's stamp. It thrilled and frightened her, for, by their language and their drunkenness, they had clearly forgotten her presence; all, that is, except Captain Richard Richards. He was transfixing her father, yet she was unable to rid herself of the strange certainty that somewhere in that domed head with its sleek covering of black hair, a third eye watched her nakedness. In a kind of desperation she sought out the reassuring face of Munro, but he too was caught, pen poised obediently over the ledger, watching with O'Halloran, Moore and Willis as the two men faced each other.

'And if you venture something truly worthwhile,' the Welsh-man added, 'I'll lay five hundred guineas against your one.'

A whistle of appreciation went round the table. Even Moore had forgotten his principles in the tension. Kemball seized the line he thought Richards had thrown him. Confused by oblique allusions and *samsu*, Kemball had hesitated. Now that no more money seemed to be involved but that some bizarre gesture of sacrifice was required, he understood. Where he was envied, the practical Jack Kemball comprehended wizardry as well as any Welshman with a megalomaniac streak.

He looked up, inspired: 'I'll wager *Erl King*'s figurehead.'

A sound that was half-sigh and half-cheer came from the assembled captains as their fists banged the table. Moore called for *samsu*. Beneath the veranda a crowd had gathered to watch the *fan kwei* bet and to gawp at the pink creature in their midst. Inveterate gamblers themselves, this point of contact with the Red Barbarians fascinated the Chinese.

But Richards shook his head, and imperiously raised a kid-gloved hand for silence.

'Add your daughter's hand in marriage and I'll stake a thousand!'

Hannah felt her heart shrink. A deathly hush fell on the men, rippling out over the crowd. Munro's head turned sharply and his indrawn breath was an outraged hiss. All eyes swivelled to Hannah and she felt the blood rush to her cheeks as her stilled heart suddenly pounded in her breast.

The subdued crowd, influenced by some intuitive reflex trig-gered by the reactions of the sea-captains, now began to chatter. Someone with an understanding of English explained what was happening. Two of the *fan kwei* were discussing the terms of sale for the big girl child. Her father wished to sell her, and the black devil wanted her for a concubine. Laughter greeted this intelligence; the beards of the foreign devils pro-claimed them closer to the animals than the Celestials, now their preference for such big-breasted sows confirmed it!

Hannah, scarlet after her horror-struck moment of bloodless fear, now paled again at her father's hesitation. She was breath-less with outrage, transfixed in expectation of some offered indignation at her shame, but her father remained silent as the seconds lengthened. She looked anxiously at Munro, never guessing that he was astounded at the proposition and that the sheer effrontery of Captain Richards had left him speechless. A soundless cry rose in her throat and she turned back to her father.

Cracker Jack Kemball was equally shocked, confronted by memories of the shady legitimacy of his own youthful man-oeuvrings. He recalled his rival's pointed remark that the only thing he himself feared was the consequences of his own sins.

For a moment Kemball rocked on the unstable fulcrum of conscience before his calculating brain fought through the fog of *samsu*. Surely Richards did not want Hannah for her looks? She was a mere girl. No, the cunning dog wanted the *Erl King* and had designs upon Hannah's shares. If he won (and it was not likely) he would come yapping at an ageing man's heels wanting to drive Cracker Jack from his own poop, God damn him! Kemball felt fury at the cool nerve of the man, but there were other things to consider.

A practical seaman, Kemball possessed the power to perceive truths drunk that would elude him sober. There was the matter of Richards's stake of a thousand pounds. Setting aside the advantage of winning it, it argued that perhaps Richards *did* desire Hannah. Once planted, the conviction grew rapidly in Kemball's mind. So public a declaration revealed to Kemball in his moment of clairvoyance that passion did indeed drive the dark-visaged Welshman.

And if he was thus moved now, what effect would be worked during the homeward race by the alchemy of love or lust? Might not Richards become prone to misjudgements, such as the over-carrying of sail? Might he not drive his ship and people too hard? Might not passion for Hannah Kemball magnify the temperamental defects every man possessed and which the lonely autocracy of command exposed?

Kemball's eyes narrowed. He found the subtle advantage falling at last to his own hand; he could turn aside the jibes of O'Halloran and seize the initiative now from Richards. This was something to make the match memorable! For all his Celtic bombast Richards had made a fool of himself and could go to the devil in his own time! He looked at his daughter. She was still to him the awkward creature that had staggered around the wildly gyrating saloon of the *Erl King* as they had crossed the

Bay of Biscay outward bound, her face green, her hair plastered stickily down her pallid cheeks. Why, look at her . . .

Hannah felt her father's eyes upon her. Disgust, humiliation and fear held her speechless. She felt that she had in some way contributed to this charade, for Munro's averted eyes spoke accusation. She tried to order her thoughts, for she knew she was being used; perhaps, remembering her mother, this was how a trafficked bride might feel! She forced herself to be calm, to remain silent, and the summoning of this resolution made her increasingly angry. She was angry with her father, and angry with Richards; aware only that whatever was about to happen she must preserve her own dignity.

And in this her father made his only misjudgement, for Hannah was no longer the sea-sick girl of the Bay, and as he willed her to silence he smugly hugged to himself, with a drunk's conceit, the knowledge that Richards really had no chance of winning. Captain Kemball allowed himself the expansive luxury of a smile.

'Done!' he said, holding out his hand.

Hannah set her face as the sea-captains jumped from their chairs and thumped the table and themselves. She hardly heard the hubbub around her as Richards solemnly shook her father's hand.

'*Da iawn*. The first to break bulk alongside a London berth is the winner. Your hat, your daughter and a hundred guineas against my thousand.'

'Make it so, Mr Munro,' ordered Captain Kemball, as Munro bent miserably over the ledger and wrote the terms. The other men scribbled their own ciphers as they made their side-bets.

'Oi'll call you ninety-two days from the Outer Bar to the Chapman Loight, Willis. Oi'm not arguing about tidal delays . . .'

'Never, nothing under a hundred at this time of year,' expostulated Willis.

They bent over Munro as the unfortunate Second Mate wrote their bet beneath the first. Then O'Halloran straightened up and they called for more *samsu* and resumed their seats, an awkward silence descending on them as they contemplated their actions individually.

41

Hannah looked round them; despite a feeling of loyalty to her father, she had ceased to be overawed by these boorish men, men who, perfect gentlemen at home, models of rectitude as they dropped their ill-gotten guineas in the parish collecting plate, would leave a young woman standing while they deliberated over their silly ships, men who would humiliate a subordinate precisely because he was a subordinate.

'Before you ask if I am willing, Father,' she remarked with heavy irony, rising to her feet, 'you have my consent. *You'll* not be beaten by Captain Richards.'

She paused, glad of the attention she now commanded, glad of the surprise on her father's face and no longer embarrassed by the whispering, pointing and grinning crowd below the veranda rail. She realised in a surge of confidence that she possessed some small advantage conferred by her sex and the moment, some brief opportunity to spike their arrogance. She looked at Richards, mustering all the hauteur she was capable of and meeting his black eyes with a level stare. She felt a sudden elation at the confrontation and the silence she had caused, poised amid their drunken sprawling. She turned to Munro:

'Mr Munro, your arm . . .' then she swung back to Richards. 'I shall be delighted to receive you, Captain Richards, when we reach London. Win or lose, sir, I shall expect you on your knees.'

3

THE cool disdain with which Hannah had left the shipmasters proved a brittle mood. Poor Munro, for whom
the idyll had been smashed by Kemball's bellow of recognition,
suffered it of necessity. But he knew that the pleasant intimacy
towards which his relationship with Miss Kemball seemed to
have been progressing, was now beyond recapture. In silence
he escorted Hannah back to the gig and the *Erl King*.

Hannah's own fragile mood sustained her only until she had
shot the bolt on her cabin door. Once she was alone it slipped
from her entirely. She flung herself upon her bunk; anger,
humiliation and frustration rolling over her in successive
waves. She was angry with her father for his rudeness, his
presumption and his lack of sensitivity. She was angry with
Munro for having walked her that way, angry with the afternoon for starting so wonderfully and ending so invasively.
Most of all she was angry with herself for feeling such a loss so
acutely. For the shipmasters had humiliated her, kept her
standing like a chattel, including her in their childish bargain-
ing in a way that affronted her sensibilities. Yet she was not
unaffected by Captain Richards's ardour though he had torn
from her the pleasurable warmth she was feeling for Munro,
and had supplanted it with something dangerous.

In the end anger and humiliation waned, leaving a bitter
residue of frustration. Anger and humiliation were imposed,
but frustration was self-generated, sustained from within and
unavoidable. It seemed to her that fate had decided she must
not yet see the world; that that initial glimpse of Shanghai was
premature. Instead she must first confront herself. The smugly
virtuous gift of the log-line to the coolie woman seemed the last
act of childhood. As her rage calmed she realised she was being

43

foolish. The abrupt dissolution of the afternoon had been circumstantial; the dreadful meeting with her father and his cronies impinged on her only in so far as it made it impossible for her to shrug off any longer her own desires. Transition from the awkward rejections of her Islington adolescence to the mild flirtations of the *Erl King*'s officers had been a pleasant experience. But even Enright, with his omnipresent sexual blandishments, had failed to penetrate Hannah's guard, and she had considered this, when she considered it at all, as a satisfactory mark of her own virtue. But today had been different; something had happened today that stripped her bare of her own self-respect, yet came to her as ready-known knowledge, an awakening to self. Like the occasion when one of the seamen had sustained a deep cut which her father had sutured and dressed, and to which she had, perforce, to act as nurse, the revelation of bone came as a shock.

She knew what it was; it was what had driven her father into the maid's bed and what had embittered her mother. Now it told Hannah the unpleasant truth that she, too, was flesh. Her strange, isolated and shielded childhood, the long period she had nursed her mother, had served to steel her against herself. As she groped towards this realisation she blamed Munro. Munro had so sweetly, so subtly, and so suddenly awakened her to the pleasure of love, that she felt he had almost deliberately prepared her for the rampant assault that had been mounted by Captain Richard Richards. Her peevishness towards Munro was a symptom of how reluctant she was to face the truth about Richards. It was only the unfortunate Munro's subordinate awkwardness among the shipmasters that gave him the appearance of a procurer. She realised now how hurt he too had been by their behaviour, and she felt sorry for him. In the end she realised it was the intrusion of Richards that had blighted what had gone before with Munro. The circumstances had all the appearance of a bad joke, as upside-down as the curious Chinese notions of beauty over which she and Munro had laughed earlier.

She calmed herself and sat up. Reaching for her hand-mirror she stared almost resentfully into it, trying to see what it was that had fired the unspeakable Richards to so outrageous a proposal. The oval face and grey eyes were as unremarkable as the

44

brown hair, her cheeks too disgustingly wind-burned for any notion of beauty, eastern or occidental. But she *knew* Richards had imagined her naked.

She could not tell what made this a certainty, or why the knowledge had so violently disturbed her. Yet even in recollection, it stirred her with a sweet, but dangerous sensation. For several minutes she sat as though waiting for Richards to materialise through the gleaming woodwork of the locked door. Then resentment flared through her, a passion to revenge herself upon Richards in some way that she knew she could never achieve. As she flung herself back on the bunk, dropping the hand-mirror, she remained unaware that she had not found the strength for her haughty departure from the Chinese inn from the anger and the humiliation the men had imposed, but from her own responsive desire to meet Captain Richards as an equal.

The night proved a long nightmare for Hannah. It was unbearably hot in the locked cabin. She lay in her shift, staring up in the darkness, listening to the noises of the ship. To the chuckle of the river as it lapped gently against the *Erl King*'s sides and the slow creak and grind of the rudder, there were added other, more animate noises that were disturbingly in tune with her own tormented thoughts.

Much of Hannah's misery stemmed from the fact that her father had had recourse to the traditional recreations of seamen after a long and arduous passage. He had gone ashore to get drunk. In doing so he had abandoned his daughter, removing from her the very real protection of his presence. Not that she was herself in any danger, though she heard a low conversation outside her door in which she detected a degree of concern for her presence on board. The restraints of watch-keeping kept half the crew on board, and while some of *Erl King*'s crew roistered ashore like their commander, the other half were mewed up on board. Mindful of every opportunity to extract an existence out of an uncaring world, the Chinese thoughtfully overcame this by providing 'flower-junks', floating brothels, each staffed accommodatingly with half a dozen girls. For those of the common seamen for whom such services constituted too expensive a luxury, a rope's end secured invitingly over the bow could induce indigent sampan women aboard to provide the same services at a more economical rate. And for those few whose moral values or whose fear of disease kept them aloof, the Chinese obligingly sold *samsu* or opium. For all her ocean beauty and A100+ classification at Lloyds, *Erl King* was worm-eaten with human weakness.

Hannah took no notice as the flower-junk bumped alongside. But the footsteps overhead and the unusual giggles piqued her curiosity, and she sat up to stare through the open porthole. Not twenty feet away was the high stern of the junk. A huge, indolent cat lay stretched out above a chicken coop whose broody inhabitants clucked quietly. Figures in the androgynous dark pyjamas of coolies hung lanterns on the quarters, and more lamps were hung over by unseen hands in the waist of the *Erl King*.

She heard the excited voices of the crew, recognising some and dreading hearing that of Munro, for she knew that she was witnessing something forbidden to white women.

'Hey, Mary, how muchee one girl?'

Light fell on an ancient face, creased and brown as tanned leather, the broad cheeks blotched by age marks, the forehead enlarged by alopecia. Although the crone's voice cracked with age, it spoke with authority as she stood alone on the deck of the junk and held the crew at bay.

'What you wantchee, Johnnie? All night, or just jig-a-jig short time?'

'How much English money for all night?'

'You give me one pound gold . . .'

A chorus of derision greeted this exorbitant demand, but the old procuress stood her ground unabashed, '. . . and I fetchee you two piece girl, velly good, velly experience, give you number-one good time . . .'

'Very well, Mary, you make a good bargain!'

Hannah heard Enright's voice and the lights caught the gleam of the crone's recognition, piercing the expanse of her broad face like dark chips of stone.

'Ah, Mr Enright, *Da-foo*, best number-one Chief Office on China coast. Take my best girls one time,' she turned to the rest of the crew, capitalising on Enright's extravagant reputation and giving vent to a little shrewd advertising by the way, 'take my best girls one time, teach them new experience. My customers velly please . . . which one you wantchee, *Da-foo*? Give you velly good time.'

The woman turned and waved two girls forward. They looked no more than children, twins to Hannah's shocked and untutored eye. They stood demurely, eyes cast down, in long silk brocaded gowns, their tiny breasts barely lifting the fabric.

'You like, Mr Enright?'

'They look too damned young.'

The crone protested. 'No, no, they velly good, velly experience, give you special good time, jig-a-jig plenty, all come together, velly nice.'

Hannah did not understand this torrent of pidgin, but there was an undercurrent of comment from the other men crowding the rail, whose grotesque shadows were thrown across the deck of the junk as graphic images of eager lust. Their patient deference to rank was growing thin and one man, more excited than the rest, called out: 'Look-see, Mary, you give us look-see . . .'

This appeal was hailed by a gleeful cheer from the others and a spittle-conveyed oath from Mary. 'You dirty li'l boy . . .'

'Suppose *I* want look-see, Mary.' The voice of Enright boomed out and Mary's chip-shrewd eyes swivelled round, knowing that she had them all in the palm of her wizened hand.

'You belong special, Mr Enright.'

She turned and said something sharply to the motionless girls. One of them looked up at Enright, then raised her hand to the loops and knotted silk fastenings that closed the gown on her left shoulder. She pulled it open, standing immobile, her slender body pale in the lamplight. The watchers on deck fell silent. Hannah drew in her breath sharply; the nubility of the girl was confined to enlarged conical nipples and a dark, pubic triangle.

'Send 'em up, Mary!' Enright's voice shattered the silence and the night was filled with renewed clamouring to see more of the merchandise. As Hannah drew back into the cabin the cat looked up, suddenly licked its haunch, then settled again.

Hannah crossed the cabin and put her ear to the door. Disgust and fascination filled her. The two girls had appeared innocent, held against their will; but accompanying Enright's

47

familiar tread in the alleyway were the giggles and chatter of two eager young women.

The slam of Enright's cabin door made her jump. Hannah flung herself on her bunk, burying her head in her pillow in an attempt to drown out the squeals and laughter, and Enright's roars of libidinous delight. She lay for a long time in an almost cataleptic state. A stream of unbidden images danced in her mind's eye, images the origin of which she had no idea, images which her ignorance suggested were impossible, but her curiosity assured her were taking place so close to her that she might witness them by tearing down the bulkhead with her bare hands. Utterly confused, frustrated, disturbed and ashamed, she finally drifted into an uneasy sleep.

Hannah woke at dawn bathed in sweat. Her shift stuck clammily to her body and had ridden up uncomfortably. She had not unpinned her hair before sleeping and it hung in coils down one side of her face. She felt this discomfort as a rebuke, and it reminded her with poignant force of the events of the previous afternoon and evening. Rousing herself, she peered from the porthole. The flower-junk had gone.

Instead the Whangpo lay calm beneath the pearl grey of the dawn sky, a pale jade green fading into a bluish mist where the wharves and godowns broke the river's margins with their harsh outlines. Ethereal as shadows, junks and sampans moved through the water. Even at this early hour the stream was crowded, for the river Chinese were truly aquatic people, and slept in relays like all sailors. Hannah breathed deeply of the morning air that always, even along the waterfront of Shanghai, smelt of the innocence of a new beginning. She had learnt to love the dawn and longed to cleanse herself of the confusions of the previous day. She dressed hurriedly, pulling a shawl across her shoulders and pushing up the dislodged braids of her hair. As she stepped out on to the dew-wet planking of the poop, she tipped her face upwards, closed her eyes and again drew in the dawn air.

Mr Munro stopped his pacing and stared through red-rimmed eyes at the uplifted profile. The wide red mouth, the firm chin and the pallid cheeks upon which the long dark lashes lay, appeared as a fantastic product of his exhausted mind.

Lusting with a fever to match Hannah's, he had only resisted his own physical craving with the thought of Hannah alone in her locked cabin whilst, to its shame, the ship slid into its seasonal debauchery. During the long hours of the night, Munro had found it impossible to sleep. He had kept the anchor watch, pacing the poop, musing on the hardships of virtue. Now Hannah's sudden appearance transfixed him; remaining motionless by the after rail, he watched her.

She shook her head and opened her eyes with a sigh audible thirty feet away in the still air. Hannah stared out over the smooth waters of the river, watching a distant junk. Then she leaned forward on her elbows, the dew cold on her skin, a mild mortification for her impure thoughts. She looked down into the water, at the vacant space alongside the *Erl King* where the flower-junk had been. Below her, floating belly-up and bloated, the coarse blue-white of its umbilical cord trailing behind it, the corpse of a tiny, unwanted girl-child drifted past.

She felt her stomach leap and the bile rise in her throat, but she could not take her eyes off the thing. It seemed like a judgement, as though it had been spawned from the scupper pipes of the *Erl King*. Her hand flew to her mouth as she gasped with horror.

'Miss Kemball, what is it?'

He was beside her in an instant and caught sight of the distended belly as it bobbed past. Instinctively he drew her sobbing body into his arms. The fragrance of her hair rewarded his own virtue even as his gaze followed the white blob drifting astern. Hannah looked up at him, her eyes full of tears.

'Hannah,' he said, deeply moved. Leaning down he kissed her forehead.

'This is a terrible place.'

He wanted to kiss her. 'This is China,' he said gently instead.

He felt her arms cautiously encircle him and they stood trying to recapture something of the previous day until he caught sight of the sampan heading towards the accommodation ladder.

'Damn!' Munro muttered, and gently detached himself from Hannah. 'Your father . . .'

She turned and saw the figure lying on the cushions as the sampan was sculled closer to *Erl King*.

49

'You'd better go below, Hannah,' Munro began, but Hannah cut him short.

'No!'

Munro was unable to retreat, held as tightly by circumstance now as he had been the previous afternoon, a helpless victim of his own obligations.

'Where have you *been*, Father?'

Hannah's outrage met Captain Kemball as his head drew level with the rail. He was pale, his eyes encircled by the blue shadows of excess.

'Been? Why ashore on business . . .'

He threw a glance at Munro; it contained no hint of reproach, but rather a prick of conscience prompting an appeal, man-to-man. Munro was not slow to seize the advantage Kemball offered. He did not want to become embroiled in a family matter and mentioned the corpse of the baby.

'You'll have to harden your heart, Hannah. This is China,' said Kemball.

His guilt thus exonerated in his own eyes, Kemball went on, 'I'm obliged to you, Mr Munro. Now, to more important matters. I've just received word that the tea is expected at Foochow soon. I've a tug ordered for eight bells. See the men are turned out with the bars shipped at the capstan and all hands ready to stamp and go.'

Munro nodded. 'Aye, aye, sir.'

Kemball made his way to the companionway, paused with his hands on the rails and looked back. 'You'd better come below now,' he said to Hannah, 'Mr Munro has work to do.'

Hannah and Munro exchanged glances, glances loaded with the conspiracy of declared lovers. Left on deck, Munro permitted himself a smile of cautious optimism.

In his cabin Kemball faced his daughter. The message from Foochow had found him with his concubine, a beautiful young woman of mixed blood who lived in considerable luxury, maintained by several gentlemen whose respective professions ensured they were never in Shanghai simultaneously. The woman managed her affairs with discretion to the mutual satisfaction of her clients. If Captain Kemball's assignation lacked the fire of spontaneous passion, it more than made up for any deficiency by the variety of its delights, the civility of its comportment and the friendship of its principals. The Captain's leave-taking had been regretful, but muted in the light of other considerations which the lady gracefully acknowledged. She retired to her bath with a handsome sum and the Captain's felicitations. He returned to his ship with his mind clear.

'I trust you were not incommoded by my absence, Hannah?' he asked, loosening his cravat.

'Not in the least, Father,' she replied, surprised at the ease with which she lied, 'I spent a quiet evening alone in my cabin.'

Kemball eyed her keenly, judged she told the truth and shrugged the matter aside.

'*I* was a little worried about *you*.'

'Very kind, I'm sure,' he mumbled, struggling with a collar stud. 'You had no cause to be.'

'You were drunk when I last saw you,' she went on, emboldened.

'What's that? Drunk?' He frowned at her, but she stood her ground and her impertinence irritated him. 'How dare you . . .'

'How dare *you*, Father,' she interrupted, no longer in awe of him and silencing him as he fought to recall the details of the previous afternoon. He had had much on his mind in the last few sleepless hours: the arrangements for the tug following the news from Foochow, and the distractions of his mistress. He forced a wan grin.

'Come, my dear, you mustn't mind me, or that dog Richards. He's jealous of the ship and hasn't a hope in Hades of beating me, surely you realised that?' He paused frowning.

'Of course, but that isn't the point . . .'

'Yes it is. The man wants your shares or . . .' He could not admit his secret conviction even as he recollected it. Sober, it no longer seemed so much a certainty. 'You weren't really upset, were you? O'Halloran thought you might be.'

'Captain O'Halloran is a little more sensitive than you, Father. Of course I was upset. I was publicly humiliated! It was *me* you were haggling over!'

Bright spots of anger burned on Hannah's cheeks now, and her fists were clenched as she leaned forward to emphasise her words.

'Oh, come now,' Captain Kemball said, lowering his voice

with an anxious glance at the cabin door. 'It was only a joke . . .'

'It was a damnably heavy joke, Father,' Hannah said vehemently, 'and I rely upon you making it quite impossible for Captain Richards to so much as *think* of pressing his suit when we arrive in London.'

And leaving her father open-mouthed, Hannah went to dress properly before the breakfast gong sounded.

'Steady as you go.'

'Steady as she goes, sir, course nor' west by west, sir.'

Kemball grunted acknowledgement and continued to stare through his telescope at the grey-green hummocks of the islets opening on either side as the *Erl King* approached the bar of the Min River.

Standing by the taffrail, Hannah watched her father, unable to find much comfort in the fact that he had ignored the matter of the lost log-line. In the few days of the passage southwards from Shanghai she had suffered from a profound sense of unease. The moment *Erl King*'s anchor had broken free of the mud of the Garden Reach, normality had returned to the ship. Her father had reverted to his former self, the men to an obedient ship's company. As the *Erl King* had been towed downstream between the levées and rice paddy fields, her seamen scrambling aloft, loosening her sails in the buntlines, all recollection of debauch had been left astern with the fading skyline and stink of the sprawling city of Shanghai. Hannah felt embittered that these men had not been transformed into something identifiably wicked, but it was not so. Even Enright, whose moral turpitude in Hannah's opinion warranted the severest condemnation, had stood on the fo'c's'le and grinned at her.

No visitation of divine disapproval had appeared to mar the operation of casting loose the tug at Woosung, where the Chinese fort and the foreign gunboats maintained an armed truce. No fateful mishap had struck any seaman as they spread the sails and swept out on to the broad yellow waters of the fast-flowing Yangtze Kiang. No hint of remorse had marred the quickening life of the ship as they swung clear of the Chusan Archipelago and headed southwards for the Formosa Strait. All on board knew a race with *Seawitch* was planned and *Erl King*'s company looked forward, not back, utterly forgetting the Garden Reach and the flower-junks of Shanghai.

But today, as they approached the estuary of the Min, Hannah felt the change that had come over herself. Though she still lacked that perfect experience that her innocence deprived her of, she was reconciled to her own raw awakening, mollified, if not fulfilled, by the certainty of Munro's devotion. As the harrowing memory of the drowned baby faded, she recollected it not so much as a manifestation of the corporate immorality of the ship, but as the corpse of her own immaturity. She had cast off the imposed sentiments of her upbringing and had come closer to the aggressive immediacy of the rest of the ship's company. It was a profound and disturbing shift in the axis of her being, but Hannah Kemball's sea-change was complete.

Under Captain Kemball's skilful direction, her yards hauled with every change of course, *Erl King* negotiated Warning Rock and the White Dogs, drawing closer to the foaming combers that roared over the shoals. To the west a high range of hills rose behind the breakers of a long bay. The northern end of the bay terminated in a sharp-peaked promontory named on the chart as Black Head. Beyond, a jumble of hills, mountains and islands formed an apparently impenetrable barrier, a China as inscrutable as the wide paddies around Shanghai had been exposed to the flooding of the great rivers that had formed it. Compared with the Whangpo, the Min was a secretive river, its hinterland rugged and withdrawn, for all the Anglicised names on the British Admiralty chart by which they navigated.

Hannah sensed a mounting tension on deck as the *Erl King* rolled and pitched amid the building Pacific ground swell, Straightening methodically from the compass, Captain Kemball shouted orders which were obeyed with impressive promptness as they picked their way through the shoals on his carefully observed transits and clearing bearings.

'Shewan had the *Normancourt* on a rock pinnacle just here,' Kemball explained in a brief aside to Hannah, as, all at once, they seemed to be in amongst the breakers. Around them the swells became pronounced, rearing on the sand bars to unstable heights and tumbling in an incessantly thunderous roar. Above this chaotic scene a white spray-mist hung over the dissolution of the huge waves. But the leadsman's chant

53

reassured them that they held the centre of the channel and they crept cautiously over the outer bar.

'Braces there . . .'

Kemball ordered another change of course, the helm was steadied and the yards swung as the men pulled in unison at the braces.

'Sharp up, and set those t'garn bowlines taut as harpstrings!'

Munro came aft, smiled at Hannah and reported to her father. 'Tug's in sight, sir.'

'I hope it's the *Undine*,' grumbled Kemball, 'I don't want that rusting heap of feebleness the *Island Queen* . . .' He raised his telescope.

Hannah could see a smoky cloud beneath the tall funnel and low hull of a small steamship clearing Woufou Island.

'It looks like *Cyclone*, sir,' offered Munro.

With a churning of paddles the *Cyclone*, its name proudly confirmed by elaborate scroll-work on the paddle boxes, rounded under the clipper's bow. Lines were thrown, the towing hawser passed and *Erl King*, furling her canvas, docilely followed the tug. The tension on deck eased.

Soon Woufou Island rose above them, its steep flanks covered in abundant and fragrant vegetation. To starboard, climbing to greater heights, the mainland dominated them. The peak of the Cockscomb soared two thousand feet above them as they swung into the gorge of the Kinpai Pass. The river swirled through the narrows, slowing their progress, giving Enright time to supervise a neat harbour stow as both watches laid aloft and spread out on the yards.

To Hannah the gorge seemed like some fantastic gateway into a forbidden land. Plants could no longer survive on the beetling crags. Split slabs of rock overhung them as the bowsprit traced the billowing smoke cloud from the tug. Wafts of sulphureous funnel gases competed with strong land-scents, as the head wind gusted fitfully through the narrows and *Erl King* proceeded at a snail's pace against the current. But at last the cliffs receded, the river banks fell away and they passed into more open country. Here the navigable channel again wound through the shoals, and they passed the walled villages of Wisong and Pitao. Hannah stared at the exotically curved eaves of joss-houses and the swarms of people on the river banks. Off Ningpo a fleet of sampans fished and the anchorage was crowded with trading junks, but finally, after towing inland for five hours, they reached Cushan Creek and the long curve of the Pagoda Anchorage, the first clipper to arrive for the season's tea.

'I am honoured to meet you, Miss Kemball.'

Hannah bobbed a curtsey at the tall, elegant Chinaman into whose gloomy trading house her father had ushered her. Lenqua was richly dressed in the brocaded gown of a mandarin. His face struck Hannah as handsome, the nose almost aquiline, the well-shaped mouth bracketed by a long, drooping moustache. He wore lacquered nail guards and a buttoned hat which enhanced his cool, dignified and almost remote manner.

'Lenqua', her father had explained as they had walked up from the boat-landing at Foochow, 'is the Hong comprador, the trading agent with whom many of us deal for our cargoes. Unlike the port mandarin, who is the Celestial Emperor's local Number-One Joss, Lenqua is honest by our standards. His honesty has made him rich.' So rich, Kemball might have added, that it was to Lenqua that the unfortunate Cracker Jack had turned for financial help when his clipper was storm-damaged in a typhoon.

What Hannah realised immediately, and what drew from her the most graceful courtesy she had yet been called upon to perform, was that Lenqua was one of nature's gentlemen. It was not, of course, something that Captain Kemball was capable of seeing in a heathen, yellow-skinned Chinaman, but it was obvious to Hannah.

'Please be seated.' Lenqua indicated a low, heavily carved chair of dark wood. She sat on its red cushion and the men followed suit. A neat, pretty woman appeared, bearing small porcelain dishes of tea and sweetmeats.

'You first to arrive, Captain John. That is very good.'

'When will the tea be down?' Kemball asked abruptly.

'Two, three, maybe four days,' replied Lenqua, 'in the usual half and full chests.'

'I'm anxious to load. Captain Richards will be here soon . . .'

'*Seawitch* leave Shanghai the day after you with *Actaeon*.'

'Huh! News travels fast. Well I must have the shingle ballast aboard . . .'

'Ballast come alongside tomorrow.'

'Good.' Kemball nodded with satisfaction and tipped a bowl of tea into his mouth, following it with two or three of the sweetmeats.

'You have good voyage to China, Miss Kemball?'

'Yes, thank you.'

'Your arrival is pleasure and honour to us. You are comfortable on board?'

'Oh, yes.' She smiled back, slightly awkward under the scrutiny of the Chinaman. Lenqua's look lingered on her for a second and then he turned to Kemball.

'Captain, there is matter of business, private business I must speak.'

'Would you like me to leave?' asked Hannah, putting down her bowl.

'No,' Kemball put out a restraining hand, 'I've no secrets from my daughter these days, Lenqua,' Kemball said blandly. 'What is it?'

Lenqua laid his tea-bowl carefully on the low table before him. He cast another long and almost lingering look at Hannah. 'I wish to go to England with you, Captain John.'

Kemball made no scruple of his astonishment. 'What the devil for?'

'I do not wish to make answer. Belong private concern. Only you ask price.'

'Who will look after our interests? You are indispensable to us here.'

'Lenqua is old man, Captain John. Sometimes old man have special fancy. Not change mind. How much? I already catch good freight rate for you, over six pound a ton, and I help you long-time . . .'

'Yes, yes . . .' Kemball frowned, thinking furiously.

'You come first ship Londonside. We hear news from Shanghai.'

Kemball chuckled and grinned. 'Well, Lenqua, what will you pay for the fastest passage?'

'What you want?'

A wolfish light had appeared in Kemball's eyes.

'I want my ship back. All of the shares . . .'

'All shares means not much profit for Lenqua this voyage.' Lenqua picked up a sweetmeat.

'You want to go to London, Lenqua, Foochow to London is a long way.'

Lenqua paused then nodded. 'My shares . . .'

'In advance.'

'But my share profit to remain payable at end of voyage.' Lenqua's eyes were shrewd behind their folds of skin.

Kemball's face split into a wide, almost boyish grin. He had intended to open negotiations for the repurchase of Lenqua's shares but had not anticipated the Chinaman would be so eager to relinquish them. 'Done!'

Lenqua raised his hands and clapped them; instantly the woman reappeared. 'Samsu,' he commanded, and they sealed the bargain with fiery rice spirit.

'Well, Hannah,' said Kemball chattily, 'we shall have a passenger homeward bound.'

'Two passenger, Captain John. Lenqua come with his concubine.'

'This is Cha Lee Foo, Hannah,' said Captain Kemball, introducing Hannah to a small, desiccated and ancient Chinaman. Plain-gowned and with an immensely long pigtail, Mr Cha lived in what appeared to be an artist's studio located above a small tea-house in a backstreet of Foochow. Cha bowed obsequiously.

'Cha Lee Foo belong Number-One Foochow painter,' Kemball continued in pidgin.

The little old man bobbed and grinned with pleasure and Hannah realised she was being introduced to the artist whose work had so fascinated her in the almost forgotten house in Islington.

'Paint in the western fashion, Missee,' the tiny man said, 'velly skilful, execute first-class, lady and gentleman portrait in oil-paint; Number-One Winsor and Newton, every ship come Foochow-side long-time.'

'I want him to paint your portrait, Hannah,' and before she could protest Kemball turned to Cha. 'You paint Missee Kemball, Cha. You do top-job, like all-same my ship. Savee?'

57

'I savee, Captain. Cha Lee Foo always do Number-One, first class proper job. This time more-beautiful from Missee,' he grinned goatishly at her.

'Twenty dollar.'

'Maybe . . . maybe . . .' Cha shook his head noncommittally.

'Twenty dollar.'

'Maybe portrait velly beautiful. Other Captain give me more dollar . . . you savee?'

Hannah looked at her father. Surely they did not know *all* about the occurrences at Shanghai here at Foochow? It was impossible!

'You do work for twenty-five dollar, or I'll kick you downstairs, you impudent rogue!' roared Kemball.

'Father!'

'Take no notice, Hannah. It's the only way to treat these villains or they'll have the shirt off your back. Believe me, John Chinaman only understands a good beating!' He rounded on Cha. 'Come on, chop-chop, no catchee monkey this fashion, too damn slow!'

The little man seemed unaffected by this intemperate outburst, but came across and pushed Hannah gently backwards. She felt the touch of his dry skin on her arms and complied until she was neatly posed in a large, ornate chair beside which a vast plant seemed to explode from a heavy brass pot.

'I'll be back shortly,' announced Kemball, 'I've more business to discuss with Lenqua. We'll dine at the club tonight.' And with that he left his daughter for her first sitting.

Such was Captain Kemball's preoccupation with preparing his ship for the loading of the tea, that he allowed Hannah to sleep ashore, joining her for dinner and remaining with her overnight in the shipmasters' clubhouse at Foochow. He had secured a chaperone in the person of Cha's woman, and saw her conducted to the artist's studio daily by Mr Talham.

Hannah suspected her father of appointing Talham to this duty as a punishment for her familiarity with Munro, and of working the Second Mate like a slave for his impudence. However, Hannah found the old proverb correct, and as she sat motionless for Mr Cha she grew fonder of Munro in his absence.

58

Beyond the shutters, open under the bamboo blinds that were rolled up during the day, were vignettes of the distant countryside; blue views of the Bohea hills where the tea grew. But they were so remote that Hannah had long since ceased to think what she saw was reality. Instead, they assumed in her imagination the character of pictures, charming but ethereal illusions wherein she and Munro wandered happily.

But these were dull and repetitive. Inevitably her mind slid from the romantic to the profane. She began to consider not Munro, but Richards as a lover. She had read explicit desire in his eyes, a sharp, demanding hunger different from Munro's worthy, conventional passion. Richards profoundly excited her and here, in Cha's studio, she sensed something of indulgence in both her presence and the atmosphere of the place. Her position as a stake in the wager only fuelled her imagination.

Deep in such dangerous thoughts she was heedless of the outside world on the afternoon of her second sitting when the whoop of a steam tug startled her to full consciousness.

'Missee please not move,' admonished Cha, his eyes swivelling from Hannah to the canvas and back in an hypnotic oscillation.

Silence again filled the room. The smell of linseed oil and turpentine mixed with the scent of joss hung heavily in the air. Insects droned soporifically somewhere beyond the opened windows. Even the *gecko*, the little fly-hunting house lizard, failed to rouse her, so long were his periods of watchful immobility. She sank back into a delicious lassitude.

Suddenly she was roused from this stupor by the pounding of boots on the rickety stairs and the abrupt appearance of Captain Richards in the doorway. His eyes gleamed with triumph.

'Get out!' he snarled at Cha, advancing into the room with his jade-headed cane raised, 'Get out!'

4

THE STILL, warm air, the buzzing flies and the strange erratic movements of the *gecko* combined with the wheezing presence of Mr Cha to induce a strange sensation of intimacy which had lulled Hannah into a mildly catatonic state. Her mind was filled with fantasies, disturbed by events in Shanghai, and mesmerised by natural curiosity.

The insidious insistence with which the Captain's image had replaced that of Munro seemed at the time a private matter; an innocent and harmless amusement at once pleasurable and painful with its reminder of ignorance. Now, however, he burst into the stifling room with a dark and thrilling aura of concupiscence.

Nor was Captain Richards's behaviour entirely motivated by his assumption of racial superiority over Cha. It had been a matter of only a few minutes' gossip to learn the hottest news of the Pagoda Anchorage, that Cracker Jack Kemball's daughter sat alone every day with Cha Lee Foo the artist. With characteristic impetuosity, Richard Richards was not the man to pass up such an opportunity when his ship had just arrived and he possessed the advantage of surprise; nor was he to remain unmoved by a more alarming consideration.

'Does that fool Kemball think the Chinks are emasculated?' he muttered to himself, tugging his beard impatiently while his sweating apprentices rowed him ashore. 'Would there be half a hundred million of them if they were? *Diawl*, had the old devil offered her any of his "sugar" coated sweetmeats? Didn't Kemball know that, just as some white men like fat women, some Chinese admired the extravagantly bulbous shapes of Western women? And Cha was a renowned goat! Everyone familiar with Foochow knew that!'

Intense anxiety and the exertion of assaulting the hill above the boat-landing culminated in his intemperate entry. Breathing hard, he raised his cane and snarled at Cha.

'Get out!'

'Sir!'

Hannah stood to meet him, an expression of outrage on her face. Sadly, it was not disinterested outrage that she felt on Cha's behalf. The truth was that, shocking though it seemed in its suspended violence, the intrusion profoundly thrilled her. But the quickness of her movement after so long a period of immobility caused a moment's dizziness. Her head spun and she sought to keep her balance. Moving a foot, she fell forward, off the dais upon which the chair stood. Her hand caught the pot stand, the bronze bowl reeled and crashed to the floor spilling earth and plant on a square of carpet. Captain Richards stepped forward and caught her.

Hannah's lapse was only momentary; she recovered almost at once, recoiling with an abruptness that indicated her own sudden realisation of her vulnerability. But it was long enough for Richard Richards to have his lust transmuted to a more permanent emotion, long enough for him to discover those intimate secrets about a woman that bind her to a man of his temperament. The scent of her hair, the sweetness of her breath, the line of her throat, the firmness of her body; all those impressions confirmed Richards in the rightness of his choice, a choice made the instant he had first seen her beside Mr Munro. And in the second before she thrust herself from him, Richards read, too, her own desire.

A less subtle man would have held her longer, mastered her as she made the first struggle of protest, perhaps tried to force a kiss upon her; but Richards did no such thing. He already knew all that propinquity could tell him.

There was a sudden gentleness in his release, a solicitude as he handed her back into her chair, that further confused Hannah. She felt herself flush.

'I am sorry if I startled you, Miss Kemball.'

The mellifluous voice caressed her with an outrageous intimacy. She began to curse her stupid weaknesses. The fire of embarrassment was accompanied by an inward melting such as she had not experienced since that day she had discovered her father with the maid. The recollection stiffened her sense of indignation, rousing memories of deception and injustice, restoring the proprieties and moral values of her mother. The relaxed softness of her mouth hardened.

'That was unspeakable, sir!'

She glared at Richards, gaining momentum as he lowered his eyes. She was aware for the first time that Cha had judiciously slipped from the room. 'Unspeakable . . . to threaten poor Mr Cha like that.'

He looked up then, with that sharp ferocity of vision that stopped seamen in their tracks.

'*Poor* Mr Cha, did you say?' he queried, his voice deep with incredulity, '*Poor* Mr Cha? Good God, girl, you do not know the danger to which you are exposed.'

He moved swiftly to one side, past the easel with its wet canvas, his gloved hand riffling among a pile of drawings on a low table until, Hannah noticed with a twinge of foreboding, his mouth flashed in a smile. He pulled out a dozen drawings and turned back to where she had reseated herself. One by one he placed them in her hands.

She was horrified. If she had any exact notion of the reproductive act it was one of bodies melting into conforming curves, the romantic desire brought to a fulfilment of perfect union. And although this concept had been modified in Shanghai to include a profane as well as a sacred desire, not even the tiny flower-girls, innocent as slaves upon a catasta, had seriously modified her image of coition.

But that at which she now looked seemed to be so shocking as to be unbelievable. Could human beings truthfully contort like this? Was such an engorgement physiologically natural? Was it pleasurable to be penetrated simultaneously? Most shocking were the expressions on the participants' faces; they seemed otherworldly, resembling nothing so much as the faces of angels.

'Cha draws them,' said Richards, his voice ominously husky and breaking what seemed an interminable silence. 'They do it there, on that couch . . .'

Hannah stared at the object of furniture. It looked so very mundane, yet the aura of licence in the room could have emanated from it. She felt an overwhelming desire to cry.

Instead she stood, scattering the drawings across the floor. Richards bent to pick them up, pausing over one and realising that he had gone too far. The face of the man, a Westerner, flung back in ecstasy, was all too familiar. He looked up at Hannah, admiring the way she fought to bring herself under control, then stood and turned to replace the drawings on the table.

'Mr Cha?' she called sharply as he turned away. 'Mr Cha!'

The old artist reappeared, casting a wary look at Richards. 'Missee?'

'Ask Captain Richards to leave . . .'

But when she turned round, Richards had already gone.

It was one of the idiosyncrasies of Cracker Jack that he took upon himself a responsibility that lay traditionally with the Chief Mate. On the all-important homeward passage, Captain Kemball was not prepared to delegate. Another Mate might have complained about this lack of trust, but not Enright. He and Kemball had an understanding: while Kemball enjoyed his courtesan in Shanghai, Enright was free to indulge himself ashore in Foochow. So it was that Kemball's energies were occupied with the *Erl King* and her cargo, and he expected his rival to be similarly engaged. He had no reason to suspect that, faced with a long passage spiced with a wager, Richard Richards would neglect his duties.

But while the *Erl King*'s Master, stripped to shirt-sleeves, personally supervised the stowage of the lead-lined chests of *bohea* tea as they came alongside in barges, Captain Richards quietly issued instructions to his officers, delegating to them in perfect confidence, and took himself ashore, aware that after Talham's daily return, Miss Kemball was alone with Cha the artist.

Hannah had absolutely no interest in the progress of the portrait. Her daily sojourn in the studio was accomplished out of weakness and a low-spirited acceptance of the inevitable, depressed further by the onset of her lunar interval. She was barely civil to her preoccupied father when they met at the club and retired early, sustained only by his progress reports and the knowledge that *Erl King*'s loading proceeded apace. Like the sea-creature she was fast becoming, Hannah wished only to leave, to be again on the vast wastes of the ocean, to leave forever the humiliation of China in the pursuit of victory. Neither she nor Cha alluded to the erotica, though the old artist must have noticed its disturbance. Hannah sat in dutiful silence, drank the tea and eased her aching muscles when Cha's woman periodically appeared and the old man rested from his painting. For five days this routine went on and Hannah, knowing nothing of the drying times of oil-paint, did not suspect that Cha was executing two portraits, the second for Captain Richards, who watched the entire proceedings from behind a bamboo screen.

Entirely ignorant of Captain Richards's concealed presence, Hannah was equally unaware that among the ships' companies assembled at the Pagoda Anchorage, it was common knowledge that she and Captain Richards enjoyed a daily assignation at Cha the painter's. This scandal formed the mainspring of gossip that season, though Cracker Jack, in the manner of all cuckolds, was unaware of it. As far as the ships' crews were concerned it added a rare and piquant spice to the news of the wager. *Erl King* and *Seawitch* had hoisted in the first chests of tea with formal simultaneity and the open secret was greeted with much glee, forming as it did a rich ground-bed for further side-bets. The exception to this general amusement was aboard *Erl King* where disbelief or a sense of desertion depended upon whether one believed the story or not. Since no one had actually seen the two together, a certain amount of doubt remained natural among those who knew Hannah. Talham, in particular, swore that the whole thing was a fabrication, trying to mollify Munro and glad that Enright was sunk in some stew and could not intervene. Not all were so generous. Among the hands disappointment prevailed. The brief spirit of romance Hannah's presence had kindled in their barren hearts had been ejected by cynicism. She was, after all, only a fickle jade; what better could one expect of a woman? They were all the same. Being seamen they retreated to the values experience taught them were to be relied upon. The result was that they worked like demons for Cracker Jack, Cracker Jack the deceived father, a hapless fool like themselves. A quiet determination seized them: they would, sure as hell-fire itself, show that Welsh bastard that philandering would profit him nothing.

65

Worst hit by this general misogyny was Munro. His depression was acute, for love had its inevitable knife in his belly. With speechless anger, Munro flung himself into the work of loading the ship with a fury that impressed his commander. He would make a damned good Mate, Kemball thought, weighing up the younger man with an expert eye. It would soon be time to ditch Enright.

It was mid-afternoon when Hannah, informed by Mr Cha that she need sit for him no longer, left the studio for the last time. Escorted by Cha's woman, her arrival at the shipmasters' club coincided with that of Captain Kemball. Kemball had never lingered on the veranda amid his cronies, having become too involved with loading his ship. Nor did he want to run into Richards with the race so close. Both he and Hannah had invariably dined in his room, but he usually arrived some time after her. This evening he explained his early arrival with the news that the ship was almost loaded, Lenqua had been summoned and a tug ordered.

'Get your traps packed, my dear. We'll go aboard this afternoon.'

Kemball looked round the bar which was empty, grinned, rubbed his hands together with satisfaction and added, 'What about the portrait?'

Hannah felt her spirits soar with the news. Almost light-headed with relief at escaping from Foochow, she could not have cared less about the portrait. 'I think it is finished,' she said.

'Picture finish, Captain.'

The high-pitched, sing-song voice of Mr Cha preceded the old Chinaman's appearance by a split-second. Neatly wrapped in palm-matting, the portrait had been dry for days. Now Cha carefully undid its cocoon and exposed the likeness. He held it before him, his button-bright eyes watching Kemball's reaction. Cracker Jack studied the portrait. It was a good likeness; he smiled approvingly.

'Very good, Cha. Number-One, first-class top-job.'

'Cha always do Number-One, first-class job, special for Captain.'

'Worth every one of twenty dollar I promise.'

'Father, you promised twenty-five!'

'Captain speak small-piece joke, Missee. Make old Cha angry.'

Kemball looked from his daughter to Cha, but Cha was his match, adding, 'Captain velly please he have beautiful portrait of beautiful daughter, he give Cha thirty dollar.'

The hand that emerged, palm upwards from the grubby sleeve of the paint-stained gown, was as small and wrinkled as a monkey's. Hannah recalled its first touch on her skin with a shudder. How could she have felt it as sensuous?

Kemball grinned again; he was in high good humour. He handed Cha thirty dollars.

'Belong good gentleman, Captain.' Cha bowed his way out, his hands dextrously counting the coins.

'Treated you well, did he? Looked after you all right?' Kemball's tone was unconcerned. A brief image of Cha's erotica flashed into Hannah's mind.

'Well enough, Father.'

'He's a clever artist,' declaimed Kemball, as though he knew what he talked about.

'I understand', said Hannah, feeling much better, 'he can execute a likeness of anything.'

'Yes, anything; clever old devil.'

'I noticed a degree of sophistication about his work,' she said relentlessly, seeking subtly to punish him for his neglect and her unhappiness.

'Sophistication? My word, yes . . .' Kemball called for another *samsu*.

'Have you posed for him yourself?'

'Yes, I told you, he painted the portrait at home, and the one of the ship.'

'What about you and the Chinese woman, Father?'

Kemball snorted his surprise into the *samsu*. He stared at Hannah open-mouthed.

'I saw some of Mr Cha's drawings, Father . . .'

'But I . . .' He flushed scarlet, bereft of words.

Hannah rose with a dignity she had not felt before. She sensed she at last had the upper hand.

'Come, it is time we returned to the ship. We have a race to win.'

The untidiness and confusion apparently reigning upon the *Erl King*'s decks struck Hannah the instant she climbed the accommodation ladder. Rope tackles she had not seen before hung from the yards and stays, piles of hatch-boards littered the waist, the white planking of the decks was defiled by black scuff marks and dark mucous gobbets of hawked spittle. What seemed a multitude of men milled about the deck and it was not until she reached the poop, turned and took stock of the prevailing bedlam that she was conscious of a degree of order.

Mr Munro was in charge. One moment she had caught a glimpse of him on the poop, then he had hurried forward and stood now on the forecastle with the Bosun and a handful of sailors. They, in turn, seemed to be gathering round the capstan, for a waving of heavy wooden bars resolved itself into the shipping of the capstan handles and the slack was taken on the anchor cable.

Over the bow she could see, too, the smoking top of a tug's funnel, belching black clouds from which a soft fall of soot descended on *Erl King*'s grubby decks to join the light dusting of tea already coating her paintwork.

The last chests of cargo were being hoisted over the side by the extra tackles she had noticed, and her sharply inquisitive mind was satisfied with identifying their purpose. Overside there was some shouting. A seaman ran to the midships bitts and threw the warp of the last junk free, and she watched it drift away on the river's current. About its mast three men tallied on to the halliards while aft a woman suckled a child, stirring a pot cooking over a charcoal stove, oblivious to the surrounding chaos.

Captain Kemball was bawling orders and Munro came aft to report the tug secured.

'Where the hell's Enright?' Kemball asked Munro.

'Haven't seen him, sir,' replied Munro, immediately attending to a sailor who had run up to ask him something about the log-line. Munro shot an accusing look at Hannah. She was at a loss to explain his hostility, unable to believe that her few days' absence from the ship could have affected him in this way.

In the waist the coolies climbed over the hatch coamings where they had been stowing the last of the tea. They were small, lean, wiry men, stripped to cotton shorts, their flat-muscled abdomens glossy with sweat. For a moment the coolies milled about the hatches, collecting from their foreman the tokens certifying their participation in the loading of the *Erl King*; later they would redeem them for cash. One of them looked aft and saw her, nudging a companion and pointing. Hannah did not know the notoriety she had unwittingly acquired in Foochow. She did not know that a nude drawing of her had mysteriously circulated among the drinking houses and opium dens of the poorer quarter. The coolies leered at her, impressed by her tall voluptuous figure.

She was rescued by the sudden order from the poop to 'Kick those damn coolies into a sampan and secure the bloody tug!'

Hannah watched the men file down the accommodation ladder, nudging one another and staring up at her as they went.

'Men no good.'

She turned. Beside her stood a small Chinese woman in a long, richly embroidered gown. Her oiled hair was drawn back from her face and decorated with tortoise-shell combs and a nameless flower. She had the small mouth of conventional Chinese beauty, though Hannah was aware that the cunning application of carmine had terminated its corners a little sooner than nature. Despite this artifice, Hannah was as uncertain of her age as to whether the strange woman spoke of all men, or more specifically.

'Me belong Lenqua's concubine,' she spoke the words with schooled enunciation. 'Me call Mai Lee.'

Hannah recognised the woman who had served tea and *samsu* at the comprador's. She smiled. 'Welcome to the *Erl King*.'

'So . . . so . . .' The tiny woman bobbed and then, as Lenqua approached and spoke sharply to her, she turned away. This odd discourtesy on the part of Lenqua seemed at variance with his former manners, particularly as he himself abruptly followed Mai Lee below. A moment later the reason became clear. Lenqua had seen what was approaching in a patiently sculled sampan, and wished his mistress not to.

A ragged coolie-woman worked the long *yuloh* at the rocking sampan's stern. At her feet, lolling in the abandonment of total drunkenness, lay Mr Enright.

'Father, Father, the Mate . . .' she pointed as Captain Kemball turned. 'He looks very drunk,' she said.

69

'Damn the man,' said Kemball, though with less vehemence than Hannah had expected. Kemball spun round.

'Third Mate!'

'Sir?' Talham, helping to ship hatch-boards amidships, looked aft.

'Prepare to get the Mate aboard!'

It was obvious to Hannah that there was nothing unusual in hoisting Enright out of a sampan by means of a rope strop. Using the same gear by which the tea had come aboard he was suspended from the main yardarm, a rope around his barrel chest, his legs swinging free, waving a bottle and kicking as he roared out a last defiant farewell to the distant town. Amidships, tailing on to the stay tackle ready to haul their chief officer inboard over the ship's rail, the seamen could barely conceal their amusement.

'Veer yard tackle, heave stay tackle,' roared Talham to make himself heard above Enright's insane bawling.

'Avast that!' Hannah almost jumped at the sudden volume of her father's imperious cry. The seamen relaxed their effort and Enright jerked, suspended between wind and water, still singing his obscene song whose words were mercifully incomprehensible to Hannah.

'Mr Enright!' Hannah realised it was the third time her father had roared the Mate's name and this time it coaxed reaction from Enright's fuddled brain.

'Ahhhh,' Enright shouted, a stupid grin spreading over his face as he stared down at the *Erl King*'s deck, 'Captain Kemball . . . it's a pleasure to see you again . . . permission to board your fine . . . ship . . .'

'Get rid of that bottle.'

'What bottle . . . are you suggesting that I'm . . .'

'Get rid of that bottle!'

Enright held up the bottle, peered into it and seeing it was not yet empty put it to his lips, making a great show of his defiance.

For a moment Kemball watched him. Then he spoke in a quieter voice, a voice almost weary with resignation. 'Now, Mr Talham . . .'

'Aye, aye, sir.' There was, Hannah noted, a matching weariness in Talham's acknowledgement and the seamen needed no further instructions. The tension they were maintaining on the rope suddenly eased, the rope went slack and Enright dropped like a stone into the Min River.

'Missee . . . Missee . . .'

Hannah looked away from the ludicrous figure of the Mate splashing feebly in the strong current. The sampan woman sculled below her, one hand held out for payment. Then her father was beside her, tossing the poor creature a coin that flashed gold in the sunshine. Adeptly the woman caught it, bit it and, grinning her satisfaction, turned the sampan aside.

With equal calm Hannah's father returned to the break of the poop.

'Hoist away, Mr Talham.'

Enright, subdued and dripping, was plucked from the flood. Half-way to the yard arm his body convulsed. A stream of yellow vomit was borne away by the wind.

'Forrard there! Heave away!'

'Heave away,' came Munro's response, followed by the news, 'Tug's fast, sir!'

A first, quavering note of the shanty rose from the forecastle, the capstan turned and *Erl King* drew up to her anchor as the dripping cable came inboard. Half a mile away Hannah caught the flash of sunlight on brass and saw the figure of Captain Richard Richards with his long glass to his eye. Was he looking at her, or at the departing *Erl King*?

'She's aweigh, sir!' Munro's voice called loud and triumphant. There was not even the slightest sign of a tug anywhere near the *Seawitch*, and half a dozen junks still lay alongside her waist. Hannah sensed a prickling of delight at the thought of the start *Erl King* had stolen on her rival.

Clouds of black smoke belched from the tug's funnel as her engineer responded to the faint jingling of her telegraph. White water ran down past the *Erl King*'s side, evidence of the churning paddles that drew the ship in a tight circle and headed down river. They were off, homeward bound with a full cargo of China tea!

Amidships, forgotten, wretched in the extremity of his depravity, Enright lay slumped. Even Hannah had taken no notice of him, so exciting had the moment of departure seemed. But as *Erl King* steadied on her seaward course astern of the tug

71

Cyclone, her father came forward from the wheel and, placing both hands upon the poop rail, looked down at the waist of his ship. Forward, on the forecastle, Munro's party had hooks and tackles over the side, fishing for the anchor, to heave it up and secure it alongside the cat-head. Clear of the river they would unshackle the cable, stow it below and plug the hawse-holes. For the time being they were occupied, for the tug's wash turned the anchor and made the ring awkward to catch with the cat-tackle.

'Look at that animal, God damn him!' Kemball muttered, forgetting the proximity of his daughter, 'I'll soon wash my hands of you . . .'

'Is . . . is he all right, Father?'

'Eh? Oh . . . yes, he's all right . . . he'll sleep it off . . .' Kemball turned aside, put his head down the companionway and called something below. A few minutes later Hannah saw the cook and steward emerge and half-carry, half-drag Enright into the privacy of his cabin. As they lugged the big man past her she caught the sharp whiff of spew and alcohol.

Gone below she spared no further thought for the man, there was too much to see. On the forecastle the anchor was swung inboard and lowered. Munro and the Bosun were sending men aft to man the wash-deck pump. The carpenter was securing *Erl King*'s narrow hatches, stretching the tarpaulins and fastening them with bars and wedges which he tamped home with his maul. A hose snaked across the deck, stiffened and then, in the hands of the Bosun, began driving its jet so that the tea stains and spittle of Foochow were washed from *Erl King*'s deck.

They were approaching the gorge now, making much faster speed than the slow, upstream slog of their arrival. The land on either side of the ship seemed to whirl past; the villages and the joss-houses, and then the rearing crags with the stunted pines and the umbral chill of the gorge. The Min ran deep and fast, serpentine and lively as it poured through the Narrows. Hannah felt something of her father's anxiety as he stood close beside the helmsman, giving the occasional order to keep the ship, jibbing in the current, in line with the tug.

From time to time acrid smoke from the *Cyclone* blew down over the *Erl King*, provoking bouts of coughing and laying black cinders about the clipper's decks. Then they emerged from the

72

gorge and the eddying down-draughts ceased. The land fell back on either side and ahead could be seen the silver glint of the distant ocean. Passing the islands the river spread wide and they were swept out on its grey surface which swirled with the eddies of its debouchment into the China Sea.

With the wind now true, Captain Kemball ordered the topsails set and the order to clew-down was given. Men raced aloft to cast off gaskets and station themselves in the tops to see the ropes ran clear. With their lower corners secured the yard-halliards were manned.

'Hoist away!'

Hannah was caught in the strange magic of departure and found herself humming to the crude words of the shanty.

'Once I loved a Baltimore girl, for love she had a notion.'

And at the third verse she was singing the chorus, her body all but responding to its urge to heave:

'Away, haul away; we'll haul away for Rosy!

She rose and fell as reg'lar as the waves upon the ocean!

Away, haul away, we'll haul away for Rosy-O!'

Forward a rasp of hanks and a white flutter marked the ascent of the fore-topmast staysail up the forestay.

'Steady now,' Kemball's voice was low, marked by concentration as *Erl King* no longer followed tamely in the *Cyclone's* wake. 'Steer east by south.'

'East b'south, sir . . . east b'south it is.'

They began to overrun the tug.

'Leggo the tow!'

There was a note of joy in Kemball's voice now. *Erl King* leaned to the breeze and the sibilant, familiar hiss of the sea seething past her gleaming sides seemed all the more welcome for the weeks of anchored idleness. Hannah too was seized by a mood of fierce joy and knew in an intuitive moment why, cut free of the trammels of the land, sailors could dismiss their aberrations there as belonging to other men.

'Gone and clear forrard!'

With a splash the spliced eye of the tow-line dropped from *Erl King's* bitts and they cast off the *Cyclone*. The tug turned in a welter of water thrown up by one reversed paddle, bucking and pitching in the sea-waves while *Erl King* gathered speed, lifting with the graceful majesty of the pelagic traveller. On the strip of

73

bridge between the *Cyclone's* paddle-boxes a tall thin man raised a stove-pipe hat in farewell, and Cracker Jack responded with a lordly wave of his own gilt-peaked cap. Replacing the cap, Cracker Jack checked the time on his gold hunter, ordered an apprentice to note it in the log and went forward with his speaking trumpet.

'Forty guineas that tow cost me,' he said conversationally to his daughter in passing, 'forty guineas and worth every penny.'

It was his last confidence. From that moment and for the next hour he gave every fibre of his being to his ship. Within minutes of casting loose the tug, the *Erl King* had set all plain sail. Within half an hour she was covered in canvas, her skysails hoisted, her studding sails drawing from their flexing booms and a Jimmie Green tucked beneath her long bowsprit.

The curses of the shore were astern of her; now she was a thing of the open ocean, and it would not have mattered if she had had coal or railway lines below her hatches. All that mattered now was speed. Looking astern the coast of China was already blue, the Min gorge hidden by distance. It was odd, she thought, that somewhere beyond that line of hills Captain Richard Richards was hastening to follow.

Mr Munro came aft and made some report to her father. Hannah avoided his eyes. She looked astern again, half-expecting the white sails of the *Seawitch* to emerge between the islands.

'No sign of pursuit, sir,' remarked Munro.

'No . . .' Cracker Jack Kemball looked at his young Second Mate and smiled. 'Let's hope the next time we see the *Seawitch* we're alongside in the West India Docks.'

The fo'c's'le bell struck once and both men swung round, staring out over the starboard bow. 'Sail ho!' sang out the lookout at the knightheads, waving an outstretched arm.

'Jackass barque, sir,' said Munro, and Hannah could see an ungainly configuration of sails white against a darker smudge.

'Damned steamer!' snapped her father, reaching for the long watch-glass nested just inside the after companionway and levelling it skilfully on the horizon. 'Hoist our numbers,' he ordered, without lowering the heavy telescope.

Talham shouted at the apprentices and they ran aft, selecting the four-flag signal that a few moments later supplemented the

74

ensign at the spanker peak and identified the *Erl King* from every other merchant ship in the world.

The stranger was coming up fast from the south, a big ship with a belching funnel of red and black situated abaft her mainmast.

'That's no coasting steam-pot of Jardine's or Swire's,' said Captain Kemball, 'd'you think . . .?'

His voice trailed off. He could not face the thought.

'She's hoisting her own number, sir . . . G . . . B . . . J . . . K . . . GBJK . . .'

They turned expectantly to Talham who fought to turn the pages of the code book in the breeze. The Third Mate shook his head.

'Not here, sir . . . must be a new ship . . .'

'Look in the supplement . . .'

'Sorry, sir . . . nothing . . .'

Kemball turned his attention to his glass again. 'She's signalling . . .' More flags were run up. There was no name, but she gave her passage details.

'Fifty-three days from Capetown,' translated Talham.

'Fifty-three,' Kemball was almost laughing, 'Fifty-three! Good heavens we did better than that in the old *Drummore*!'

'I can read her name, sir . . . the *Glencarron*.'

But Captain Kemball was not listening. He was still full of the euphoria of relief. 'For a moment,' he muttered, half to himself, 'I thought the damned French had dug their confounded canal!'

5

'YOU see, my dear, at this season of the year, we are opposed to the prevailing monsoon.'

Hannah leaned against the heel of the ship and stared down at the chart spread before them. Her father traced their intended track with the needle-point of the brass dividers.

'We shall have to beat our way down the South China Sea, so . . . across to Cochin China, then down to the Borneo coast, near Tanjong Api . . . then I shall have to decide whether to slip through the Gaspar Strait, or go the longer route . . .'

Kemball waved the dividers airily to the eastward, imparting the impression that he had not the slightest intention of doing anything of the kind. 'Once through the Sunda Strait, then the Indian Ocean is ours.'

The phrase rang in Hannah's ears: 'The Indian Ocean is ours.'

It was so lordly, so imperial and so apt for such a ship as she now knew the *Erl King* to be. Beyond the narrow strait between Java and Sumatra, barred by the volcanic island of Krakatoa, the Indian Ocean stretched limitless beyond the margin of the chart.

'You will not see much of me from now on, I'm afraid . . . you won't mind, will you?'

Hannah looked at her father, sensing a shift in his feelings towards her. She thought perhaps he regretted the clumsy incident in Shanghai, and realised the extent of his neglect in Foochow, that he was sorry for his preoccupation with the ship. But his next remark disillusioned her. His solicitude proved mere off-hand courtesy.

'It's more than the wager,' he said, picking up his cap, 'from now on all my attention will be devoted to the ship.'

Hannah bit her lip. She had been about to say 'I thought it already was,' but her father had moved to the companionway door.

'You can shift into my cabin,' he called, and was gone with a clumping of boots on the wooden steps.

Hannah looked down at the chart. The hachured coastline with its hills and walled villages, its conventional signs and lines of soundings, marked the track of the Royal Navy's survey ships. Her finger traced the intended track of the *Erl King* to the bottleneck of the Sunda Strait. She was sailor enough now to know they could not take the line a crow or a seagull might fly, but must tack west, then south against the monsoon blowing up from the south-west. Across the chart the light flooded in through the skylight and she looked up at the curve of the spanker and the sharply braced mizen topsails. For a few moments she felt her father's abandonment, not so much as a desertion but as a sense of her own uselessness. She was here because she was a dependant, a chattel and an encumbrance; to be tolerated, used as she had been in Shanghai as a source of amusement, but not to get in the way. Yes, that was the root of her father's disinterest: she must not get in the way.

'You're not feeling queasy are you, Miss Kemball?'

Munro's tone irritated her, confusing her feeling of guilt towards him and stinging her to a sharp reply.

'For God's sake stop calling me Miss Kemball as if . . .'

'I'm sorry.' Munro's burr had an edge of hostility in it. 'Did you enjoy your stay in Foochow?' he asked coldly, adding, 'They tell me you found Captain Richards's company amusing.'

'What else did they tell you, Mr Munro?' she flashed back at him, straightening up and glaring defiantly.

'That he enjoyed your company daily,' he muttered.

'*What?*' She was genuinely shocked. 'Was that what you heard?' He nodded. 'And you believed it? You believed I had some sort of a tryst with Captain Richards every day? What kind of a woman d'you think I am, one of those painted things you had aboard in Shanghai?'

'I did no such thing . . .' Reciprocal indignation flared in Munro.

''Scuse me, sir.'

Osman pushed through from the pantry, wanting to raise the table-fiddles and lay up the saloon for dinner. But more than the table lay between Hannah and Munro. Munro turned away.

'Please Miss Kemball . . .' Osman nodded at the spread chart, 'would you put it in the chartroom?'

She looked at the scrawny man before her dressed in a grubby vest. His impudence infuriated her. Even this scruffy specimen was ordering her about now! She ignored the steward and turned aft, into her father's cabin, and shut the door behind her. Let him take the chart up.

Dinner was no longer the convivial meal it had been on the outward passage. The officers came and went with a purposeful speed, almost bolting their food as they made for the deck or their bunks. Even Enright affected to ignore her and it took Hannah some time to realise this attitude had nothing to do with her, but was a consequence of their desire to keep the ship sailing as fast as possible. As for Captain Kemball, he remained on deck where a canvas hammock-chair had been rigged up. Here he dozed as he kept an ever-watchful eye upon his charge. For Cracker Jack there were no watches below, only a long vigil punctuated by cigars brought for him from the humidor in the saloon by the apprentices.

As she had sensed once before as they entered the Min River, the mood about the deck was almost tangible; a tautening of expression, a fussing over trifles that possessed a new intensity. There was an acute awareness that the helmsman's task was paramount; and that the officer of the watch was ceaselessly vigilant, mindful of the ship and her gear, the wind and the state of the sea, and of Cracker Jack himself.

But on the second morning out of Foochow Hannah woke to find the *Erl King* no longer heeling over, her ears no longer filled with the sound of water rushing past the hurrying hull. Instead the tall ship rolled awkwardly and from aloft came the slatting of slack canvas and banging of blocks. She dressed and went on deck. Cracker Jack's affirmations of *Erl King*'s ability to ghost through a calm were more than justified. Despite the flap of barely filled sails, the ripple of a wake stole past her side, but the low swell of a distant storm upset more than the equilibrium of the ship.

'Damnation,' her father muttered as he paced up and down. 'I don't recall a calm hereabouts in this season before . . .'

He grunted a 'good-morning' at his daughter.

'A calm, Miss Kemball, and a low mist with it,' said Enright, who had the watch.

'But we still make some progress, don't we?'

'Yes . . . the log . . .' and he gave her a long, steady stare, 'gives us two or three knots. But aloft', the Chief Mate jerked his head in the direction of the main truck, 'we're chafing everything away.'

'It's this damned swell,' snarled her father.

Hannah watched the faint ripples on the surface of the sea flutter and die as tiny breaths of wind ruffled it, but beneath these minimal disturbances, the low undulations of swells, the residue of large waves hundreds of miles away, passed under the *Erl King*'s hull with the regularity of pendular motion. They seemed to gather on the edge of visibility, suddenly appearing mysteriously out of the mist as though their manifestation was being performed by some spirit antipathetic to the *Erl King*. The thought made her shudder. And then she heard something, something so eerie, that the thought suddenly seemed but a prelude to reality.

'What's that?'

The lugubrious note, low and vibrant, sounded from somewhere to starboard, born on the first puffs of a breeze.

'Eh? Oh that, that's only fishing junks.' Kemball, preoccupied, was curtly dismissive.

'They blow fog signals to each other, Miss Kemball,' explained Enright, 'on conch shells.'

'Oh . . .' Her feeling of gathering evils was swept away by rational explanation.

'Here's the breeze . . . steady your helm there!' exclaimed her father, suddenly animated, and the mist lifted, revealing the bat-wing sails of two junks a quarter of a mile to windward, bearing down on them.

For perhaps five minutes the sails filled, the *Erl King* leaned a little and gathered way. Instantly the mood about the deck lightened, the watch ran to trim the braces at Enright's shouted order and only Hannah saw the junks alter course, maintaining their convergence with the clipper.

80

Then the wind died, leaving them ghosting again, barely moving as her father gave vent to his spleen.

'God damn and blast it!'

'Father, those junks . . .'

'She's not steering, sir!' The helmsman's cry drowned Hannah's anxiety.

'What the hell d'you mean, she's not steering?' roared Kemball. The *Erl King* always steered, even in a calm. Everyone knew that!

'She's coming back, sir!' Enright bellowed a warning and explanation in the same sentence. From leeward, where the mist still hung, the breeze had backed and now came at them with a steadiness of purpose. *Erl King*'s lofty sails had felt it before their own senses.

'Braces there!'

'Let her pay off, damn you!' Enright and Kemball shouted frantically, trying to keep way on the clipper whose fine hull would drive backwards if she were allowed to gather stern-way.

'Headsail sheets there! Back 'em to port!'

'Aye, aye!' Cries of acknowledgement were drowned in a sudden roar. Hannah felt the hot wave of an explosion tug at her, spinning her round and throwing her aside. She heard herself screaming with shock through a sudden, temporary deafness. Enright's face, contorted with something between rage and fear, went grimacing past her field of vision. With a sickening jolt she crashed into the mizen fife-rails and clung wildly to the lines that ran vertically aloft from the hardwood belaying pins. Looking round her she saw the loom of the nearer junk's sail, felt the lurch as it ran alongside and then, as in one of her feverish nightmares, the snarling faces of twenty or thirty Chinese swarmed over the *Erl King*'s teak taffrail. She seemed to confront them defenceless and quite alone as her hearing returned with their horrible yells.

From somewhere below her came a command, drowned in the roar of a second explosion. 'Fire!'

The sound jerked her out of her shock. She could cling supinely to the ropes, her legs giving way beneath her in surrender, or save herself. A dash to the companionway and she could go below. She took a deep breath.

A third roar coincided with several things happening at once.

As Hannah moved towards the door of the companionway Munro emerged. Catching sight of her he called her name.

'Hannah! Go below!' She felt him thrust her aside, one hand wielding a knife. There was a dull gleam of steel and a China-man jerked backwards. Munro darted forward and, as she stepped into the shelter of the companionway, her father and Enright at the head of a gang of seamen were pouring over the raised centre of the poop, jumping the saloon skylight, yelling savagely and brandishing extempore weapons, knives, capstan bars, belaying pins, as they rallied against the pirates.

'Fire!'

Another explosion followed, and this time Hannah, sheltered in the companionway opening, was rooted to the spot by curiosity. Beyond the break of the poop the brass cannon mounted behind a washport fired into the junk. An Astbury's patent breech-loader, it was quickly recharged once ammunition had been brought to it.

Cheering began to break out and Hannah saw the shape of the junk's sail alter as it sheered off. Beyond it, its partner also turned away. On the poop the *Erl King*'s company were shouting abuse and cheering at their defeated foe. So quickly had things happened that men were still running aft, laggards from the watch below only now reaching the deck, buttoning trousers and cinching belts.

Gingerly Hannah stepped over the sea-step and back on deck. Her eye was caught by the dark stain of blood on the teak planking and its brighter spots on the white paintwork.

'All right there . . . belay that nonsense!' Kemball reasserted his authority. The fuss was over, there was a race to win. The men turned forward and Kemball leapt up on the saloon top to cast an eye aloft. It seemed to Hannah, as she adjusted herself to the knowledge that the bloody, murderous little encounter had lasted but a few minutes, that old Molloy had remained immobile at the wheel for its entire passing.

'Can you steer her? How's your head?'

But Captain Kemball never heard the answers to his queries. As Molloy studied the compass bowl before him and Kemball looked impatiently aloft, only Hannah saw the blue-white mushroom of smoke that marked the pirates' Parthian shot.

Cracker Jack Kemball crashed from his vantage point, spun

round by the impact of the jingal ball that struck him above the heart, to fall full-length at his daughter's feet, striking his temple on the ring-bolt in the deck.

Horrified, Hannah watched the last, shuddering exhalation of her father's life.

'Man that is born of woman hath but a short time to live,' intoned Enright. Grief and shock played a part amid the turmoil of Hannah's thoughts as she stood weeping at the rail a few feet from Astbury's patent cannon whose assiduously polished muzzle now bore the blueing of explosive gases. And yet, through her tears, she sensed the incongruous in Enright reading those majestic words out of her father's own Book of Common Prayer.

'He goeth up like a fore-topmast staysail . . . and cometh down like a flying jib . . .'

She looked up, sensing mockery. But all heads were bowed and over Enright's shoulder she saw the thin, pedantic scrawl of her father's handwriting. This was a sea-funeral, read by a seaman on the deck of a ship, and it was appropriate that it was in the vernacular.

'Therefore we commit his body to the deep.' Enright paused and nodded. The Bosun and an able seaman lifted the platform upon which, under the fluttering bunting of the red ensign, Captain John Kemball's mortal remains lay shrouded in a spare skysail, weighted with pigs of ballast lashed to his feet and (though Hannah did not know this), the last stitch of his winding sheet passed through his nose as tradition demanded.

'We commit his body to the deep,' Enright repeated and the platform was angled steeper. Hannah felt a hand touch her arm and looked round. The rosebud mouth of Mai Lee looked up at her.

'Missee . . .' it whispered. Hannah smiled bravely back. There was a sigh from the gathering of men. They turned their caps awkwardly and Hannah heard the mumbled comment, 'He doesn't wanna go . . .'

And then the hummocked red ensign subsided upon the planks. There was a faint splash and Cracker Jack was gone.

The finality of the moment hit Hannah with an almost physical violence and she felt herself wracked once again with irresistible sobs. Enright was rushing the last words of the prayer, leading a now restless crew in a pathetically mis-muttered version of the Lord's prayer that was itself shattered by the staccato splutter of exploding fire-crackers. Above them, at the break of the poop, Lenqua held a bamboo wand from which the highly unstable balls of mercury fulminate dropped, driving off the devils which might be hovering over his friend's last resting place.

'Get forrard,' Enright was growling, 'main braces there!'

They swung the yards on the main mast, refilling the tem-porarily backed sails, backed to check *Erl King*'s way while the last respects were paid to her Master. The clipper leaned again to the wind, braced sharp up, the spray whipping away to leeward from her bow as her racing cutwater dipped and rose and dipped again, wetting the figurehead's fancy boots long before Cracker Jack's corpse hit the coral heads, spun slowly, then gently subsided with a stir of sand until the sea should give up its dead.

'Miss Kemball . . .'

The knock came again at the cabin door and Hannah woke to full consciousness. It was late afternoon and she had fallen asleep after the funeral. She felt dreadful, her clothes twisted about her body, her hair in disorder. But she had shaken off the worst ravages of grief and, swinging her legs over the leeboard of the bunk, she tucked her hair up.

'Come in.'

It was Osman, the officers' steward, respectable in his white jacket and wringing his hands with obvious anxiety.

'Beg pardon, Miss, I, er . . .'

'It's all right, Osman, thank you . . . I'm quite all right now . . .' She managed a wan smile, taking his awkwardness for a condolent ineptitude.

'It's . . . er, Captain Enright, Miss Kemball . . . he, er, wants the cabin. I've been told to move you back into the one you had before.'

It came out with such a rush that Hannah took a moment to grasp the significance of what Osman was saying. She had no real objection to reverting to the small cabin she had inhabited until their departure from Foochow, but it was Osman's shift in Enright's status that finally jerked Hannah back to the present.

'*Captain* Enright?'

'Well, yes, Miss . . . he's in command now . . .' Osman's Adam's apple bobbed uncomfortably up and down.

'Very well. Leave me for half an hour then come back and I'll be ready to move . . .'

She needed time to think, to digest the import of what Osman had said, for, setting apart the wager, the details of which had shrivelled in her consideration to puerile irrelevancies, the accession of Enright to command of the *Erl King* altered a great deal more than her own status on board. For a moment she experienced a sensation of pure, unreasoning panic. She was alone, quite alone in the world, aboard a ship in the South China Sea with a drunken and lecherous man who knew no moral scruples and whose only temperamental rein had been severed by her father's death.

She steadied herself with a glass of brandy from her father's unlocked tantalus. The spirit soothed her, fired her resolve, and the tiny practical desire to find the key to the tantalus so that she might lock it, set her mind to more pragmatic considerations.

'If ever anything happens to me,' she heard her father saying to her, 'sack Enright.'

She must not leave the tantalus to Enright, and there were other things, personal things, that she would not leave to be rummaged through by the detestable man. Galvanised into sudden activity she began a systematic looting of her father's effects, binding them up in his bed sheets. At the end of half an hour, she ordered Osman to transfer the odd-shaped bundles to her own cabin. She made no attempt to eat in the saloon and the officers left her to her grief. Behind her locked door, opened only to Osman who brought her soup and fresh baked bread from the galley at sunset, Hannah Kemball discovered her father's legacy.

It was a curious antidote to grief. An anodyne in which she discovered more of the innermost thoughts of her father than is given to most children.

Sometime in the small hours of the following morning she completed her survey. She sat and contemplated her father's belongings, bending forward from time to time to put an article on one or other of three piles. On her left were odds and ends of paper, old clothes, his razor and toilet case. In the centre a selection of his newer garments, garments that she thought she should keep, his greatcoat, for instance, his cap, reefer jacket and some sea-boot stockings. On her bunk lay a small pile of papers, a few leather-bound volumes and a revolver. Fifty rounds of ammunition gleamed dully in the light of the oil lamp that swung in its gimbals from the bulkhead.

She tied up the unwanted clothes in a sheet and put them by the cabin door. Her father's best clothes she hung in her own locker, squeezing them in beside her dresses, fighting back the desire to submit to tears as she smelled the odour of his cigars pungent in the heavy melton coat and the doeskin of the reefers. Then, pouring herself another glass of brandy before locking the tantalus, she sat and took up a pen, dipping it in the inkwell of a handsome writing-case that she recalled her mother buying her father for a present years earlier. Very slowly she drew a folded document towards her. It was of waxed linen and bore the heavy crowned motif of the Board of Trade. The ink of its details was fading, but her father's hand of but a few days earlier was clear, amending the details of the *Erl King*'s owner-ship: of the sixty-four shares allowed to British tonnage all had reverted to Captain John Kemball, Master, even those mort-gaged to Lenqua, ship's factor at Foochow.

Except, of course, those already owned by Hannah.

She turned the document over. On the reverse of the Certi-ficate of Registry were two names. The first was that of *Erl King*'s original ill-fated Master, the second, that of her father.

Below it Hannah carefully wrote in her own.

'Now you may do your worst, *Captain* Enright,' she said, and raised her glass symbolically to the portrait done by Mr Cha that rested on the cabin settee and showed the face of a girl who no longer existed.

Either the brandy or the turmoil of her thoughts, or a combi-nation of both, drove Hannah on deck, for she could not sleep during what remained of the night.

The steady south-westerly breeze was warm. Braced sharp up on the port tack, the weather luffs of her deep single topgallant sails steadied by their bowlines, *Erl King* raced to the westward, stretching out towards the distant coast of Cochin China somewhere over the rim of the world in the darkness ahead. Above the deck the tall columns of sails glowed in the night, and the mast-trucks moved serenely against the alternating backcloth of cloud and stars. The faint creak of the ship's fabric, the working of a rope, the occasional cough or snatch of song from the watch, seemed only to emphasise a kind of awed silence from the score of men whose duty kept them from their beds. And overside rushed the endless music of the sea, the hiss and slap of waves and wake, throwing their eerie light up on to the lower courses and the passaree that dipped beneath the forward studding sail boom as the phosphorescence boiled aside from either bow of the ship.

She seemed, this magnificent creation of man's ingenuity, truly to possess some magical quality, embracing the power of the wind in contrast with the roaring, stinking iron-clad implacability of a steam locomotive. Hannah knew why the ship had been called *Erl King*, and why her father had loved her beyond the simple affection of a man for his trade. And with that thought came another, something that had been started down below with her signing of the Certificate of Registry. *She* had been handed the command; now, at this moment as she stepped out on the deck and felt the breeze and the response of the ship to its energy; it was her father's last farewell.

'Hannah?'

Munro loomed out of the night and leaned on the rail beside her. She half-turned, seeking the dark shape of her father's canvas chair.

'Enright doesn't keep the deck like Cracker Jack, Hannah . . .'

She felt the touch of his fingers tentatively upon her arm.

'Has he a mind to keep on with the race, Mr Munro?'

He withdrew his touch. 'Aye, I think so . . . Miss Kemball.'

She turned her face, yearning to kiss him, but the parameters of their formality had been set. By her. She could see his face faintly in the intermittent glow of the phosphorescence.

'Mr Munro . . . I need your help . . .'

She sensed him stiffen. 'Aye?'

'Enright is not to command . . . I presume he has taken it upon himself to do so?'

'Why, yes . . . but . . .'

'I am sole owner of the ship, Mr Munro . . . *sole* owner . . .'

'But Miss Kemball . . .' Munro's tone was apprehensive and Hannah saw his predicament.

'Forgive me,' she said, 'but I don't mean you to take charge, that would place an intolerable burden upon you, faced continually with the back-stabbing of Enright; no, I intend you all to remain in your present ranks . . .'

'But somebody must assume . . .'

'I know. And I know you all to be men of ability, otherwise my father would not have had you tread this deck, men who are more than capable of carrying out your duties to my father's satisfaction. So I am taking command of the ship, Mr Munro, and that is why I need *your* help and your loyal support – if only for my father's sake.'

Munro no longer lounged upon the rail. Hannah remained leaning upon her elbows, watching the seething water rush past and the welter of the bow waves resolve themselves into the smooth grey line of wake that vanished into the darkness astern.

Munro walked aft, considering the bizarre proposition. He was no fool. Something had fuelled that slanderous gossip in Foochow. Whatever it was it had drawn a toughness out of Hannah that he had suspected lay in her the moment she threw the log-line to the begging coolie-woman in Shanghai. It was not to be wondered at, perhaps; she was, after all, Cracker Jack's daughter, and she would have her work cut out to keep Enright in order. The thought brought him to the helm. He grunted at the helmsman and turned forward again. Faced with a choice between Hannah and Enright, Munro's sympathies lay with the girl. And she had asked him for help . . .

She could exercise no more than a temporary command without interference from the Board of Trade. The *Erl King*'s next Master would be the choice of the owner, ironically Hannah herself. She could scarcely fail to be aware of her father's opinion of Enright. Not even Hannah would make the mistake of appointing him! Munro's loyalty might therefore pay a better long-term dividend than he could have expected.

And yet he needed to know how she really felt about him after the agonies of Foochow. He leaned beside her again.

'Miss Kemball, I shall do as you ask, not for your father's sake, but for the afternoon we might have spent in Shanghai.'

She turned her head towards him. 'I suppose we all wish the clock could be turned back sometimes, Mr Munro. For myself one such occasion occurred yesterday morning; another would be that afternoon in Shanghai.'

'Miss Kemball,' he began again with an awkward formality, 'I am oppressed by the thought that you do not understand how I feel . . .'

'Please stop. I think I do understand. But it is not appropriate . . .'

'So the matter rests there between us?'

'Yes.'

'Very well . . . Ma'am.'

She turned away for the companionway, not knowing whether Munro's proper manner was ironic or genuine. She paused, one foot on the sea-step.

'Mr Munro?'

'Ma'am?'

'Please tell Mr Enright of my decision when you call him for the morning watch.'

6

ENRIGHT.
Hannah spent the rest of the night sitting in her cabin, dozing intermittently, her thoughts brooding upon Enright and his likely reaction to her assumption of command. These were interspersed with semi-conscious images of her father and his admonition:

'If anything happens to me, sack Enright . . .'

With her father's death that passing remark seemed invested with the power of prophecy, yet the past months gave her little cause for comfort. She recalled Enright in the aftermath of the alleged fracas with the rebellious seaman. Enright breaking the points of the seamen's knives, Enright at the break of the poop threatening 'belaying pin soup' to a second unwilling sailor, Enright selecting the twin flower-girls and Enright ducked from the yard-arm . . .

She heard the clump of steps on the companionway as one bell rang overhead and was answered by the lookout on the fo'c's'le. It was one of the apprentices sent down by Mr Munro to turn Enright out of his bunk for the morning watch.

Hannah was fully awake, her heart pounding. Soon Enright would be informed of her action, but she heard nothing more, not even after eight bells had signalled four in the morning and the change of watch. Above her, on the poop, Munro would be deciding what to do. But surely, faced with the news that she, Hannah Kemball, had ordered him on deck, Enright ought to have reacted angrily? Surely he should have risen and demanded an explanation. She sat bolt upright, her ears alert for any tell-tale sound that explained what was happening. Then she heard a second set of steps, heavier this time and recognisably those of Munro. She rose and went to her door, quietly

91

drew the barrel bolts and, cracking it ajar, listened. Munro knocked sharply on the Mate's door and called out:

'Mr Enright! Mr Enright, it's past eight bells and you're to relieve me on deck . . . Mr Enright . . . ?'

She thought she heard the creak of Enright's cabin door being fully opened and then:

'Oh, Christ . . . Enright! For God's sake, Enright, get up!'

Pulling a shawl about her shoulders, Hannah stepped out into the narrow alleyway and met Munro coming out.

'Well?'

'He's been drinking,' Munro jerked his head, 'he's in a stupor . . .'

'I see . . .'

'I'll call Talham.'

'Yes . . . no!'

She caught his sleeve, thinking furiously. Circumstances gave her an advantage over Enright at this moment. Beholden as she would be to all their skills, this was a moment not to be lightly cast aside. On the one hand she might need Enright's experience, but on the other she must destroy his ability to challenge her. So long as she had Munro as an ally she thought the former could be sacrificed to gain the latter.

'No . . . wait . . .'

But Munro took her grip for something more intimate and had caught both her elbows, pushing her gently back against the veneer of the bulkhead. The dim light glimmered, throwing her face into sharp relief. Munro's body stirred her and she yielded. Desirous though she was of securing the *Erl King*, this was a stolen moment, one that had been interrupted twice in Shanghai. After grief and upheaval, nothing seemed sweeter, more desirable or more appropriate than this small token of surrender. After a long moment she pushed him gently backwards.

'Hannah . . . I love you . . .'

'Please, no more now . . . not now, not again . . .'

A sense of panic seized her. Who had charge of the deck? Suppose they were caught in this compromising position? All her authority would evaporate before it was truly secured!

'Please . . . later, not now, not while I have to . . . to run the ship . . .'

'You don't have to run the ship . . . I can . . .'

'No! You don't understand, it's impossible. I have to do it . . . perhaps in London things will be different . . . I need your help . . . if you truly love me prove it . . . please . . .'

A note of desperation in her voice and the speed of her thoughts gave her speech the conviction that pure artifice would have denied it.

'You mean to keep on with the race?'

'With your help, yes . . .' The words were out of her mouth before she had given them any consideration, and yet the race was all to these men.

The appeal in her eyes was irresistible. Munro bent his head in acquiescence. For a long moment physical passion and personal ambition vied in them both, and the resolution of the dilemma cemented the alliance that both were intelligent enough to admit. He put his hands up and took her face in them, pressing his lips on her mouth again.

'Very well . . . I will!' He stepped back and jerked his head again at Enright's cabin door. 'Then what do I do about him . . . Ma'am?'

The heavy irony made them both smile.

'Give me a moment to get on deck. Is there an apprentice up there?'

'Yes, young Harrison's just out of his bunk.'

'Very well. I'll send him down. Between you, get Enright on deck . . .'

He suddenly grinned, a boyish, complicit expression that gave her the courage to move away from him, to make for the ladder in the knowledge that, from this moment, Munro or not, she was truly on her own.

As she stepped out on the deck she called the young man's name.

'Harrison?'

'Miss Kemball?'

'Go below and help Mr Munro get the Chief Mate on deck.'

'You mean Mr Enright?' The boy's tone was incredulous.

'Yes . . . go on, jump to it!' She walked aft, heading for the dull glow of the binnacle light and willing her eyes to acquire night-vision.

'How's your head . . . what course are you steering?'

'West a-half south, Miss.'

'It's Molloy, isn't it?'

'Yes, Miss Kemball, Jack Molloy, been with your father these six seasons and very sorry that . . .'

'Yes, thank you, Molloy, that's kind of you.'

'We all feel the same, Miss, specially now that the race . . .' The voice trailed off.

'The race is what?'

'Well, er, sort of forfeit, like, Miss.'

'Who says it's forfeit?'

'Well, I, er . . . I supposed . . .'

'Well don't suppose, Molloy, and tell the fo'c's'le not to suppose anything until they hear different.'

It surprised her how in her keyed-up state, as her heart beat after the encounter with Munro and in anticipation of a show-down with Enright, she found it easy to be brutally frank with this man.

'Yes, Miss Kemball.'

Molloy's voice was full of uncertainty. Quite suddenly she sensed she had him at a disadvantage and seized the initiative, subconsciously awaiting the moment when she would do the same with Enright, practising upon the unfortunate helmsman the venom she must produce for the delinquent Chief Mate.

'Don't "Miss Kemball" me anymore, Molloy. Call me Ma'am, for I'm taking command of the ship now my father's dead!'

And she took three paces forward, leaving an astonished able seaman staring after her.

Hannah could see everything about the deck now. Her eyes were adjusted to the darkness and she saw the huddle of men at the break of the poop, men aware that something odd was going on, that there was no officer on watch and that she, Miss Kemball, was on deck at an unusual hour.

'What are you staring at?' she said, working herself up to a furious pitch that seemed somehow to come easily to her as the moments passed. 'Take a turn at the pump, and get some water boiled on the galley stove . . . make some tea.'

She watched the vaguely hesitant huddle of men break up, heard a low murmur of resentment terminated by the remark, 'I'll not refuse a cuppa tea at this hour, not from anyone.'

'The old bastard wouldn't have suggested *that*,' said a voice as they moved forward. Then behind Hannah, coming up through the companionway they heard a groan, a groan that turned itself into a roar, and then Munro and Harrison half-dragged, half-supported Mr Enright on to the poop.

'What the bloody hell do you think you're doing? Damn you . . .' the voice was still slurred, but clearing as conscious-ness dawned upon Enright's reluctant mind.

'Hey, damn you . . . Harrison, what the hell's going on? What d'you think you bastards are doing . . . ?'

Enright jerked free, pulled himself upright and stared about him. He shook his head and glared at Munro, then he suddenly lurched forward, his fists balled.

'Munro, you mutinous bugger! D'you mean me to keep a watch? I'm in command! I told you yesterday you and Talham would work watch and watch.'

'*I* told Mr Munro to bring you on deck, Mr Enright.'

Enright's advance on Munro stopped before it was under-way. He turned, staggered slightly and faced her.

'*You?*'

'I'm taking command of the ship . . .'

'You're *what*?'

'Taking command . . . you may retain your rank as Chief Mate . . .'

'Who the hell d'you think you are? What right have you to . . .'

She raised her voice, her falsetto tone slicing through the deep outraged protest of Enright's bass. 'I'm taking command because I own the ship, because it was my father's wish that I did so and because *you*,' she poured all the accumulated venom of her frustration, of her grief, of her hatred for the position Enright and his ilk had forced upon her, into the pronoun. With it she conveyed a depth of accusation at his ineptitude that exceeded even her wildest intentions. 'Because *you* are in-capable; drunk and incapable, Mr Enright, and since you remain incapable of keeping your watch you may go below again, and sleep off your stinking drunkenness.'

Enright grasped the rail, swayed open-mouthed, unsure of the reality of the moment, then turned, tripped on the sea-step of the companionway and vanished below. They heard the slam of his cabin door.

95

Hannah expelled her breath. 'Thank you, Mr Munro.'

'I'd better stay . . .'

'No, Harrison can call Mr Talham, he can stand the morning watch.'

'Very well . . . Relieve the wheel and lookout,' he called to the men milling once more about the break of the poop,' and attend to your duties. D'you hear me?'

'Aye, aye, Mr Munro, sir.'

'Ain't she a bleedin' chip off the old block!'

'I'll go below then,' Munro said. 'Are you sure you'll be all right?'

'I'm fine. Please go below now, Mr Munro.'

'Very well, Ma'am,' and she could see him smiling.

Enright woke to the knowledge that he had a hangover and had suffered a vivid nightmare. With the persistence of some dreams, the details of the nightmare remained to haunt him, clear details that slowly revealed themselves not as imaginings, but as true incidents. It took him some time to realise fully what had occurred during the night, and only when he discovered his barked shin, caught on the brass lip of the companionway sea-step in his precipitate descent, did the extent of his humiliation fully dawn on him.

With sudden ire he leapt from his bunk, only to be reduced to a pathetic crouch, as his aching head dissuaded him from violent action. Slumped in Captain Kemball's chair, he brooded upon his fate, too far gone in dissipation to seek justification for his drunkenness or to muster arguments by which he might retrieve the situation.

So Hannah Kemball had seized the ship. That was a fact and appeared to have been condoned by the connivance of Munro. It followed, therefore, that Munro was in cahoots with Mistress Kemball; a self-seeking alliance; that much was clear!

But Munro had no Master's certificate, he was licensed only to sail as First Mate, though he occupied the Second's berth aboard the *Erl King*. Ownership or not, Miss Kemball's act and, more significantly, Munro's, were mutinous. The reflection made him growl with anger, but Enright jumped to no hasty conclusions. He *had* been drunk last night, and therefore an air of legitimacy might be imputed to the actions of

96

Munro and the girl. Furthermore, ownership was nine points of the law . . .

He pulled out his watch, for he had fallen asleep all-standing, dressed in his day clothes in emulation of Cracker Jack. They would call him soon, call him for his watch . . . but if he took his place on the poop first, he could provoke a further confrontation with Mistress Bloody Kemball and that without the interference of Munro who, he knew, still slept. Rising, he dragged a comb through his hair, pulled on his cap and was about to go on deck, when another thought struck him.

'She doesn't own the ship . . . not all of it . . . and she can't have made herself Master . . .'

He cast about the cabin for the ship's papers, but found only the cargo manifest. Had Munro told Hannah about the Certificate of Registry? Surely she had not signed it? He would get Osman to secure it later, purloin it if necessary. And he must see Lenqua, Lenqua's friendship was going to be all important . . . in the meantime, as behove a prudent and diligent Master, he should check the progress of the ship. The thought brought a smile to his face. He flipped open the lid of his sextant box, lifted the instrument and made for the cabin door.

'At least the clever bitch can't do this!' he muttered to himself as he went on deck.

Hannah had gone below after Talham had come on deck, but she had not slept. She tried to, aware that she would be tired later in the day, but after the momentous events of the night, she was too excited to compose herself and sat in her cabin, reading through her father's papers.

Amid the official documents she came across three notebooks filled with columns of figures that were, she knew, his sightbooks. In their margins were notes and remarks relevant to the daily navigation of a clipper. She found too his journals, extraordinarily private accounts of his doings at sea written in his neat but powerful script in leather-bound and hasp-locked books, the keys for which she had discovered on his belt. Her father, it seemed, had paid large sums of money for red jade in Shanghai, a substance which Hannah had never seen and which she assumed her father had traded in on his own private account. There were also notes on his officers in which it

97

gave her a warm glow of pleasure to read, under a recent date at Foochow: *Munro shaping up very well, a most competent, diligent officer worthy of advancing vice Enright.* This allusion to her adversary made her turn back to an earlier page, to see what her father had written about Enright's return to the ship after his recent debauch. She found it, its brevity confirming her in her assumption about her father's opinion:

Enright returned in his customary drunken condition. Ducked as usual from the yard-arm to the amusement of all hands. Cannot long tolerate this, one example might have retrieved him, but he is a lost cause. Resolved to discharge him Londonside.

Hannah knew that 'Londonside' was pidgin parlance for in, or at, London, and discharge was plain enough. If she felt she needed any further justification for acting as she had done, she had it now. Indeed, she reflected, she had been lenient with the man, allowing him to retain his rank and pay until the end of the voyage.

She looked up. A pale daylight was filtering in through the porthole. Beyond the cabin a faint chinking told where Osman had started his daily round in the pantry. Going to the cabin door she opened it and called him.

'Miss Kemball?'

'Would you see if Mr Enright is awake?'

'He's on deck, Miss, went up about half an hour ago . . .'

The news alarmed Hannah, for she knew the lack of fuss boded ill. Enright occupied on deck could mean only an undermining of her authority. But there was one advantage . . .

'Osman . . .'

'Yes, Miss?'

'I want all Mr Enright's effects moved out of my father's cabin. I'm moving back into the place, d'you understand?'

Osman looked unhappy. 'But Miss, Captain Enright . . .'

'Damn Enright, Osman, and don't call him "Captain"; I've taken command of the ship. I give you five minutes to clear the place.' She turned back into her cabin, gathering up all her own and her father's belongings. Osman stared open-mouthed after her. He had never heard her swear before.

Osman was not the only member of *Erl King*'s crew who was surprised at the change that had come over Hannah Kemball.

98

It was assumed that Miss Kemball, incapacitated by grief, would keep to her cabin and leave the business of the ship to those competent to carry it out. Despite the fact that she was Cracker Jack's daughter, her taking command came as a complete surprise.

Molloy went forward with the story at the end of his trick at the wheel, and by that time all the starboard watch (who had witnessed the scene with Enright) knew the substance of it, as did many of the off-going watch who had not then turned in.

An initially popular acceptance, based largely upon the discomfiture and humiliation of the detested Enright who they saw as a real threat to their collective well-being, replaced itself in the cold light of morning with the consideration that Miss Kemball was neither competent nor tried in the matter of commanding a sailing ship. The fo'c's'le fell to a debate of pro and contra. A few partisans supported Hannah on the grounds that she seemed to have the support of Munro, who was counted a good man. The bulk reluctantly sided with Enright if only because all of them had ventured money on the outcome of the tea-race with the *Erl King*, and to oppose the traditions of the sea seemed contrary to their interest.

'There ain't much chance o' winnin' with Enright as Skipper, but there's none at all with a slip of a girl, no matter *whose* daughter she be.'

'Munro's a canny lad . . .'

'Aye, he's a canny lad, but he doesn't know how to carry sail . . .'

'You think Enright does? Enright drunk is a bold man, but that ain't any good to you nor me. Happen the girl an' Munro'll make a job of it.'

'A *job* isn't enough to beat Dandy Dickie Richards . . .'

And so the argument went, back and forth, whispered on deck in the shelter of the lee bulwarks as the duty watch peered aft in the growing daylight to see what was happening on the poop, and muttered below as the off-going men turned into their bunks.

Enright's appearance cradling his sextant and searching the sky for the sight of a star amid the racing cloud had the effect of a sudden thunderclap. Enright was a man of intelligence and cunning. He knew he had only a few cards to play, and while they were good cards, the fact that he possessed a mere handful made him careful. Had he not had a thunderous headache he might have acted with more precipitous haste, but curiously the hangover made him pause and think.

He knew he was not popular and that, although it was likely that the conservative element of the crew would not tolerate a woman in command, the rivalry of Munro was more threatening. The fact that Munro did not possess a Master's certificate cut little ice with the crew, who knew him for a competent seaman. Enright knew, too, he had first to wipe the stain from his own character by a surprising display of conscientiousness, one that might put the lie to the suggestions of drunkenness falsely trumped up by Miss Kemball, who had had him dragged from his bunk in the middle of the night. Enright had long ago learned the value of telling a big lie long enough to be believed.

'Sir . . . I . . .'

'You what, Mr Talham?' asked Enright, holding up his sextant and searching for Arcturus in the index mirror.

'I, er, nothing, sir.'

'Have you taken the stars?'

'Er, no, sir . . . there is too much cloud, I didn't think . . .'

'You would have made the effort if Captain Kemball were still alive, wouldn't you, eh?'

Enright lowered his sextant and wiped a streaming eye before fixing it upon the handsome young officer.

'Yes . . . yes, I suppose so.'

'No bloody suppose about it.' Enright raised the sextant again, grunted with satisfaction, concentrated a moment and marched into the chartroom, counting the seconds, to time his observation on the chronometer. A few minutes later he reappeared, seeking another star with which to cross his sight of the first.

Apparently successful, he returned to the chartroom to work out the calculations, poking his head out to shout:

'Send the boys aloft, Mr Talham, to overhaul the buntlines! And don't wait for me to tell you everything! The bloody *Seawitch* will be catching us and overhauling us if you don't pay attention to your duty!'

100

By breakfast, as the watches changed again and the men mingled while the muster was called, the word was that the race was still on, and that Enright appeared to be the Master.

Hannah had less time to consider the implications of the sea-change that seemed to have come over her. The transformation that had astonished Osman and Enright was not as abrupt as they imagined. The truth was that for months Hannah had been at more than a disadvantage by being a woman, for she had been in a totally strange and unfamiliar environment. Those few intimates of her mother who troubled to call while Mrs Kemball wasted away had noticed a firmness of purpose and capability about Captain Kemball's daughter as she had nursed her mother through the last weeks of her life. Though frustrated of outlet, those same energies had been employed passively on the outward passage, and while the men had thought her merely a decorative female, an ornament to her strutting father, Hannah had not simply watched them at their labours out of idle curiosity. There was a logic in all things done at sea, not always readily perceptible, it is true, but Hannah quickly picked up enough to know why, at a given time, men let go this rope and pulled in unison on that. Once she knew the names of the sails, she could identify the main upper topsail halliards from their namesakes that served the main topgallant. Likewise she knew a brace from a lift and a tack from a sheet. Of course the complexities of ordering men from one task to another, of putting up the helm, of judging when to haul the yards on each mast, indeed of when to do any of these things in a rough sea, were beyond her. But she was very far from being the ignorant chit of a girl that men like Enright took her for, for despite his wide experience of women, Enright knew little about them as sentient beings. The charade of his concern in fixing the *Erl King*'s position, necessary though it was to the good management of the ship, was about to fail in its purpose of impressing Hannah.

Dawn disturbed her from a fitful doze over her father's journal. She closed the book with a feeling of sadness. She could not really say that she had grieved for her father, for she had not known him at that impressionable age when the strong bonds of familial ties are made. In the stultifying atmosphere of her

101

middle-class home his remote figure had been paid a ritual 'love', composed for the most part of dutiful respect and grateful sentiment. The product of this inculcated emotion was reverence to an image, an image that had shattered irreparably the afternoon she had caught him with the maid. But she felt a sadness at his passing because her own loneliness and isolation were now complete.

The attack of the Chinese pirate junks, a thing she had been warned about in an off-hand way with assertions that they never overcame a determined resistance and only attacked in expectation of easy pickings, had happened so quickly that it still seemed a dream. She had heard from the officers, speaking round the table, of other attacks in which the only casualties had been the Celestials, and that Captain Kemball had died from a chance shot, a fluke of sheer bad luck.

The assertion only served to make Hannah think that she was an instrument of fate, for how else could such an event make any kind of sense? Here, alone in the midst of the South China Sea, aboard a ship full of men, she had to have the chief command, or submit . . .

Then she thought of Munro's kiss, and the hard thrust of his body with a delicious melting that she knew, another time and in another place, would lead to the complete surrender of herself . . .

Munro was Munro . . . it almost hurt to think of him . . . but Enright was a different, more dangerous animal, feral in purpose, to be whipped before he bit . . .

Hannah had already accepted the burden imposed by command. The response to responsibility was already implanted. Even as Munro had kissed her she had been aware that no competent officer trod what she already thought of as *her* poop; and now, in the grey dawn, she realised through inherited instinct that the *Erl King*'s position on the terrestrial spheroid was important. Galvanising stiff limbs, she too made for the chartroom.

What caused caution in Enright, debate and contention in the fo'c's'le and qualified admiration in Munro, caused little sensation in the half-deck where the apprentices, with the casualness of most young men, took life pretty much as they found it. They

102

were young enough to consider themselves immortal, and therefore not threatened by any lack of experience at *Erl King*'s metaphorical or actual helm; and poor enough materially not to concern themselves over-much at the outcome of the race. On the other hand there was a trifling matter of honour, and Cracker Jack's impetuous departure from the Min River had deprived them of participating in the customary regatta of ships' boats and establishing themselves as cocks of the walk.

Bent over the upper yards as the sun broke through the cloud lowering over the eastern horizon they were therefore carefree, as they overhauled the buntlines.

It was the boys' task, light work, requiring nimbleness and agility, high above the clipper's deck, but it was not selected for the apprentices on that account. It was especially their task because it was a *detail*, an apparently trifling task, but one that taught that economy in small things was beneficial, and that later, as officers themselves, they had constantly to consider such trifles in the management of a sailing ship.

'What d'you think then?' asked one, of his watch mate.

'What about? This race?'

'No, Cracker Jack getting shot like that.'

'He was an old man . . . bad luck on Hannah . . .'

'Get that nancy Talham out of the half-deck.'

'Yes . . . d'you think we've much of a future in these ships?'

'What makes you ask that?'

'I reckon the future's in steam . . .'

'That's only because you saw that bloody steam kettle the other day.'

'They said that steam couldn't get to China . . .'

'They said the bloody earth was flat.'

'Beat you down.'

'You go if you like, I'll hang around for a bit.'

And the younger of the two, a boy of seventeen named Gordon, hitched himself over the main topgallant yard and watched the sunrise. While his mate, impelled by the fragrant aroma of the saloon coffee, went in search of breakfast.

Hannah knew that since the funeral of her father they had been lucky with the weather. The wind had held steady, allowing the *Erl King* to hold her course, neither taking in, nor making more

103

sail, steering a little south of west, full-and-bye for the coast of Cochin China, where, with skill and patience, they would work the land and sea breezes, dodging the prevailing monsoon to edge the *Erl King* southwards.

It was the fruit of progress. Sixty years earlier the lumbering East Indiamen would never have left in midsummer, at the height of the contrary wind of the south-west monsoon, but would have waited until the fall of the year, after the typhoon season and the onset of the favourable north-east monsoon. But *Erl King* was a masterpiece of the ship-builder's art whatever the scandal of her genesis, and she cut to windward with the spirit of a thoroughbred. Hannah arrived in the chartroom just as Enright straightened up from his calculations. Enright stared at her. The fresh air and the need to concentrate had all but blown the fumes of debauchery from his mind.

'Good morning, Miss Kemball,' he said with the aplomb of a man who has slept with a clear conscience.

'Mr Enright . . . you have obtained a, er, fix, have you?'

Enright smiled, a curiously predatory grin. 'Indeed. Such things are within even my competence, Miss Kemball,' he said sarcastically, adding, 'as it is with every master mariner.'

'I'm very glad to hear it, Mr Enright. It was why I intended to keep you on as Chief Mate. You are the best man for the job.'

He looked at her sharply, sensing irony, but he could find none in her eyes. The flattery threw him off-balance and she knew it.

'Let's hear no more nonsense, Mr Enright, about who commands. The ship is mine, I own it, you are its Chief Mate and will continue to be so. Where do you put us?'

She turned to the chart. Enright was speechless. The cool effrontery of the girl robbed him of suitable reaction. Had she been a common seaman he would, with a bull-roar of rage, have struck her to the deck. But she was a woman, and her hair fell across her face and the eyes into which he had been looking had . . .

'We should sight the coast by nightfall.'

He stared at her. The dividers marched across the chart, held in her slender, competent fingers.

'What speed do you estimate we are making?'

She looked up at him, and he felt those eyes on him again,

arousing him and, inexplicably, at the same time making him realise the extent of his earlier humiliation.

'Be so kind as to heave the log, will you?'

And she stepped out on to the deck with a nod and a smile for Talham and the helmsman.

Enright brought his heavy fist crashing down on to the chart table so that the lead chart weights jumped. There was only one way he could get even with the bitch! Only one way, and by Christ he would make her pay and pay with interest! Snarling he followed her on deck. Opening his mouth to order Talham to heave the log he was interrupted by Gordon's cry from the masthead:

'Sail ho! Three points abaft the starboard beam! Looks like *Seawitch*!'

7

THE strange vessel was hull up and visible from the poop by late morning. News of her sighting spread quickly through the ship and few of the men below could sleep. There was a brief period of debate while watchers on *Erl King*'s poop studied her with telescopes. By six bells in the forenoon there was no doubt in anyone's mind that she was the *Seawitch*. By the time the eight bells of noon were struck, she was no more than two miles astern of the *Erl King*.

Hannah, by now adept with a long watch-glass, studied the *Seawitch*. Her heart beat with excitement and concern, for she could see no reason why Richards's ship should be overhauling them. Both clippers carried 'all plain sail' from courses to royals, with spencers and staysails set between the masts, and flying jibs high above the ends of the dancing bowsprit jib-booms. Both, as far as she could tell, lay at a similar angle of heel, so that neither could be said to gain advantage from a greater symmetry of their underwater form as they advanced through the blue, white-capped waves of the China Sea.

From time to time she heard snatches of comment, remarks about studding sails, or so-and-so being a steadier hand at the helm than another, but, as the day wore on (and no one felt much like going below to eat), the wheel was relieved by successive helmsmen and none seemed able to hold off the inexorable advance of the *Seawitch*.

In the end, Hannah could contain herself no longer. 'Mr Enright!' Enright jerked his head from his glass. 'What is it?' he grunted with ill-grace.

'Can we do nothing about being overtaken?'

'What would you have me do? Eh?' He moved closer to her, menacing her with his bulk. 'What would you have me do? Set

107

stuns'ls? Very well, I'll set stuns'ls, and when our lee rail's driven under and we've lost a knot and that Welsh goat has waltzed past us, I'll take them in again. So what would you have me do, Mistress Kemball, since you have the honour of command?'

'I was right, wasn't I, Enright,' she snapped back. 'If you'd taken the command yourself, you'd have thought of nothing better to do than to stand here and let Captain Richards "waltz past" you!'

'That's as may be, and who knows? Certainly *you* can't answer better! But as long as I'm Mate, don't expect me to bail out skippers who don't know their business. D'you hear?'

They were shouting, and the wind whipped their words to leeward, but the ferocity on their faces was plain to all and the helmsman, no more than twenty feet away, heard every word, storing them up to regale his cronies on the second dog watch.

'Damn you, sir! I'll bring you to heel if it takes me forever to reach the London River!'

'Don't you be too bloody sure, girl, and don't presume to tell me my business. Owner you may be, but that doesn't mean a thing, and gives you little title on the high seas . . .'

Fuming, she turned away. Munro was coming aft from the companionway. He nodded at her. 'I've plotted the noon latitude and run up the Mate's longitude. We should sight the coast by midnight . . . Hannah, Miss Kemball?'

She swept past him and was about to go below when she drew aside from the companionway. She held out a hand and assisted Mai Lee on deck, the tiny, bound feet insubstantial for the job of bracing even so small a body as the little Chinese woman's. It was her first appearance since they had left the Min River, owing to her prostration from sea-sickness.

Hannah helped her to the rail. The woman looked about her, then at the black hull and towering white pyramids of gleaming canvas above, as with water streaming from her rising bow, then foaming out as her dolphin striker lunged at the surface of the sea, *Seawitch* slowly came abeam of the *Erl King*.

'That belong Captain Richards ship?'

'Yes,' said Hannah.

'Ah . . . she . . . she more quick than this ship?' The dark, swimming eyes beneath the smooth folds of skin looked concernedly at Hannah. Hannah nodded. 'Yes.'

'Ahhh . . . Lenqua speak all same . . . you can no go more quick?'

'No . . .'

'Captain Kemball would know something to do.' Lenqua joined them, his heavy brocaded silk robe fluttering in the breeze alongside that of his mistress.

'What would he do, Lenqua?' Hannah asked with fast disappearing civility.

'Captain Kemball, he would play trick.'

'By God, he's right!' Munro had overheard.

'What d'you mean?' snapped Hannah, almost irritated beyond measure.

'Here, let me take the wheel . . .' Munro turned aft, spun round again and asked with a slight grin, 'with your permission?'

Hannah caught the smile and thought him boyishly handsome. She nodded. 'All right.'

'What the hell are you going to do?' Enright called, as Munro stepped on to the teak grating that straddled the screws and quadrant of the steering gear.

'Give him a spoke, Mr Enright, give him a spoke . . .'

Munro eased the helm a little, passing two spokes through his strong, brown fists. *Erl King* fell off the wind half a point, heeled a little more and slowed a trifle. Along her lee rail the roil of water foamed aft in a long white and green curve. In the waist men ran forward to ease the braces, but Munro roared at them.

'Hold fast there, don't start a burton! Let's see who has the nerve.'

Hannah could see details on the *Seawitch* clearly as the westering sun threw *Erl King*'s shadow over the heaving welter of water that ran between the two ships that were now neck-and-neck. *Erl King* would be in silhouette with the sun brilliant behind her, peeping through the slits between her sails and making the observation of similar details on *Erl King* difficult. But the same light picked out small things on *Seawitch*'s deck. Someone had pointed out the tiny alteration of *Erl King*'s course and Hannah clearly saw Richards, his black beard prominent against his pale face, move to the weather rail to survey them. He still wore grey, a grey worsted pilot jacket and a stove-pipe hat of the same colour. The sight of him inexplicably thrilled Hannah. She was defying him! She suppressed a desire to leap up and down with excitement, gripping the smooth teak taffrail with white-knuckled fists. They were getting closer! The gap between the two ships was suddenly narrowing fast; the white waves trailing back and outwards from *Erl King*'s racing cutwater crashed and foamed into those running off from *Seawitch*'s port bow.

'Haul your wind, Kemball, damn your eyes!' The roar of Richards's prodigious voice rolled to windward.

'For Christ's sake, Munro! Are you mad?'

Enright was suddenly pale and Hannah, caught in her dependency between the expertise of the two men knew not whether to take alarm from Enright's anxiety or to support Munro's insane yet obviously effective action. From his bellow, Hannah knew that whatever it was that Munro was doing it was shaking Richards, for he was shouting again.

'Damn you, Kemball! Hold your course . . . I'm overtaking vessel . . .'

'And must keep bloody clear!' roared Munro, quoting the Rule of the Road at Sea as preached at the Board of Trade and learned by rote by every aspiring officer.

'Especially when passing clumsy old ships run by women,' remarked Talham facetiously, blushing when Hannah frowned at him and Enright, thinking the remark a jibe at himself before Hannah, snapped, 'Shut your mouth!'

But Munro's trick worked, for as *Seawitch* came up on *Erl King*'s starboard beam she fell into her lee and lost the advantage in speed she had found. Unable to overtake her rival, the relative position of the two ships became static, until Munro's ruse, when his alteration of *Erl King*'s helm caused her to cut across *Seawitch*'s bow, confronted Richards with a dilemma. With fully half his ship overlapping *Erl King*, Richards risked an entanglement of the lower yards that could, in an instant, result in the dismasting of both ships. Alternatively he too would have to ease off the wind, dropping back, with *Erl King* continuing to steal his wind.

'Kemball, you black-hearted devil, mind your helm or I'll see you in Hades . . .'

'Thank God the breeze is steady,' someone remarked.

'Aye, an' young Munro's got the nerve for it,' said another.

Hannah threw a glance aft. Munro stood braced on the grating, leaning to meet the heel of the ship, playing the spokes a little, his face a curious mixture of absolute concentration and strange rapture. He was watching some sail aloft, judging the response of the ship from the luff of the mizen topsails, Hannah thought, though she was not quite competent to be certain.

'Shall we let him know, Miss Kemball?' asked Talham in an obvious attempt to reingratiate himself.

'Let who know what?' asked Hannah, turning to watch *Seawitch* again.

'About . . . about your father . . . Captain Richards thinks he's still . . .'

'Alive?'

'Yes . . .'

'Does it matter what Captain Richards thinks?' she said dismissively, still thinking of the look on Munro's face.

'Jesus Christ!' Enright looked aloft as *Erl King* heeled to a stronger gust of wind. The crossjack yardarm caught something and Hannah was aware that the two ships were impossibly close now, the *Seawitch*'s fo'c's'le overlapping the *Erl King*'s poop. The dripping crossjack yard had plucked the weather forebrace of the *Seawitch* which, taut though it was, rippled in oscillating sine waves from the contact.

'Kemball . . . !'

Richards was forward, not fifty feet away from Hannah, his black eyes glowing like coals.

'Why the devil's not there! Is he below drunk? Eh? D'you hear me? Are you all drunk?'

The two ships lurched together again and suddenly Richards turned aft, disappearing from sight as *Seawitch* heeled away from them. No one had responded to Richards's angry hail, and then he had put up his helm. *Seawitch* fell suddenly astern, was gone from the forefront of their vision like a parted curtain, and Munro had recovered his helm, holding *Erl King* close to the wind while, three cables, four, half a mile behind them, *Seawitch* again took up the pursuit.

And then, inexplicably, as if the impartial, invisible laws of physical science that moved the two ships had shifted in favour of the *Erl King*, or perhaps because the wind and sea, for

111

undiscovered reasons of their own, had their own game to play with the fates of the two ships' companies, *Erl King* drew steadily ahead of her rival. That was the position at darkness.

Enright opened the door of Lenqua's cabin. The old Chinaman lay propped up on the bunk. Mai Lee's right arm was about his head; her left hand held a basin into which the old man spewed. The cabin reeked of vomit and Enright wrinkled his nose in contemptuous disgust.

'What you want?' Mai Lee asked defensively, humiliated on Lenqua's behalf. Enright ignored her.

'Lenqua?' he growled. Lenqua raised his head. His face was sickly green and covered with the sheen of perspiration.

'What for you come here, Enright?'

'How many shares d'you own in this ship, eh?'

Lenqua frowned, then a thin smile of comprehension crossed his pallid features. 'Lenqua not have any shares in *Erl King*. All go back to Captain John. Now he is dead, all belong Missee Hannah . . .'

Enright stood dumbfounded. He turned abruptly and slammed out of the cabin. Behind him Lenqua's laugh turned into a gurgle as he retched again.

In the saloon Enright bumped into Osman.

'Did you find it?' he asked the steward. Osman nodded, and held out the thick fold of the ship's Certificate of Registry. Enright snatched it and flipped it open. What he saw infuriated him further; Hannah's signature lay beneath that of her father.

'God damn the bitch!' he swore, then turned on the cowering Osman, dropping the certificate on the saloon deck. Aiming a kick at the steward Enright made for his cabin. 'Bring me a bottle,' he ordered.

'Yes, sir,' said Osman, adroitly avoiding Enright's boot and recovering the certificate from beneath the table. Returning the purloined paper to its rightful place, Osman went to find a bottle of gin.

'But she's faster than we are. How else could *Seawitch* have . . . ?'

'Look, Hannah, please, listen to me for a moment.'

'My father was foolish . . . heavens, no, he was drunk when he made that ridiculous bet!'

112

'You want to give up the race?' Munro asked curtly.

She wanted to humiliate Richards, wanted to see him on his knees, but the stake was too high and the odds shortened with her father's death.

'Yes . . . no . . . I don't know.' She paused. 'I can't win, can I? Not now that we know for sure that *Seawitch* is the faster ship . . .'

She stared astern where, in the moonlight, *Seawitch*'s pyramid of white canvas glowed dimly in the night and the ruby eye of her port sidelight shone steadily.

'But she isn't. Not necessarily. That's what I'm trying to tell you.' Munro, officer of the first watch of the night, calmed his incipient exasperation and tried, for the third time, to make Hannah understand.

'Look . . . it's all a question of relative motion. *Seawitch* overhauled us because, although we left the Min ahead of her, she can't have been far behind. My guess is that Richards was damn near ready to go when we were but, for whatever reason, he left after us. Your father ran offshore and into an unseasonal belt of calm. He had absolutely no way of knowing that it was going to be there, but Richards either ran further to the westwards, hugging the shore and holding the wind, or he followed our track and did not experience the calms. It happens, and it'll happen again. I've seen ships in sight of one another being affected by different winds . . . you learn to live with the perversity of natural law at sea, Hannah, you have to, you've no alternative . . .'

'Try not to lecture me.'

'I'm sorry, but the fact that he caught us up does not necessarily argue that, in exactly similar circumstances, *Erl King* is the slower ship.'

'But this afternoon does . . .'

'No it doesn't,' riposted Munro, verging on irritation.

'How on earth do you explain . . .?'

'For God's sake, Hannah, how the dickens can I explain if you keep interrupting.' He blew out his breath and fell silent.

'Go on,' she said at last.

'Right. Try and recall exactly where *Seawitch* was when young Gordon spotted her.'

'Right behind us.'

'Exactly. Right astern of us. And the minute they spotted us they must have known it was *Erl King* . . . the excitement must have been intense aboard *Seawitch*. How would Captain Richards react to the opportunity of overtaking us? You know him better than I . . .'

'Oh, if you're going to go over all that again . . .'

'No, I'm simply asking you a question.'

'Well, of course, he'd jump at the chance. He's showy . . . flamboyant . . . but he caught us up, so he must have been faster – I mean to have come over the horizon . . .'

'Hannah, how much attention, real attention I mean, the concentrated kind of undivided attention, do you think any of us paid to the steering and sail trimming with you and Enright and your father's death and all the rest of it . . .?'

'All right, go on with your hypothesis.'

'He has maybe half a knot advantage over us due to our problems, but to overtake us he needs more than that, particularly if, as happened, we start to pay more attention to what we're doing. So he eases off the wind a little, frees off to gain extra speed and instead of coming up on our windward quarter, taking our wind and sweeping past us . . .'

'He comes up on our lee side and you saw him off.'

'Something of the sort,' he said, lowering his voice and feeling her hand press his arm in the darkness.

'Thank you,' she said simply, 'but do you think we stand a real chance, with Enright? It was good of you not to make trouble . . .'

'None of my business, but I'd watch him, he's too quiet for all his raving this afternoon. Keep your cabin locked and . . . Hannah . . .'

'Yes?'

He seemed to hesitate. 'We *can* do it.' It was not what he had intended to say but her hand pressed his arm again.

'She's luffin', sir!'

Munro turned away, almost running aft to peer into the binnacle and then up at the sails.

'Keep her off, man, keep her off.' He moved quickly to the break of the poop, gripped the rail and stared forward. 'Fo'c's'le head! D'you see anything?'

'No . . . nothing ahead, sir.'

114

'Keep a sharp lookout!'

He returned to the binnacle then again raised his voice. 'Hands to tack ship . . . stations to tack ship . . . lively there!'

The watch, hunkered down in odd corners about the deck, waiting their turn to relieve wheel and lookout as the double rings of the bells tolled the passing of the watch, suddenly quickened. The waist was full of dark and moving shadows, caught suddenly by the moonlight.

Thinking something was wrong, Hannah found her left hand was clutching at her shawl and her right gripping the rail. She too went forward, peering ahead, under the curve of the main and fore courses, but she could see nothing beyond the darkling sea and the faint bar of the horizon.

'Braces . . .'

'All ready . . .'

'Heads'l sheets . . . stays'l sheets . . .'

'All ready, sir.'

'Stand by to 'bout ship!'

Hannah knew the wind had fallen lighter as she and Munro had talked, for the rush of the wash was less urgent . . .

'Ready about, down helm!' Munro commanded.

Erl King began to turn, coming upright as she spun into the wind and suddenly she was a-quiver, her jibs flogging and the vibration running through her fabric.

'Mains'l haul!'

The whirr of ropes through blocks and the creak of parrels swiftly followed as the men at the midships and after braces let go the starboard and hauled frantically on the port braces. Above Hannah's head the yards and sails on main and mizen came round, hard on the stays.

The spanker boom ran across, clunking on the short, iron horse as the shock absorbers cushioned the travel of the lower sheet block. On the fo'c's'le, like sprites in the moonlight, a handful of men trimmed the jib sheets.

'Haul foreyards!'

Thrown aback by the manoeuvre, and left a moment longer to press the ship's head round on to the new tack, *Erl King*'s foremast yards swung and she lay over, swiftly gathering way on the new tack.

'Haul taut bowlines . . .'

Munro came aft to set the new course. 'Keep her full, Ferlin, don't lose an inch now, because by God this is a chance . . . Good, that's well, steady so . . .'

Hannah watched his face in the yellow glow of the binnacle light, intent on the gently swinging compass card while Ferlin, a short, wiry old man with ridiculously small hands, looked aloft, passing a spoke from port to starboard, meeting the swing of the ship and coming back a little, until he had the *Erl King* sailing like a witch.

'And now, I think, stuns'ls . . .' said Munro, rubbing his hands with quiet satisfaction. 'Pass the word there,' he called forward, and the men coming aft after coiling the braces and hauling down the tacks, started preparing the studding sails.

'It'll take a moment or two with just the watch . . . can you still see *Seawitch*?'

They both stared astern. *Seawitch* seemed to be farther away now, still holding a course that was more westerly than south.

'What . . . ?'

'The land breeze', explained Munro, 'coming off the coast twenty miles ahead of us will give us a good slant to the southward during the night. There'll be baffling winds at dawn and then, when the sun gets up, we'll haul all the yards again and carry the land breeze until sunset.'

'I see.'

Hannah continued to watch in the soft glow of the moonlight as the ship, *her* ship, spread even wider wings, extending the sweep of her fore and mainsails by lee and windward studding sails, by a large passaree below the fore bumpkins and the long, tapering sleeve of a 'Jimmie Green' below her bowsprit.

'Got all the washin' out now, Miss,' remarked old Ferlin as he came forward after his trick at the wheel. Hannah smiled after him, in high good humour herself, for nothing could match the magic of the night.

She had almost forgotten her father, so wrapt was she in new adventure.

Hannah awoke with a start, aware that something had alarmed her and caused her heart to slam uncomfortably in her breast. A pale grey light filtered into the cabin through the side scuttles and the deckhead bull's eyes. *Erl King*'s fabric creaked gently,

116

the hiss of water racing past the hurrying hull filled the still air with its muted insistence, but otherwise no untoward noise disturbed the silence.

And then she heard it. The sound of someone breathing, carrying with it the sharp stink of alcohol.

Wide-eyed she twisted round. Enright was bending over her.

He reached out and wrenched off her bedclothes. Her shift had ridden up round her waist and the violence of her turn exposed her to him. Gasping with shock she drew up her legs in an attempt to cover herself as he hissed her to silence.

'Shhhh . . .'

His left hand was on one knee and she fought to keep it pressed against the other, feeling his strength. The movement of his right hand seemed to paralyse her. She was holding her breath, her lungs full, ready to vent them in a scream of fear, anger and outrage. But something stopped her, and her eyes followed his right hand, flickering from it to his face, to the leer and the wet lips.

'There . . . quiet . . . don't make a sound and I promise you'll enjoy it.'

Her eyes closed as he bent over her, arching his back as he moved on to the bunk and drove forward. Hannah felt the rasp of his loins along the intimate inside of her thighs, felt the revulsion as his full weight came upon her and his right hand slid from her mouth to clamp hard over her breast.

The breath came out of her now, exhaled as she straightened her legs with a powerful thrust. At the same time she twisted with all her strength. Her descending knee struck Enright, sending a searing agony through him. Thrown half off her, he rolled away, his legs flailing, his buttocks off the bunk, its leeboard in the small of his back. As he bent with the reflex of genital protection he pivoted on the leeboard, tipped over the fulcrum and crashed to the deck.

Gasping for breath, Hannah kneeled on the mattress, her hands frantically fumbling under the pillow. In a moment she would scream, and the temptation to submit to the release was almost overwhelming. But something told her the reaction would render her helpless, as though screaming was an end in itself and the shriek of hurt was defence enough. Alongside this instinctive urge ran a powerful will to hit back, to suppress the

117

weak mechanism as a futile, inflaming sham. It would not stop a man like Enright, but only provoke him to violence.

Her hands sought under the pillow as panic rose in her throat. Enright was on his feet again, reaching out to grab her, his shrunken member an obscene wrinkle of suspended flesh.

'You bitch!' he spat, through clenched teeth. 'I'll show you who's master.'

Hannah pulled her hands clear of the pillow and sat up, one leg braced against the leeboard, the other tucked beneath her and her back ramrod straight against the bulkhead. Her shift was a mere remnant, torn and rolled about her waist. She thrust out both arms directly in front of her, clasping the butt of a pistol.

Enright swayed, his advance arrested at the sight of the gun. Only a few inches separated his grasping hands from the long barrel. It was wavering and he stared into her eyes. She was unable to stop them welling with tears. He could see she was cracking.

'You wouldn't . . .'

He leaned forward, one hand held supplicatingly for the pistol. The first sob wracked Hannah and she lowered the gun. He sensed triumph, responding with a renewed tumescence. Tears began to course down Hannah's cheeks and she started to slump sideways in defeat.

Enright was grinning when the gun went off.

8

DESPITE the fatigue of duty Munro slept badly, waking fully the instant he heard the report of the gun. Thinking something had carried away aloft he was out of bed and into his trousers in seconds. Flinging open his cabin door he stepped out into the alleyway, cannoning into Enright. The Mate recoiled from the impact, then without a word of explanation, pushed past. Munro caught the reek of drink.

Light from the saloon skylight shone wanly on the alleyway deck, illuminating a dark trail of blood that ran into the saloon. The door to Hannah's cabin opened, banged shut, and swung open again. Munro understood. He negotiated the saloon table in a moment, meeting Talham at the bottom of the after companionway.

'What's happened?' asked the Third Mate.

'Get back on deck!' snapped Munro, pushing at the door as it swung to again.

Hannah had dropped the gun and fallen back on to her pillow. The corner of the sheet was drawn inadequately over her. Her body shook violently and the sound of crying came from her buried face. Munro paused on the cabin threshold, uncertain what he should do, to take Hannah in his arms or to strike Enright, whose door slammed shut even as Munro hesitated. He caught sight of Mai Lee coming aft, shuffling her ridiculous little feet and supporting herself against the motion of the ship with a hand pressed against the bulkhead. She wore a white robe and looked like a wraith.

'Lenqua ask if everything all right?'

Munro swallowed with relief. 'Please, you look after Miss Hannah. Chief Mate make trouble . . .'

'Chief Mate very bad man.' She pushed past him and closed

119

the cabin door. Still irresolute, Munro stood for a moment bracing himself against the saloon table. Recalling the gun and the blood he went forward again, turned the handle on Enright's door and finding it locked, put his ear to the pannelling.

'Mr Enright? What happened? Are you badly hurt?'

From within came a whimpering interspersed with grunted oaths. Munro knocked and raised his voice. 'Mr Enright? Are you hurt?'

The feral noises ceased, there was a pause, then 'Munro?'

'Yes . . . are you hurt?'

'Go to hell.'

Munro shook the door handle. 'Mr Enright . . .'

'Go to bloody hell, Munro!'

Munro paused, looking aft again, at the door to Hannah's cabin beyond the saloon table. Across his line of sight the brass lantern swung gently.

'Are you still there?' Enright growled.

'Yes. Is there anything I can do?'

'Damn right there is. Don't jump to any conclusions . . . now go to hell and leave me alone.' Munro sighed, then went back by way of the forward companionway. Talham met him as soon as he stepped on to the poop.

'What the devil's going on?'

Munro looked about him. The watch, milling in the waist, stared aft, their expressions full of curiosity, blank receptiveness waiting for him to fill in the details for which their hunger was so obvious.

'There's been an accident below,' he explained in a voice just loud enough to carry. 'Mr Enright was cleaning a pistol and it went off.'

'Hope he shot his bollocks off,' Munro heard someone say.

'What would he be cleaning a pistol for?' asked another.

'Drinkin', shouldn't wonder,' offered a third.

Munro turned aft, his hand on Talham's elbow; the fo'c's'le rumour-mongers could make what they liked of his lie. Probably both Hannah and Enright, for vastly different reasons, would welcome it. He stopped, half-way between the break of the poop and the able seaman at the wheel. Talham stopped too, the two officers facing each other. Could he trust Talham? Should he confide the truth in the Third Mate?

'What on earth was Enright doing cleaning a gun at this hour?' Talham asked.

'I don't know,' replied Munro, perceiving the lie had taken root and offered him a course of action he could not have embarked upon alone.

'That's what worries me, Charlie. He doesn't like what's happened, doesn't approve of Miss Kemball taking command . . .'

'Do you?' Talham asked sharply.

Munro shrugged. 'She *owns* the damned ship, and she'll need help to get through the voyage. I want my wages and pay-off . . .'

'More than a ship-owning wife?'

Munro looked fixedly at Talham. They were friends and colleagues of a sort, men thrown together by circumstances more than inclination, 'Board of Trade acquaintances' the cynics called such relationships. He could not lie again, for it was not in anyone's interest, least of all his own.

'Would that bother you?' he asked.

'Not in the least,' Talham said smoothly, 'she's not my type . . .'

'No . . .' said Munro, eschewing any speculation as to what Talham's type might be. 'Are you with us?'

'Against Enright?' asked Talham, his urbane expression clouding.

'If he's against us, perhaps . . .'

'And he must be assumed to be hostile to you if he's servicing a revolver,' Talham said, adding, 'I assume it was Old Man Kemball's and he got it when he occupied the after cabin.'

'I suppose so,' replied Munro, helping the assumption become fact in Talham's perception.

'I was an apprentice on the old *King of Man* when Preacher Johnson went mad. He came out of the saloon brandishing a Colt revolver and shot the man at the wheel; roared it was the will of God and the archangel Gabriel had just paid him a visit to tell him to rid his ship of the ungodly. He missed the Mate on deck by a whisker and it took three seamen to bring him to his knees.'

'What happened to him?' asked Munro, considering the necessity of getting possession of the pistol.

'We trussed him in his cabin and the Mate took over the ship, but Preacher burst his bonds, bellowed he was Samson reincarnate and went over the side. We were in Drake's Passage at the time, with a following sea running mountain high . . .'

Both men fell silent, then Munro said, 'Let's keep our minds on this passage then, Charlie, and see if a couple of greenhorns like us can't whip Captain Richards and his *Seawitch*, eh?'

'I applaud the notion,' grinned Talham.

'Good,' said Munro, smiling back. Then he turned and went below.

'Missee? Missee Hannah . . . this belong Mai Lee . . .'

Lenqua's concubine put her small hand upon Hannah's shuddering shoulder, stroking it gently, clucking and crooning to the distressed young woman and gradually causing the sobbing to subside.

Mai Lee caught sight of the tantalus and poured a measure of cognac.

'You drink . . . make better.'

Slowly Hannah turned, wiping her face. Mai Lee bent over her and she caught the whiff of the brandy. The Chinese woman's eyes were dark with concern as she held out the glass.

'You drink . . . make better,' she said again.

With a shaking hand Hannah took the glass, propping herself up on one elbow. The cognac hit the pit of her stomach like fire. She shuddered again with an involuntary violence that was accompanied by a rising gorge and the strong desire to retch. But the moment passed and she kept the brandy down, following it with a second and then a third sip.

'Chief Mate very bad man.' Mai Lee stroked Hannah's hair. The lightness of her touch after Enright's ponderous weight was wonderfully soothing. She closed her eyes, trying to arrest the renewed flood of tears.

'You cry . . . make better,' advised Mai Lee, her hand continuing to smooth Hannah's hair. 'Chief Mate very bad man, eh?'

Hannah nodded, sniffing back her tears and finishing the cognac. She dragged the corner of the crumpled sheet across her eyes and looked up at Mai Lee. Uncertainty must have been obvious upon her face, for Mai Lee, taking the glass, inserted a phallically suggestive finger into it.

122

'No! No . . . nearly . . . he tried to.'

Mai Lee nodded and put down the glass. 'Missee Hannah,' she asked, 'you have other man? You make jig-a-jig with other man? Mr Munro, maybe?'

Hannah shook her head. 'No.'

Mai Lee smiled. 'Ay-ah . . . I savee. This belong first time . . . very frighten.'

'Yes . . . yes, he touched me, but . . .'

'I savee.'

Mai Lee's head nodded vigorously, her face smiling and her smooth, oiled black hair catching the daylight as it flooded through the skylight. Beyond the door Osman could be heard preparing the saloon for breakfast.

'You talk . . . make better.'

Hannah began to talk, rapidly, making no concessions to Mai Lee's imperfect command of English; she talked as though to herself, exorcising the memory of Enright's attempted violation, and all the while Mai Lee stroked her hair, soothing her. When she had finished and grown silent, Mai Lee stood back.

'More-better now, eh? You not be frightened next time. Next time you go with Mr Munro. Much more-better. Mr Munro make love proper fashion . . . you like.'

Hannah protested her virtue, but Mai Lee nodded and smiled. 'I get water now . . . you wash . . . make better . . .'

And smiling and nodding she retreated from the cabin.

With daybreak the winds fell light, as Munro had predicted. It was almost mid-morning before the sea-breeze stirred and the watch hauled *Erl King*'s yards to the shift. It was mid-morning too before Munro had an opportunity to speak quietly to Hannah.

'Miss Kemball . . . I am aware of what happened last night . . . of the circumstances . . .'

'Please, Mr Munro,' Hannah whispered insistently, drawing her shawl about her shoulders, 'I do not wish to discuss the matter, I only want to know what has happened to Enright.'

'You can dismiss him from your mind. He has locked himself in his cabin and is as drunk as a lord,' Munro hurried on, impatient of interruption. 'Please, I *must* speak of it, but only briefly. It is common knowledge about the ship that something occurred. I have put it about that Enright, having obtained your father's pistol during his occupation of the after cabin, shot himself by accident . . . you see, you are not implicated, Miss Kemball, not in the imagination of the ship.'

'Nor is Enright . . .'

'Well, he is, to the extent of raising the question of what he was doing with a loaded pistol . . .'

'But not in attempting to . . . to . . . please God don't talk about it again.'

'Bear with me, Hannah, try to act normally . . . for your own sake . . .'

Hannah ceased to tremble with the memory. She felt an overwhelming rage and suppressed it to an explosion of invective aimed at the unfortunate Munro.

'Act normally? Good Lord! Don't patronise me! Do you know what that *animal* tried to do?'

She stared up at him, her face pale with two spots of colour on her cheeks and her lips strangely, seductively red. The image of her distressed nakedness upon the after cabin bunk swam into Munro's consciousness and he drowned it in anger of his own.

'Yes . . . I know what he tried to do and I'm not patronising you. Good God, Hannah, can't you understand . . . ?'

'I understand that I'm not safe . . .'

'For God's sake, Hannah, you don't think that I . . . ?'

'How do I know, *Mister* Munro? How do I know that you wouldn't attempt the same thing?'

Munro fell back as though whipped. For a long moment he stared at Hannah and she dropped her gaze before the hurt pride in his eyes, hurt pride that was swiftly replaced by something more frightening, a kind of fierce hostility.

'I need the gun, Miss Kemball,' Munro said icily, 'as though I had removed it from Enright . . . and then perhaps you would be kind enough to give me my orders.'

His apparent hostility roused her. She drew herself up to face him. 'The pistol is the possession of the Master, Mr Munro, and my orders are to confine Enright permanently in his cabin and get *Erl King* into the London River before the *Seawitch*.'

Leaving Munro staring after her, Hannah went to her cabin.

Long afterwards Hannah recognised that Enright's attempted rape was pivotal in the outcome of the voyage. Quite circumstantially it defined the roles of several people whose actions were to have a direct bearing on events. But at the time it seemed, for all of them, coming so soon after the murder of Captain Kemball, that affairs had reached a very nadir. For Hannah, shocked, mistrustful and lonely, the ensuing day was one of utter misery. It had never been her lot to experience such solitary despair, for flickering about the edges of her sense of injury was an insistent image of licentiousness.

'I promise you'll enjoy it,' tempted Enright still, whispering at her through the air of the darkening cabin. And as the seductive mystery confronted her again, another voice cautioned her from the very depths of the South China Sea: 'If anything happens to me, sack Enright.'

As darkness fell upon the ship Hannah finally slept at last, behind the locked doors of her cabin and unaware of Munro hauling the yards to catch the land breeze.

Osman had conveyed fact forward to the galley. As a result of his menial status it had fallen to his lot to swab Enright's blood off the scoured planking of the officers' alleyway, and in doing so he had discovered the 'true' course of events, settled them to the satisfaction of his own mind, and later regaled the cook with the details.

'He'd taken Cracker Jack's big Colt from the cabin when he was in there, d'you see, before Miss Hannah threw him out . . .' Here Osman giggled, still enjoying the discomfiture visited on the bullying Enright by the girl.

'Threw him out she did, just as if he were of no account . . .'

'You already told me that,' remarked the taciturn cook, 'tell me what happened this mornin'.'

'Well, Enright got the gun, see, and was on his way aft with it. He got to the saloon, right up to the after cabin door when . . .'

'What was he doing that for?'

'What?'

'Going to the after cabin?'

'Why to establish his rights as Captain. Ain't right the girl becomes the Master, is it?'

'Doesn't make much difference to me . . .'

'Don't you want to win this race, then?' asked Osman, nonplussed.

The cook shrugged and threw a dirty swab into a large iron pan, his pudgy arms wobbling like a barmaid's as he swirled it round.

'Longer the voyage, more the days; more days, more dollars. Go on.'

'Strange cove you are. Anyway, he must have pulled the trigger an' injured himself. To cover up, he ran forward and locked himself in his cabin.'

'So he's locked himself in his cabin with a gun and he's drinking himself insensible, is that it?'

'Yes,' declared Osman with a grin of triumph.

'With a little help from Osman, his devoted steward whose main task is lowering bottles down Enright's bloody ventilator.'

'Well, we have a little arrangement . . .'

'You keep that maniac away from my galley . . . and now you can bugger off yourself, I've work to do.'

The cook shook his head behind the ejected Osman. 'More likely the bloody mate was trying to roger the girl,' he muttered matter-of-factly. 'Still, she's bloody asking for it on a ship.'

He humped the pot on to the stand beside the pump and drew up a gallon of water, grunting with the effort of hoisting the filled pot on to the stove. Sniffing, he began peeling onions, pitching them whole into the pot. Women were always trouble; trouble on board, trouble ashore. When a man wore his brain in his bollocks what could you expect? And there was enough trouble on the ship with the Old Man dead, the Mate dead drunk and a deadly bit of stuff causing havoc down aft, without stirring up more. So when the hands came at noon, banging their kids and holloaing for grub he told them Osman's version of events.

Thus did Enright, lately the dominant factor in the corporate thinking of the fo'c's'le, pass into at least temporary oblivion, sunk in drunken stupor amid the bottles so assiduously supplied by the faithful Osman.

For Munro, too, that day proved a turning point in life, unrealised at the time because his personal preoccupations were those of a wounded man whose pride had suffered a certain amount of damage. This was mitigated, however, by considerations of sympathy for Hannah after the ordeal to which she had been exposed. Unable fully to understand the depth of her sense of outrage and invasion, his own sympathetic nature strove to console her, crystallising into an inexorable resolve to prove himself worthy of Hannah and of the responsibilities her plight had thrust upon him.

The oaths with which Enright had turned Munro away and which had accompanied subsequent visits to his cabin with food, had persuaded the Second Mate that Enright was not seriously hurt. The longer the Mate could be confined in his cabin, the better it suited Munro, who had more pressing concerns which would not be easier with a sobered Enright interfering. Of one thing Hannah had left him in no doubt, Enright was *persona non grata* and out of the running in the hierarchy of the clipper. Munro had known Masters confine themselves, quite voluntarily and usually at the beginning of a voyage, for up to a fortnight, leaving the management of their ships to their subordinates.

Munro had ascertained the extent of Enright's injuries on his first visit, a cautious affair with Talham in support. They had found Enright stupid with drink, lying in his own filth and, with Osman to help, had succeeded in cleaning him up a little. The bullet Hannah had fired from her father's revolver remained in the bird's eye maple panelling of the after cabin, for it had scraped Enright's hip and the back of his left hand. The hip wound was superficial, no more than a nasty graze, but in passing the hand it had grazed an artery, releasing the copious flow of blood which Osman had swabbed from the alleyway and Mai Lee had thoughtfully removed from the cabin deck. Enright had staunched the wound with a torn shirt-tail bound tightly around it, and left it in place while he sought consolation with a bottle of gin.

This loss of blood and the swift ingestion of raw spirits reduced Enright to a stupor, the condition in which Munro found him. Satisfied that no lasting damage had been done and having cleaned up the Mate, Munro had a padlock hasped to the door, and arranged for Osman to supply food with himself or Talham in attendance.

The truth of Enright's assault upon Hannah Kemball, of his incapacity and the distress of his victim was related to Lenqua by Mai Lee. It roused the old Chinaman from a stupor as profound as that into which Enright was subsiding. Lenqua's desire to reach England had taken little consideration of the vastness of the sea, or of the unevenness of its surface. Despite long and profitable association with the *fan kwei*, despite an acknowledgement of their technical achievements, Lenqua remained at heart a Celestial. To a man who had seen the steamships of the Red Barbarians force the forts of the Bogue and enter the Pearl River in defiance of wind and tide, the awesome powers they commanded were undoubtedly impressive. But they in no way invalidated the deep sense of superiority he felt in all his transactions with them. Had not Captain John himself asked Lenqua to arrange a few matters to the detriment of Captain Richards before leaving Foochow? Now Enright's vulgar behaviour merely confirmed the rightness of his thinking: it was true that the *fan kwei* were lower than the rutting animals.

Nothing since their departure from the Min River had served to persuade Lenqua otherwise. The sea-sickness that had struck him as they lifted to the first swells off the White Dogs had not affected the *fan kwei*; the perilous labours of the seamen aloft gave every sign of being beneath the peasants of his home province in their grinding tedium, and as for the food, it was worse than a man of ancestry would throw to his pigs!

In the circumstances he did what only a civilised man could do and, as the nausea in his stomach showed no sign of subsiding and he could not enjoy the Thousand Delightful Ways with Mai Lee, he took to his opium pipe. In the darkened cabin he uncoiled the dreams of solace that surpassed the erotic pleasures of a woman.

Only twice did he rise from his bed; once to pay his respects to Captain John, and the second time to establish what was going to happen in the aftermath of Enright's assault upon Captain John's heavy-uddered daughter.

On the morning after the shooting, attired in his second-best robe, with his small round hat, button and peacock feather, he went unsteadily aft to see Miss Kemball whom he understood to have taken command of the *Erl King*. He found the situation mildly puzzling, for the *fan kwei*, he had discovered, regarded women much as he himself did. But he made no attempt to understand the conventions that allowed Hannah to assume such eminence, being more concerned for the bargain he had struck with her father, and this preoccupation overrode any disapproval he felt.

Hannah was not in her cabin. Perspiring slightly with the effort of retaining his equilibrium in the gently swaying saloon, Lenqua made his way cautiously to the foot of the companion-way and thence to the poop-deck. What he was confronted with there caused him to consider the entire world set upon its ears. It was enough for a Western woman to inherit wealth; but when she assumed the character and appearance of a man, his ancient heart yearned for the dry warmth of a south-facing hillside among the bones of his ancestors. Unseen, Lenqua returned to his bunk and the solace of his pipe.

Twenty-four hours after the attempt on her virtue, Hannah Kemball was a changed woman. In the hours between her father's death and Enright's attack, the alteration in her outlook had been profound. She had already assumed command and, as a result, her attitude, bearing and mode of address had altered with it. Her outward appearance, however, had remained the same. She still pinned up her hair and wore a dress. She still had to clap a hand to her head when the wind lifted the brim of her bonnet and threatened to wrench it from her head.

But the day after Enright's attempted rape she had forsaken these distinctions, these signs of her womanhood. A person periodically clapping a hand to her headgear at every gust of wind could not be taken seriously as even the token commander of a clipper. Instead, she moved about the decks in a simpler, more masculine attire. She wore a waistcoat beneath one of her father's pilot jackets, her bust accommodated within the capacity intended for his barrel chest. She had discovered a pair of ducks that fitted her hips, though they flapped about her calves with a nautical abandon she was not sure was quite proper for a commander. She had rolled her hair into a small-crowned cap, the peak of which bore the laurel leaves of a Master's rank, and only her feet remained feminine, in a pair of frivolously bought dancing pumps that she might otherwise never have worn.

Inspecting herself apprehensively in the dressing mirror screwed to the locker door, she had wondered whether, instead of respect, she was about to promote ridicule. She settled the matter by thrusting her father's revolver into the waistband of her trousers. As she closed the locker door her face showed a grim determination, a frosty glare that, as she stepped from the companionway and faced forward, intimidated Lenqua and precipitated his hasty retreat.

Hannah ignored the wide-eyed surprise of Molloy at the wheel, and walked to where Talham lounged negligently on the forward rail. Behind her Jack Molloy drew his breath noisily through a gap in his teeth.

Gordon, the junior apprentice, was sand-and-canvassing the taffrail, his mate buffing the brass binnacle. The boys stopped work and gawped at the passing Hannah. She glared at them and, though they exchanged grimaces, they bent to their work suppressing their sniggers.

Talham was staring indolently down at the able seamen in his watch who were engaged in scrubbing the main-deck.

'Mr Talham,' she called.

The insolently good-looking face broke into a grin. 'Good morning, Ma'am,' he said ironically, sizing her up. '*Très de rigueur*, if I may say so . . .'

'It's more than I can say for your buntlines, Mr Talham! They're taut as a fiddle string . . . you boys,' she turned to the apprentices, 'up and see to it . . . and cast a look round for the *Seawitch* while you're about it.'

Gordon and his companion were in the main rigging in a trice, scrambling aloft like monkeys while Talham blew out his cheeks and turned forward again.

Hannah stood beside him. Spreading her legs, her hands on her hips drew apart the pilot jacket. The blued butt of the heavy Colt caught Talham's eye.

'Stand up, sir, and don't ever lounge on my poop again.'

Talham opened his mouth in a protesting smirk. Surely the damned girl could not be serious?

'I mean it, Mr Talham. I'm of a mind to command, not play at the matter. I rely upon you to attend to details like the buntlines, that's *your* field. D'you understand me?'

Talham managed a discomfitted nod.

130

'What speed are we doing?'

'I'll have the log hove when the boys come down.'

'And remember, Mr Talham, your wages depend upon my opinion.'

'Yes, Ma'am.'

And Hannah turned away to hide her smile as the shadow of worry crossed Talham's amiable features.

'And Molloy tells that she told Nancy Talham that his wages, an' our wages depend upon her opinion . . . and what does she know about ships I asked meself?' whined Osman, picking up the saloon soup at seven bells.

'And *what*, I asks *my*self, do you know about women?' replied the cook maliciously.

Osman paused, aware that the cook had had the parting shot. Then he turned at the galley door and put his head round it again.

'They can usually cook,' he said, grinning at his own wit.

'Aye, and empty piss-pots . . .'

9

HANNAH'S metamorphosis was timely. Blue skies and blue seas accompanied their passage from the coast of Cochin China to that of Borneo; lighter winds with studding sails set, and a ring-tail laced to the leech of the spanker, conferred a yachting atmosphere upon the ship. Paint-brushes licked the scars of coastal cargo-work, adding to the effect, while a light-hearted mood prevailed.

Hannah's confidence increased, she paced the poop or sat in her hammock-chair, emulating her father, and her very presence kept the attention of *Erl King*'s company upon their business. Fluky winds needed constant sail trimming, and she was quick enough to detect a lifting sail luff, or a lowering of cloud that signalled the chilly shower and blustering short-lived squall that could descend upon them quickly. She remembered her father's advice, too, taking the wheel alongside Molloy, and learning the tricky art of luffing, shaking the wind while it lasted, gaining a cable to windward in the process.

'Chip of'n the old block,' was Molloy's satisfied verdict when, with a katabatic suddenness, such a squall rolled off the Great Natuna Island and sent the *Erl King* bowling along at sixteen knots with Hannah alone at the helm, her hair torn from below its preposterous cap, only to head the ship, so that she bore up to meet it instinctively. Molloy had gone forward delightedly, damning all the fools in the fo'c's'le that had nothing better to do than complain no good would come of having a woman aft.

'Wish she were my daughter,' he said shortly, kicking off his boots and turning in.

The coast of Borneo lay visible off the port bow next morning, lifted above the horizon on the illusion of refraction. Low and monotonous, the mangrove swamps stretched southwards

133

from Tanjong Api. With every sail spread the *Erl King* sliced
the deep blue of the sea into crisp white bow waves and curled
them astern. A flat wake boiled out from her counter into which
sea-birds dipped for tiny morsels, and the watch cheerfully
holystoned the decks. Scraps of song floated aft from the galley
where the cook banged and scoured his pots and pans. As the
wash-deck party worked aft, the hot sun burned off the water,
leaving the steaming teak decks white, with the pitch in the
seams soft to the touch.

Finishing his breakfast Munro went with Osman to Enright's
cabin. The steward bore a tray of coffee and biscuit. Munro
opened the padlock and flipped the hasp fitted by the carpenter.
Stepping aside, he ushered Osman into the cabin. The Chief
Mate seemed to shake less now, but he was weak and his eyes
were sunken and red-rimmed. More than a week's stubble
added to the impression of gauntness, heightened still further
by the pallor of his complexion.

''Morning,' said Munro with a smooth formality. Sunk in
this pathetic state, Enright was robbed of all the intimidation he
had mustered earlier. Munro and Osman heaved him into a
sitting position.

'We're in sight of Tanjong Api this morning, making good
time. Eat your breakfast and Osman'll shave you. You'll feel
better . . .'

'Go to hell, Munro,' Enright growled. 'You don't gull me, I
know your bloody game, you yellow-bellied bastard. Do a man
out of his rights, eh? Wait till I get ashore and this scandal is
exposed . . .'

'Hot water, Osman, if you please.'

Munro waited for the steward to disappear. 'Enright, the
ship's company think you shot yourself accidentally . . .'

'*What?* That bloody tart . . .' Enright began with returning
spirit.

'Shut up! Just shut your mouth and listen.' Munro poked an
angry finger at Enright's face. The Mate pulled back with such
violence that his head struck the bulkhead and Munro could see
he was shaking again.

'You went aft to rape her. *I* know that's the truth of the
matter, but you might find a scrap of decency in you to
see mine's the better story for Miss Kemball.' He paused,

134

allowing Enright to grasp the importance of what he was saying.

'Her word against mine . . .'

'And it's a better story for you, too, for Christ's sake. God knows why you were in possession of the pistol in the middle of the night . . .'

'I was the Master,' Enright said, 'I *am* the Master.'

'You're a drunken wreck, Enright, for God's sake. If you shut up and lie low you might get a discharge without proceedings being taken against you, but if you make trouble I'll not answer for the consequences. Now eat up, or are you too palsied to manage to pour yourself coffee?'

Munro had not meant to jibe so cheaply, and disliked himself for doing so, but Enright was beyond the remorseful stage. Now he justified his actions by self-delusion, convincing himself he was the victim of conspiracy, of other people's malice and the self-seeking ambitions of Mr James Munro.

Trembling he bent over the breakfast tray as Osman returned with a bowl of water.

'Hurry up now,' said Munro impatiently. He was tired and wanted an hour or two in his bunk.

'Gaspar Strait or the Karimata?' Enright suddenly said, looking up from the biscuit he was buttering. Munro ignored the question.

'Gaspar or Karimata Strait?' Enright repeated.

'Mind your own business,' snapped Munro wearily.

'The Gaspar is quicker, but the Karimata is safer.' Munro and Hannah leaned shoulder to shoulder over the chart, studying the archipelagos that dotted the ocean between Borneo to the east, Sumatra to the west, and Java, lying like a huge breakwater, ahead of them. Hannah stared at the narrow gap between the west end of Java and the southern tip of Sumatra. A dozen miles wide, divided by the volcanic island of Krakatoa, the Sunda Strait was the gateway to the west, to the fair southeast trade wind and the favourable sub-tropical current of the southern Indian Ocean.

'Moreover,' went on Munro, picking up the brass dividers, laying them against the scale of latitude and encompassing twenty minutes of arc, 'we will be making a night passage.' He stepped off the twenty minutes as nautical miles from the neatly pencilled cross marking their noon position. The tropical darkness falling like a curtain at six o'clock in the evening would find them north of Pulo Belitung. To the east of the island lay the comparatively open water of the Karimata Strait; to the west, enticingly direct, lay the Gaspar Strait; narrower, dotted with reefs and with a fearsome reputation for the inexperienced and unwary. 'So I think, discretion being the better part of valour, I advise we . . .'

'My father always used the Gaspar,' Hannah said, 'I've read it in his journals.'

'Yes, but . . .'

'Which way will Richards go?' she pressed.

'Why, the Gaspar . . .'

'Exactly.' Hannah's air of finality irritated Munro. He felt his lack of experience keenly and he was aware it seemed like lack of nerve.

'Look, darkness is coming on . . .' he protested reasonably.

Hannah picked up the dividers and stepped off her own rhumb-line. 'If we are *here* by sunset,' she picked up the pencil, marked the spot and laid off a course, marked an alteration and continued the line clear to the south, 'we could be through by midnight.'

She had learned enough, Munro thought with undiminished irritation, to be dangerous. Now she was calling the shots. The Gaspar Strait could be a death-trap.

'I can't take accurate bearings at night, not off these islands . . . it's not a simple matter of theory . . .'

'It doesn't have to be theory. There's a trick. My father used it, it's mentioned in his journals and I remember him telling me something about it outward bound.'

'A trick?' Munro said, inwardly damning Captain Kemball's legacy of his journals. Resistance to a night passage of the Gaspar Strait rose like bile in his throat.

'Well, a "wrinkle"; isn't that what you call them, these professional tricks? Something about taking a bearing of the sun when it's at right angles to the course you want to steer . . .' Hannah looked enquiringly at Munro. His mouth, opened to protest the necessity of having to override her 'tricks', shut like a gin trap.

136

'Good God!'

'Does it mean something to you?'

Dumbly Munro nodded. 'Yes . . . yes, of course it does. The old devil, begging your pardon, but he used to make me take a lot of azimuths, compass checks, as we approached this area . . . of course! He wanted to know exactly what his total compass error was, so that he could take a sight when the sun bore at right angles to his rhumb-line for the Strait.'

'I'm afraid I don't understand . . .'

'The rhumb-line, the, er, course we steer, can also be a Sumner Line, the line of position determined by a sight of the sun. He used to take a series during the approach to the strait, working the ship east or west.' Munro's expression was alive with excitement and satisfaction. 'I often wondered what he was up to!'

'You mean this line, this Sumner Line . . .'

'Is coincident with the course line, or as near as you can get it . . . you'd have to be damned good to get it right on the nose, but you *could* correct for a few miles easting or westing, I suppose.'

'You suppose?' Hannah frowned. The enthusiasm had drained from Munro's voice. He recalled himself and looked at her.

'Yes . . . it could be done, but not by us . . . me . . . it's too risky. If I make a hash of it . . . it needs practice . . .'

'You could do it though, couldn't you? I mean the calculation seems standard enough.'

He shook his head. 'You don't understand the risks.'

'I'm asking you.'

'No . . .'

'*Please.*' Her face was imploring him and already he knew he would do it. She knew, too, for there was the hint of a smile playing about the corners of her mouth, tempting him to devilment, to foolhardiness . . .

'I'll clear an anchor away . . . just in case,' he said, leaving the chartroom where his better judgement had been seduced.

Talham thought he was mad and said so, but Munro felt a surge of confidence. He worked four sights with sextant, chronometer and almanac as the sun westered from the meridian.

With carefully reckoned runs between and a handful of distant compass bearings to verify his calculations, he had Talham calculate a series of azimuths. As the sun reached the desired bearing he took his final sight and found the ship was six miles east of the intended track.

'Not bad,' he muttered, flicking the pages of his traverse table, applying a correction to bring *Erl King* on to track within twenty miles of the entrance to the strait.

'Are you standing on?' asked Talham.

'Yes . . . a man in the chains and a lookout aloft . . .'

'What if the wind falls or heads us?'

'We anchor until daylight.'

'I don't think the end justifies the risk. The bloody woman's turned your head.'

'Mind your mouth!' Munro swung round on Talham. The younger man shrugged resignedly and turned aside. Munro went aft and stood beside the helmsman.

'Steer small. Concentrate on the compass; I'll worry about the sails. If she shakes, we trim the yards. Your job is to hold her on course.'

The sun set in a blaze of scarlet and gold, flecking the high cloud long after its disappearance. The sea turned green as jade, ruffled by the light airs that wafted the heavy scents of dense vegetation from the islands that loomed in the distance. Aloft, at the change of the dog watches, all hands doused the light weather sails, shortening the *Erl King* to a swiftly manageable state, and stowing the studding sails in the tops, ready to be hoisted again at daybreak.

Beside the helmsman two apprentices read the log. One held a lantern, the other noted the figures for units, tens and hundreds. Munro came aft again and took the figures. Everything had to be done with meticulous care; this was no time for mistakes, for they could result in the loss of the ship. On deck, hardly a word was said, and when it was necessary to pass an order, it was done quietly. Even the leadsman's chant seemed muted.

'Here comes the *terral*,' said old Molloy, feeling the sudden heel of the ship and tug at the helm. From aloft the slight, flogging shiver of a luffing topgallant was insistent.

'Braces there, lively now . . .' Munro's voice was thick with anxiety. The click of braces in blocks drifted aft, together with the grunts of men hauling them.

'Two – six, that's well . . . belay.'

After ten miles, when Munro estimated they had regained their track, he made an alteration of course. The wind was a steady breeze now, fragrant with hibiscus and frangipani. With braced yards *Erl King* stood south into the waiting maw of the Strait.

Around them the sea responded to the rising breeze, rippling with sharp-peaked waves that spat phosphorescent fire and creamed back along the clipper's sides in a dazzling glow. Aft again, Munro found that he could read the log by its eerie luminescence. Pacing forward again he cocked an ear for the leadsman. 'By the deep nine!'

'Now!'

The apprentices leaned outboard and read the log yet again.

'Nineteen, sir.'

Impatiently Munro paced the poop. Hannah stood in the darkness, motionless in her support of him, though he did not notice this manifestation of her concern. For Hannah the second thoughts came after she had committed Munro. She did not care to examine her motives for insisting on the night passage of the Gaspar Strait, recognising only that it was a complex amalgam of revenge and something more frightening still. Behind her obduracy loomed Richards, and Enright, even Talham and Munro, upon whom, in some strange way, she felt she had turned the tables.

'Now!'

'Twenty-one, sir!'

'Twenty-one,' muttered Munro as he passed her silent figure, dark and inconspicuous as she pressed herself out of his way, against the mizen rigging. Twenty-one miles from the last alteration of course put them close to the next. She looked out on either side of the ship. There was no moon, but the soft brilliance of the stars lay upon the Strait and she sought the dark swirls, the Scyllas and Charybdises that lay in wait for the ship's incautious keel.

'Now!'

'Twenty-three . . .'

'Braces there, ease tacks and sheets, wind drawing forward. Steer sou' b'west a half west!'

'Sou' b'west an a half west it is, sir.'

Molloy swung the ship, checked her and steadied on the new course. Munro looked forward and aloft as the cry 'All's well, light's bright' marked the endless routine of a voyage.

'Sommat to starboard, sir,' sang out the masthead lookout. Munro was on the rail in an instant, Hannah too stared out on the beam. Was that a curl of sea breaking sluggishly on a reef? She could not be sure.

But the leadsman went monotonously on, *Erl King* slipped through the deep water, never having less than eight fathoms beneath her, and by midnight the call of 'No bottom' told them all that their daring had paid its dividend. They passed into the Java Sea with only one hundred and eighty miles between them and the Sunda Strait.

Somewhere forward a man began to sing.

> 'I thought I heard the Old Man say,
> Leave her Johnny, leave her,
> It's time for you to draw your pay,
> And it's time for us to leave her . . .'

Plunging his hands deep into his pockets Munro stopped his pacing abreast the mizen rigging. 'Well, Miss Kemball?'

'Well, Mr Munro?' She thrust herself forward from the rigging and faced him. 'The men are happy that we're through the Strait.'

He laughed, an unforced mixture of relief and mild contempt for her lack of understanding.

'The men are happy that we're homeward bound.'

10

'IT WOULD be an advantage to take on board fresh fruit and vegetables. The native boats bring it out to us . . .' Munro sensed resistance in Hannah and sought to win her to his way of thinking. 'We've been lucky with the wind,' he pressed on, 'and we were damned lucky in the Gaspar Strait.'

'Don't keep *on* about it,' snapped Hannah. Munro could read the indomitable will of Cracker Jack in the set of her jaw and cursed himself for capitulating to her over that damned night passage. The success seemed to have turned her head, given her a pride she had no right to. She was all for pressing on, into the Indian Ocean and the long haul to the Cape of Good Hope.

But at the moment Krakatoa loomed ahead, its sharp volcanic heights dark against the blue sky, while to starboard the green tumbling jungle of Sumatra rose above the red-roofed and white-washed buildings of Anjer, gathered under the horizontal tricolour of the Dutch. A dozen miles to port the equally verdant coast of Java stretched away to the south-east.

Anjer stood at the gateway to the Indian Ocean, on the threshold of the steady driving force of the trade winds and the long, low pelagic swells in which records were made by the ships whose noon-to-noon runs became part of legend. An hour's pause for cabbages and mangoes, for a sweet-tasting durian or a cool melon, would scarcely delay them after a twenty-two-day passage from the Min River.

'An hour at the most . . . look the *praus* are already coming off to us.' Munro pointed at the approaching boats, dark canoes paddled energetically by turbanned natives.

The watch below crowded expectantly, looking aft and awaiting the order to back the sails on the mainmast. Hannah looked aloft. The white pyramids stretched upwards, spread

athwartships by the passarees and the studding sails. With a
stern wind *Erl King* barely heeled, running for the open ocean
beyond the Strait.

'This is Anjer?' Lenqua appeared on deck like an apparition,
his face grey and Mai Lee trotting anxiously in his wake.

'Yes, this is Anjer, Lenqua,' explained Hannah, a trifle
impatiently, then, recalling her manners, 'I trust you feel
better?'

'A little,'

'Miss Kemball . . .' prompted Munro.

'Very well,' she nodded, 'no more than an hour.'

Triumphant, Munro swung forward to order the ship
hove-to.

'Please, Ma'am,' Gordon was dancing in front of her to
attract her attention, 'shore station's signalling. Can we report
ourselves to Lloyds?'

'Yes, of course,' Hannah replied, 'make our numbers and let
them know we're twenty-two days from Foochow.'

Hannah turned her attention to the *praus* now closing the *Erl
King*. They bobbed and surged alongside and Munro and
Osman were already negotiating for fruit and vegetables.
Hannah watched for a while, then turned to the apprentices
who stood among piles of brightly fluttering bunting.

'We've reported to Lloyds, Ma'am,' said Gordon, folding the
flags.

'Thank you . . . can we ask for news of the *Seawitch*?'

Gordon scratched his head. 'I . . . I'm not sure,' he replied
uncertainly.

'They're still signalling,' snapped Munro, turning from the
rail and berating the apprentices. Hannah lifted her father's
pocket-glass. The flagstaff with its crossed yard stood on a slope
of lush green turf alongside a white-washed, red-tiled building
with Flemish gables. Surrounding it the houses of the settlement spread out, almost merging with a native *kampong*. The
horizontal tricolour of the Dutch ensign flew from the mast,
and several hoists of brilliant flags rose beneath the red and
white pendant of the International Code.

'That's *Seawitch*'s number,' someone said, and Munro's attention entirely deserted his over-side transaction as Gordon
looked up from the code-book.

'Hoist close up!' ordered Munro, taking Hannah's offered telescope. With a jerk of the halliards, *Erl King*'s answering pendant rose in token of comprehension.

Down came the four flags, then up soared another hoist.

'Three flags, a tackline, first and second substitute . . .'

They deciphered the signal completed after a further three-flag hoist but the gist of it was swiftly clear. *Seawitch* had passed Anjer a full day ahead of the *Erl King*.

'Cast loose there!' bawled Munro, throwing off the aftermost *prau* painter in his haste. 'Main braces there, jump to it! *Seawitch* is ahead and I want your shirts in the rigging if we're to catch her!'

Gordon scooped up the last of the flags and Hannah turned aft to stand by the wheel. She had learned it was the best place to assume the semblance of command without interfering in the management of the ship. She held the rail to steady herself. A yard from her hand the wheel of the log-line began to turn. The white hemp line drew tight as *Erl King* gathered speed, then the wheel ceased to turn and the gentle curve of the plaited rope drew taut. She looked astern. A man in one of the *praus* had caught hold of the log, he was standing up, his boat towing astern of the clipper as he shook his free hand and demanded money for the goods upon the *Erl King*'s deck.

'Shake him loose, Miss,' advised Molloy at the wheel, who had seen what was happening. Hannah leaned outboard and grasped the rim of the regulating wheel, shaking it so that her effort snaked up and down the line.

The native shrieked even louder, catching the attention of Munro, come aft to make an adjustment to the course.

'Get rid of him,' he snapped, turning to stare into the binnacle.

'Yes, but how? I'm shaking the thing for all I'm worth!'

Munro swung round, his face suddenly angry. 'God damn it, woman, shoot at him – that's what the gun's for, isn't it?'

Hannah stared open-mouthed at Munro. 'Shoot at him?'

'Yes. Over his head, alongside him, just so he feels the wind of the slug.'

'But . . .'

'You're too late, Miss,' sniffed Molloy, and Hannah, still holding the regulating wheel, felt the sudden loss of tension.

Glancing astern she saw the flash of the *kris* and the white snake lying in their wake.

'Bloody hell!' swore Munro, 'That's the second log-line you've lost us!'

'I don't understand,' snapped Hannah, angry and confused, as she and Munro consulted the chart. 'We left *Seawitch* astern off the Cochin coast. How did Richards get her to Anjer in twenty-one days?'

'Twenty,' said Munro, still exasperated at the loss of the log. 'Remember he left the Min after us.'

Hannah sighed, sagging upon her elbows. 'Then the thing's impossible. He has already won.' She felt her eyes swimming maddeningly.

The anger went out of Munro. It was unjust of him to blame her for not opening fire a second time with that revolver.

'Look, he's better than us. More experienced and with a full crew. We are short-handed aft here, and I think some of the guts has gone out of the men. We can throw in the towel and make the best of a bad job, get her home as soon as we can . . .'

'No! No, I'm not giving in that easily.' Hannah sniffed with sudden resolution. 'I'm sorry about the log-line.'

'Oh, it wasn't your fault.'

'Thank you,' she gave him a wan smile.

'There *is* something we can do to improve our chances,' Munro said thoughtfully.

Hannah listened while Munro explained, then nodded her formal approval. Both of them went on deck, Munro to go forward and call the 'idlers' together, Hannah to keep watch upon the poop. Molloy was still on the wheel.

'Beg pardon, Miss . . . Ma'am.'

'What is it?'

'Well, beggin' your pardon, Ma'am, but seein' as how that darned *Seawitch* has got ahead of us an' I'm standin' 'ere thinking how we could maybe catch her up, it occurs to me, like, that you an' Mr Munro might stand a bit of advice like . . . if you takes my meanin', Ma'am.'

'Go on . . .'

'Well, Miss, I once see Old Barney Brown, him as was Master of the *Brisbane Star*, emigrant ship, back in the 'fifties.

144

He was a flyer, Miss, and he got wind of the *Southern Cross* bein' about two days ahead of us. He comes aft to the wheel where I was doin' my trick, Miss, jus' like I'm doing now, an' he says to the Mate, who was standing alongside o' me, jus' like you are, "Mister," he says, "this wind's going to hold for several days." Runnin' our easting down we was, you see, Miss, steady wind, steady course and the yards squared away for a run dead to loo'ard. "With the seas astern of her," he goes on, "she'll scend . . . want to bury her bow a touch, Mister. So you fill the boats with sea-water, and maybe stretch an old sail 'neath the skids, and lets get her a smidgin by the stern." An' we did, Miss, an' we gained more'n a knot an hour by it.' Molloy smacked his lips together and nodded with conviction.

'Thank you, Molloy . . . and you think the trades'll give us the same situation . . .'

'Not the same, Miss, but like enough. If you don't mind my saying so, Miss . . . beg pardon, Ma'am, you catch on fast.'

'Thank you.'

Hannah walked forward to study the boats on the skids. They would have to turn them over, for they were stowed keel up, but the thing was possible. As she neared the forward end of the poop she came across Osman. The steward was intent upon lowering a thin line made of spunyarn down a narrow tube let into the deck. Beside the tube, removed from its greased exterior, lay the red and white cowl ventilator that gave air into one of the cabins below the poop. By its location she knew it instantly for Enright's.

'What are you doing?'

Osman jumped. He had not seen Hannah's approach, his nerves were stretched to breaking point by the necessity of making this delivery during daylight. Hitherto, he had been able to carry out the supply of bottles to the Chief Mate under the cover of darkness. But so insistent a demand had Enright made that this interim delivery was necessary.

'Cleaning the ventilator, Ma'am,' said Osman, surrendering the yarn to Hannah with a guilty look.

'Osman, you bastard, lower it, damn you!'

Enright's voice accompanied the retrieval of the bottle up the trunking. Lifting it clear Hannah held it. Gin, a pint bottle of best London gin.

'Osman, you bugger, lower that bottle . . .'

Hannah bent to the vent. 'Mr Enright, be quiet. There will be no more bottles for you. Now please be silent.'

There was a long pause, long enough to persuade Hannah that Enright had docilely taken her advice. Then a long howl of rage and agony came from the vent. 'Put that thing on,' ordered Hannah, pointing at the cowl. Osman did as he was bid but its bell-mouth pointed towards her, amplifying Enright's moaning into an eerie sound that seemed to pursue her as she went to the ship's side and tossed the gin bottle over.

'Stuff a flag into that thing,' she snapped at Osman, 'and don't you dare give Mr Enright a drop more drink. D'you understand?'

'Yes, Ma'am.'

Enright's howling carried the length of the *Erl King*'s waist and into the deck-house where the petty officers lived. They sat, solid, ageing men, on their scrubbed teak bench and listened to the young Second Mate. By and large they liked Munro, trusted him and sympathised with him. This was their third voyage together and the young officer had done nothing to upset their good opinion.

Munro had finished his explanation of the ship's plight, and he now looked round the trio, seeking their agreement. Bosun, Carpenter and Sailmaker looked at each other. They were three of the *Erl King*'s so-called idlers (like the cook and steward) who got their names by being allowed all night in their bunks.

'Well, sir . . . I've no objection to standing watch . . . but I can't do everything I'd do if I was busy all day with my routine jobs, now can I?'

'No, Chippy,' Munro replied to the Carpenter.

'And the same goes for me, sir,' said the Sailmaker. 'It's all hunky-dory until you start carrying away gear.'

'It's the same for all of us, and it may be necessary to take any one of you out of the watch routine if it becomes necessary. But we need experienced men to keep an eye on the deck, though the next few days should be plain, trade-wind sailing, routine stuff to help us settle down. If Mr Talham and I have to work watch and watch without some assistance we can manage, but we can't crack on sail, and then this race is lost . . .'

146

The three men stirred uncomfortably. It was clear they had laid side-bets of their own. Judging by his anxiety, the Carpenter's was a considerable one.

'And if you crack on sail, then we're going to risk carrying away gear.'

'I think that's a risk we must take. We've all got something at stake I believe.'

'Too bloody right,' said the Carpenter gloomily.

'How much, Chippy?' asked Munro.

'Half my bloody pay-off.'

Munro whistled. 'That was a bit rash, wasn't it?'

'He got three sheets to the wind Foochow-side,' explained the Bosun dismissively.

'Well, what about you, Bosun?'

'I've got a few bob on the outcome . . . not to mention my pride in the old hooker.' The Bosun slammed a broad palm on the table that made the crocks jump.

'What about *you*, sir?' enquired the Sailmaker, the oldest of the trio. 'I'll bet *you've* got most to lose, eh?' he added slyly.

'More than my pay-off,' grinned Munro ingenuously. 'Look,' he added, 'I know what you're thinking: "Those back aft are in it up to their necks and once again we've got to bale them out." That's right, isn't it?' The petty officers stared unmoving at the table and mugs before them in silent assent. 'Well it isn't quite like that. Captain Kemball's death was a murderous consequence of piracy, but we can't put the clock back. Miss Kemball's taken command in name and with Enright sick . . .'

'And howling like a banshee . . .'

'Wants his wet-nurse, the bugger.'

'He ain't sick, he's demented . . .'

'He's wounded and he won't let anyone near it. He may be suffering worse than . . .'

'Good riddance,' said the Sailmaker. 'If Enright's in this you can count me out.' The old man stood and wagged a stubby forefinger at the protests of the Carpenter, 'And I don't give a button about your pay-off, Chippy, I told you you were a sozzled loon at the time, but Enright struck me once, and I ain't forgiven him.' And he sat again, crossing his arms with a nod of finality.

'We'll do it for you and Miss Kemball,' agreed the Bosun after a moment's consultation. 'And the ship,' he added.

147

'*And* a consideration of the winnings,' suggested the Carpenter hopefully.

'If there are any.' The Sailmaker made a sour face and drew a pipe from his pocket.

'I shall insist that Miss Kemball makes some acknowledgement of your loyalty when you sign off,' said Munro. 'I think you can rely on my having enough influence for that. Very well, and thank you.'

'Don't mention it,' said the Carpenter, scraping his unshaven jaw when the Second Mate had left them. 'Looks as though I'm scuppered.'

'Your own bloody fault,' said the Sailmaker, tamping tobacco into the short-stemmed briar.

'You'd be all right if we won,' murmured the Bosun, raising one eyebrow significantly.

The Sailmaker snorted. 'Bloody ship's only as good as the bugger driving her from the poop.' He struck a match and his features disappeared behind clouds of smoke. 'Munro's no driver,' he shook the match until it died, 'don't have no experience. Wouldn't have come down here asking for us to hold his bloody hand if he had.'

'Well, we'll hold his bloody hand, then,' said the Carpenter with enthusiasm, 'hold his bloody bollocks for him if it saves my pay-off.'

The south-east trade wind settled the balm of routine upon the *Erl King*. Day succeeded day of perfect sailing weather, with the ship reeling off the knots, producing day's runs in excess of three hundred miles and steering a course as straight as the flight of an arrow. Covered with a mighty spread of canvas from her waterline to her lofty, gold encircled main truck, *Erl King* swooped through the deep blue seas of the Indian Ocean with the grace and loveliness of a thing manufactured exactly for the purpose now demanded of her.

About her decks and aloft, the watches attended to the routine duties of maintenance and husbandry; splicing, whipping and pointing ropes, overhauling gear, winding baggywrinkle about clew and buntlines in the endless war on chafe; oiling spars and slushing top and topgallant masts so the yards would slide upon them when the time came to take in sail.

Parrels and trusses were inspected and greased, worn gear replaced, paint-work touched up and bright-work revarnished. *Erl King*'s brilliant brass fittings were polished and buffed, then covered with a film of grease to protect them from the heavy weather expected off the Cape of Good Hope. These tasks, interspersed with meals and sleep, made up the daily routine of flying-fish weather, its progress marked by the striking of the ship's bell.

Such halcyon days blurred and then faded the memory of Hannah's ordeal. Her suggestion that they fill the boats and an old sail added a mensurable one and a half knots to *Erl King*'s speed. For five hours she ran at seventeen fantastic knots, and for five days she rarely logged less than fifteen, tramping the miles under her keel and tearing off its reel the old-fashioned log-ship that Munro had made up in lieu of that lost at Anjer.

At noon, armed with her father's sextant, Hannah quickly learned how to calculate their latitude from a simple meridian altitude, and although she failed to master the more complex theory behind the computation of longitude, she made a passable effort at determining it. Subtly, without knowing it, she drew closer to Munro, sharing with him his keen interest in driving the ship.

Munro, absorbed with this taxing business, unconsciously distanced himself from Hannah, mindful, for all his masculine pride, that she was the inheritor of the ship. Moreover, Munro had paid for his professional knowledge, incomplete as it was, by a distinct lack of experience in other matters. There was an uncertainty in his attitude to young women of his own class, for he was still a relatively young man. Physical intimacy, even of the comparatively innocent kind indulged in at Shanghai, was therefore laid under a taboo.

This undemanding relationship made a joyful end out of pure companionship, melting that mistrust with which Hannah had, perforce, embraced all men. But it did not remove that private and ambivalent reaction she felt, an ambivalence that grew strangely more insistent as the shock of her encounter wore off and which was kept alive by her growing friendship with Mai Lee.

When not occupying her father's canvas hammock-chair suspended in the mizen rigging, when not learning the rudiments of navigation or discussing the passage with Munro or Talham, when not eating or sleeping, Hannah had taken to playing cards with Mai Lee. The little Chinese concubine was an inveterate gambler and an adept card-sharp. In their intimate *soirées*, alone in the saloon while Munro and Talham worked or slept, and Enright remained locked in his cabin, they brought an oddly inappropriate atmosphere to the poop of an ocean-going clipper. Hannah found she was acquiring a curious and vicarious experience from her conversations with Mai Lee, for the concubine possessed none of the inhibitions thought proper to the demeanour of a lady, and Hannah possessed them in too great an abundance to interrupt Mai Lee's shameless recollections.

There was, however, a charmingly inoffensive explicitness in Mai Lee's chatter, an almost childish quality that robbed the practical value of her information of any taint of impropriety. Indeed she dealt with sexual mechanics with the ease with which other women discussed recipes. Mai Lee, her feet tight-bound by an ambitious mother, had been sold into prostitution at an early age. Trained in the oldest profession, her expertise, imparted with unconscious humour, did much to rob Enright's assault of its long-term effect on Hannah.

But it did rekindle those longings that had tortured her as long ago as Shanghai, when flower-girls and Munro's kisses had disturbed her dreams and her father had disrupted her first real flirtation.

'How long-time you savvy my father?' she asked Mai Lee.

'Oh, long-time. He belong number one makee jig-jig my friend, Shanghai side. Lenqua take me Foochow, my friend stay Shanghai, belong concubine for Capting Kemball.' Mai Lee looked at the girl. 'You no worry. Same like your mother.'

Bewildered, Hannah asked, 'What was her name?' The odd idea occurred to her that she ought to know, had a right to know, the name of her dead father's mistress.

Mai Lee shook her oiled head. 'Very' diff'cult you say. I know English words,' she announced triumphantly, with a proud puckering of her rosebud mouth. 'Her name mean "Red Jade".'

'Red Jade!'

Hannah's mouth fell open as Mai Lee nodded. Now she

knew the reason for the disbursements made for red jade in her father's accounts!

'You savvy why I belong Lenqua?' Mai Lee went on as, for the umpteenth time she produced a hidden trump to trounce Hannah's harboured ace. Hannah shook her head. 'Because Lenqua belong gentle man proper. Never make me jiggy-jig if no want to.' Mai Lee pursed her mouth and stared at Hannah over the fan of her cards; Hannah was transfixed. 'You savvy Mr Munro belong all same Lenqua. He belong proper gentle man. More-better you make Mr Munro Number One.' And selecting a low trump from her hand, Mai Lee led. Bewildered still further, Hannah allowed herself to be beaten yet again. Nodding knowledgeably, Mai Lee swept the accumulated tricks into her hand and dealt once more.

'Believe me, Missee Hannah, Mai Lee speak true.'

And it brought Hannah's thoughts disturbingly full-circle, catching her in a whirlpool that seemed unavoidable. She glanced upwards at the skylight. Munro's footsteps pacing the poop overhead sounded unnaturally loud. The nature of the two women's conversation would doubtless have dismayed Mr Munro, though he had acquired a similar, and more practical knowledge of these matters himself, from a woman of as dubious an origin as Mai Lee.

And then, above the creaking of the hull that passed for silence below decks, Hannah heard the lugubrious tones of Enright. The moaning ululation reached a crescendo that was swept into the crash of breaking furniture and subsided at last into a diminuendo of weeping.

Always, it seemed to Hannah, that the dream shattered upon the reality of Enright.

Time had no meaning for Enright, and consciousness, by bringing with it recollected humiliation, no value. He had submerged himself in the oblivion of drunkenness, unheeding of the outside world until the interception of his supply by Hannah on the forenoon of their passing Anjer. Deprivation had dragged him reluctantly back into their midst. His howls of miserable resignation were replaced during the next few days by the alternating sounds of vandalism and post-alcoholic remorse. Whimpering entreaties, even abject apologies, could

151

be heard coming from beyond the padlocked cabin door. But these went in cycles in which this cowering composed the bottom of the revolution, provoking a rapid reaction, a reassertion culminating in violent language and noises of destruction. Shortly before sunset the following evening Munro, recognising the symptoms of withdrawal would worsen and could no longer be ignored, knocked on Hannah's door.

She was playing cards with Mai Lee and looked up at Munro's entrance. 'Yes?'

'I need something from your father's locker.'

'What is it you want?'

He was already inside pulling open a drawer, and she felt offended at the arrogance of his action. He lifted a hard canvas roll wound by a leather belt. 'I beg your pardon, ladies,' Munro said, and disappeared as abruptly as he had arrived. Understanding of his errand dawned on Hannah a few moments later when a louder shout came from the alleyway. Assisted by the Bosun, Munro entered Enright's cabin. It was in near darkness and filled with a nauseous stink. The Mate, pitiable in his extremity, had again fouled himself; the stench of excreta, sweat and vomit filled the air. Both men gagged and swore as they searched the cabin for its occupant.

The movable items of his cabin furniture, a chair and the door of his locker, an oil lamp and a small glass-fronted bookcase lay smashed on the deck. Glass, splinters and still more empty bottles added to the mess.

They found Enright huddled into his locker, shrunk in self-effacement. He was whimpering, the pale oval of his face glistening with tears, his black hair plastered lankly on his head. His unwounded arm, trembling slightly, stuck incongruously from the locker while the door lay in matchwood. Munro bent forward and grasped the outstretched hand.

'Out you come now . . .'

With sudden, frenetic energy, the arm seemed to whip like a lash. Munro was flung backwards, striking the base of his skull a painful blow on the bent oil-lamp bracket.

'Hell!'

Like a huge, obscene jack-in-the-box, Enright shoved himself to his feet, spewing a frenzied torrent of invective.

Recoiling from the shock of Enright's eruption, the Bosun

recovered himself. The shaken Munro saw a powerful, tattooed forearm, fist bunched, slam into Enright's belly. The big Mate jack-knifed forward, his head falling on to the Bosun's ascending knee. Enright's head lolled back, eyes closed, the body beneath falling sideways, then spreading out inert, with spasmodic tremors passing through it.

'Waited a long time to do that,' said the Bosun, snatching the canvas roll from Munro's feeble grasp. 'You all right?'

Munro shook his head to clear it. 'Yes, I think so . . . Christ! Here, let me help you.'

'The bugger's got DTs,' grunted the Bosun, as both men struggled with the unconscious Enright. It took them ten minutes to pass the strait-jacket over his arms and lash him, heedless of his bandaged hand. When they had trussed him they lifted Enright on to his bunk.

'Thanks, Bosun. It wasn't quite what I had in mind when I asked for your help.'

The Bosun nodded, still panting heavily, then he looked down and kicked the leg of a chair angrily aside.

'Bloody mess he's made.'

'Osman can clean it up. By the look of things he's been supplying more hooch.'

'Reckon that's him finished then,' remarked the Bosun, casting a final look at the felled Enright. 'No more being cock o' the walk, you bucko-bastard.'

'He gave us precious little option.'

'Stupid sod.'

Erl King rushed headlong to the westward, trending a little south in her course, carrying the steady, fair wind from Anjer to the Mauritius. Flying fish, in fear of their lives from albacore as much as the shadow of the ship, lifted from the wave at *Erl King*'s fleet cutwater; dolphins rushed in from either quarter to leap and gambol in the curling wash, or bow-ride before the slender pressure wave her advancing hull made in the ocean.

In the dog-watches, when Hannah and Mai Lee were known to be playing cards, the men stripped off and floundered in the half-filled sail, slopping backwards and forwards as *Erl King* lifted to the following seas. As the sun set and the watches rotated through the dogs, the strains of an accordion and a penny whistle floated aft, accompanied by cracked, inexpert voices attempting the lilting bitter sweet melodies of the sad, longing sea-songs: 'Shenandoah', 'Leave her Johnny'.

Far above their heads, above the thirty-five thousand square feet of wind-driven canvas straining at its bolt-ropes, the gold-encircled mainmast truck turned lazy arcs against the darkening sky.

11

'A CHANGE in the weather, Ma'am,' said Munro, peeling off his sou'wester and blowing the accumulation of spray off the end of his nose before leaning over the chart alongside Hannah.

'Did you get "stars" this morning?' she asked.

Munro shook his head. 'No . . . but this is my D.R. for eight o'clock.'

He picked up the dividers and placed their point on the neatly pencilled circle marking their position by dead-reckoning. They were south-west of the Mauritius now, stretching down into the temperate latitudes of the southern hemisphere where the depression tracks roll round the world and blustery, wet, changeable weather is to be expected. Ahead of them, a great barrier to their westward progress and on account of which they found it necessary to dip southwards towards the Antarctic pole, lay Africa.

'It seems odd that we have to go *round* Africa,' Hannah said wonderingly.

'Well we can't go through it,' replied Munro shortly.

Hannah went out on deck. A sheet of spray drove over the weather bow and streaked aft, catching her cheek with a painful, aching chill. The lurch of the deck sent her staggering to the rail. After the easy motion of the last week the sudden veering of the wind came as a shock. Gripping the rail, Hannah stared aloft. Gone were the studding sails and the flying kites. Even the royals were furled and the *Erl King's* single topgallants were reefed. All the yards were braced sharply, those on the mizen sharper still to hold her as close-hauled as possible.

Munro came and stood beside her.

'No more flying-fish days,' she said.

'No,' he agreed. Gone were the blue seas with the white caps running up under their port quarter, gone was the easy, scending roll, the gentle slap-slap of buntlines against the gracefully bellying white canvas, and the responsive whip of studding sail booms. No bosun birds trailed over the wake, no dolphins gambolled about them, and no flying fish lifted from their bow. Instead the sea was grey-blue, the colour of wet Islington roof slates, Hannah thought with a start, wet roof slates with a thin sunlight upon them. The wave-crests, curling with more purpose than hitherto, held a grey menace, while the wind, heading them now, had a spite about it that promised more in the coming days.

'No,' repeated Munro, 'but she's making nearly twelve knots . . .'

'And that's good?' asked Hannah, accustomed to fourteen or fifteen in the trades.

'Aye, that's very good, close-hauled on a wind like this.'

'Will it worsen?'

There was anxiety in her voice now. She had seen the sea state much worse than this, with the ship burying her lee rail and nothing set above the upper topsails; but then her father had stood where they stood, and she had shaken her hair in the gale and embraced the wind as something elementally splendid. This morning the mantle of responsibility lay upon her shoulders, though she looked to Munro for guidance. It was clear he too was feeling the weight of it.

He shrugged. 'Perhaps. The glass is still falling, but less than it was.' Hannah chided herself. She should have noticed that, it was an elementary enough matter.

'Are you . . .' she began awkwardly. 'Do you . . . ?'

'Do I what?' Munro turned to face her.

'Do you think we are carrying too much sail?'

'She's all right,' answered Munro shortly, his abruptness sure indication that the same question preoccupied him.

Munro stared intently aloft and watched the sails, the same sails that had gleamed white in the trade wind sunshine and now reflected the monochrome grey of sea and sky. They strained at their bolt-ropes, their clews tugging at the lifting yardarms. It was a matter of experience and judgement that told a shipmaster when to reduce sail, when to reef and when to furl, and although there was an established sequence of short-ening down a full-rigged ship, Munro knew captains favoured diversions from these procedures to suit the idiosyncrasies of their own vessels.

At that moment Munro felt the want of experience keenly. Munro as Second Mate had known most of the answers and been quick to criticise and float ideas of his own. That quality, recognised by Cracker Jack, had marked the potential in him. But, as Captain Kemball also knew, it had to be exploited wisely, nurtured alongside a growing experience, developed with a sense of caution without the latter killing initiative. If the thing was done properly it produced that equilibrium of daring and circumspection that the fo'c's'le might call wizardry, if the fo'c's'le bothered to put a name to it, but which was better known as confidence. There were many shipmasters who were sail-drivers, slave-drivers, bombasts and wind-bags, but few possessed the confidence and ability that produced a crack clipper Master such as John Kemball had been. As long as a man of Kemball's stamp dozed in his hammock-chair, or curled on the chartroom settee, men like Munro could push their luck and cut their teeth, learning all the while, reined in by the pre-scient appearance of their commander with his, 'Very well, Mister, I'll take her now . . .'

But Munro no longer had a mentor. As he looked aloft seek-ing signs of strain or chafe, he reflected that this was the first real blow of the homeward voyage. The contrary monsoon in the South China Sea had been relatively moderate; fickle, even, allowing Richards to get ahead of them by standing offshore. *This* was the testing time.

The thought of the *Seawitch* somewhere ahead of them stif-fened Munro's resolve. He turned aft and stood next to Molloy on the helmsman's grating. Without a word Molloy relin-quished the wheel. Munro felt the kick of the rudder through the worms of the patent steering gear. He eased a couple of spokes through his hands, feeling the clipper's response, watch-ing the distant jib-boom beneath the gore of the courses scrape across the rim of the world. She was beautifully balanced, still racing like the thoroughbred she was. He smiled at Molloy. The old man grinned back.

'Full an' bye, sir?'

'Full an' bye, Molloy, as long as she'll stand it.'

'Aye, aye, sir.'

He went forward again. Water was still draining out of the boats on the skids, the last of the temporary 'ballast' pumped into them after leaving the Sunda Strait. The sail had long gone. Hannah wedged herself into the hammock-chair.

'You'll not find it so comfortable now,' he remarked, as Hannah jerked to and fro at the extremity of each lanyard.

'I don't . . .'

She tried to struggle out of it, finding it difficult. Munro caught her wrist and pulled her clear. They swayed together as *Erl King* dipped then lifted, climbing over a large sea which broke on her bow and sent a shudder of protest through the hull. Instinctively Hannah turned her face away, towards Munro. The spray whipped aft with a sibilant hiss and Hannah found herself pressed against Munro. His arm curled about her as *Erl King* dived again. The green water poured seething over her rail, surging aft in a foaming wave, knocking down two men and filling the lee side of the main-deck half-way to the rail. The wash-ports slammed open as the ship shook herself clear of the burden. Gasping, the two seamen hoisted themselves to their feet as clouds of steam accompanied by loud abuse poured from the galley.

'How's your helm?' roared Munro at Molloy.

'She's fine, sir, jus' fine.'

Munro shook himself and looked down at Hannah. 'She'll stand it,' he said, letting her go, aware of the gaze of the men in the waist.

'Look!' said Hannah, as if covering some private embarrassment. The piebald crescent of a Pintado Petrel swept across the wake and rose, wings motionless, so close that they could see the faint tremble of its feathers as the wind stirred the lifting surface of its wings.

'Cape pigeon,' said Munro.

'And there too,' she pointed, and Munro saw the tiny feet of dabbling storm petrels, diminutively dark birds, Mother Carey's chickens, so tiny and fragile, as if seeking shelter in the hollows of the wave troughs. They watched as a cascading crest tumbled down the smooth surface of a wave, vindictively threatening the questing birds. But they lifted easily from the avalanche of foam, pecking at the tiny life-forms that stirred in the welter of its passing.

Bosun Harris struggled up from the waist. He looked soaked, despite the rope yarns at his wrist and the twist of flannel towelling round his neck, but his grin was approving.

'You're driving her, sir.'

Munro nodded. The Bosun's approval was a small chip of consolation.

'But I think we'd better rig lifelines fore an' aft . . . oh, an' I don't intend to try up-ending them boats . . . not in this sea.'

'Very well, Mr Harris . . .'

Harris nodded at them both. 'Ma'am,' he said, his right hand just touching the black peak of his sou'wester.

'I don't think he approves of us gossiping,' said Hannah perceptively, turning and going below.

Munro looked at the dull overcast. The sun's earlier appearance had been short-lived. There would be no latitude at noon. Harris came up from the main-deck. The watch were already stretching out the lifelines, taut wires that ran from poop to fo'c's'le providing a ready hand-hold for men working at braces and halliards. He stood beside Munro and looked aloft.

'She'll stand it, Mr Munro, don't you worry.'

The starboard watch rapped their mess-kids on the bare pine of the fo'c's'le table and waited for the pan of stew from the galley.

'I can stand anything but a buggered-up meal,' remarked Dando Douglas, a thin wiry man in his early thirties along whose bare forearms a tattooed tangle of snakes writhed around an elongated anchor.

'And love back aft,' added Gopher Stackpole, sucking at an empty pipe and spitting the result skilfully into the spittoon.

'Love?'

'Aye, Miss Bleedin' Kemball and young Munro . . . if he wants to win this bloody race, he'd do well to keep his mind on the job . . .'

'I thought you meant Enright . . .'

'He's still comatose,' added a third, gentlemanly man with an educated accent. 'The Duke' sat beside them, looking at a small leather pouch. It was his third voyage aboard the *Erl King* and they still knew no more about him than on his first. He never went ashore and always waylaid the various missionaries who occasionally ventured aboard, to solicit a few books. These were incomprehensible to his mess-mates, as a consequence of which they welcomed his opinion on most things except seamanship.

'What do you make of *that*, Duke?' asked Dando, looking anxiously up at the companionway for the first sign of dinner.

'Enright's silence and inactivity?' he shrugged. 'Munro's got him lashed in a strait-jacket and he's coming round to being half-sane, I imagine. I doubt they'll rehabilitate him entirely, he's too much of a recidivist, but dried out he'll be as cunning as a weasel.'

'Cunnin', eh,' muttered Gopher, not knowing what a 'recidivist' was.

'Yes, he's biding his time . . . he can afford to, but we haven't heard the last of him.'

'I wish we'd heard something of the *Seawitch* . . . you got anything bet on the race, Duke?'

The cultured able-seaman smiled and' shook his head. The three men looked up as a shaft of grey light lanced down from the slammed open companionway doors. Seconds later, Ordinary Seaman Bailey stood before them, oilskins streaming and stew pan steaming.

'Come on, you lubbers, rise and shine, hands off cocks and on socks, dinner's on time . . .'

Gopher banged on the bunk-board nearest the table and the rest of the watch, grumbling and scratching, turned out, dropping down in various states of undress to crowd the benches and scrabble for the stew.

'Cook says this is the last of the cabbage, an' it's onions and spices from now on.'

'Should have stopped and victualled proper at Anjer . . .'

'Quit moaning . . . what else did Cookie say, eh?' asked Dando, eager for the news of the day, for the ship's galley was like an oasis in the desert, a place where tracks crossed and news might be sought.

'Port watch reckon there's something afoot between Munro and Miss Kemball.'

'Christ, they *are* sharp. We sha'n't catch Dickie Richards with that load of lumpheads on deck. Jesus, Duke, how many of

160

those fucking dumplings are you having?' Dando asked despairingly, having lost first turn with the ladle.

'At least three, my dear fellow,' replied Duke urbanely. 'Or possibly four.'

'That leaves three for the rest of us.'

'I hope you are good at division. What about our oriental friend, Lenqua?'

'Cook says Osman told him that he's back in his bunk . . .'

'With his bint?'

'Cook didn't say . . . just said he'd only had seven meals at the saloon table since we left Foochow.'

'Well, they don't need to eat as much as we do . . .'

'As much as *you* do.'

'I shall ignore that remark, Gopher. Tell us, Bill, what precisely put our colleagues in the port watch on to the trail of romance today?'

'Well, Munro had his arm round her on the poop, like,' said 'Bill' Bailey.

'Lucky bastard,' said Dando, spearing a dumpling off Duke's plate.

There was no such conviviality in the saloon. Like the fo'c's'le it was lamp-lit, despite the hour being that of noon, for the wind-whipped rain that hardened the canvas and drew taut the sheets and braces had produced a dull overcast. Like the fo'c's'le the saloon creaked and groaned and thrummed to the tension in the rigging and the working of the straining hull, but there was no half-shouted banter. Instead a decorous silence reigned as Hannah, Mai Lee, Mr Talham and two of the apprentices sat down to the same stew as the starboard watch were enjoying. The proprieties of class distinction filled the air, not with gossip, but with the courteous formalities of good manners and the chink of cutlery on crockery as the little English dining-room, ministered over attentively by Osman, bucked and heeled its way to windward, into the winter of the southern hemisphere.

'It grows a little colder, I think,' remarked Hannah.

'Aye, Ma'am, and we may experience a shift of wind, a backing to the south-west perhaps . . .'

'That would help . . . Mai Lee, are you well?'

Mai Lee normally toyed with her meal. Unaccustomed to Western cooking, particularly that served on ship-board, Mai Lee had always picked at her food like a bird, but now she dropped her cutlery with a clatter, and half-rose, one hand supporting herself on the fiddled table, the other clasping her breast.

'Mai Lee!' Hannah rose, oversetting her chair, Talham was half on his feet, while Osman quickly removed the chair behind the swaying Chinawoman.

Hannah caught her and, nodding at the after cabin door, led her through as Osman opened it. In the sanctuary of the cabin Hannah sat Mai Lee down, kneeling before her small, bent figure. Tears cascaded down the painted face, and sobs wracked her thin body.

'Mai Lee, what is it? What belong matter?' Hannah turned and poured a thimble of brandy from the decanter in the tantalus. Mai Lee was fond of a nip, she had learned. Gratefully, and with a shaking hand, Mai Lee took it. Again Hannah kneeled before her, looking up at the tired face. Not for the first time, Hannah wondered how old the concubine was.

'Mai Lee?'

'Lenqua,' Mai Lee said at last, 'Lenqua is very sick. Maybe he die soon, we no come Londonside . . .'

In the saloon the two apprentices and Talham finished their meal in silence. The stew was followed by duff, and they ate with the appetites of young men. When eight bells struck above their heads, Osman was still pouring their coffee.

'Serve a tray on deck, Osman,' snapped Talham, whipping his napkin from his neck and grabbing his oilskin.

'Yes, sir,' replied Osman wearily, as the two apprentices were compelled to follow the Third Mate's example.

On deck Talham exchanged the saloon gossip for the course and took over the watch. 'How's she taking it?' he asked Munro, dismissing the plight of the Chinawoman from his mind.

'She'll stand it; the wind's backed a touch and she's logging twelve and a half. We'll leave her as she is for the night if the wind doesn't freshen by sunset.'

Talham nodded. 'Very well . ... stew and duff,' he imparted, 'last of the cabbage, but the Cook's been lavish with the sultanas.'

162

'Lavish?'

'Well, for him, yes . . .'

The two men exchanged grins and Talham took over, nodding to the Sailmaker who was to share the afternoon watch with him.

'She'll stand it, Sails,' he shouted down to the main deck.

'*You're* telling *me*? I made the bloody things! Of course she'll stand it.'

'If the wind doesn't freshen by sunset.'

The Sailmaker nodded, then went forward to muster the watch.

Munro paused at the companionway. When the starboard watch was mustered he nodded dismissal to his own men. He cast one look at the grey, rain-filled sky and tasted salt on his lips. He was hungry and tired, and if the wind did not freshen he was going to let the ship have her head.

And the wind had not freshened at sunset. But neither had it fallen.

Munro, Talham and the bulk of the seamen were working watch-and-watch, four hours on and four off, with the two dogs worked between the hours of four and eight p.m. to revolve the watches. The petty officers, in order that they might attend to those essential duties of their ranks, kept a different watch rota, four on deck and eight off, making up the extra four hours on routine maintenance. No one worked less than twelve hours and Cracker Jack Kemball had had his own system, devoting much time and effort to preserving wear on his gear, so much so that Munro judged he could live off the fat of this prudence.

Erl King drove south and westwards into the night. Her pyramids of canvas rose ghostly against the sagging overcast, the paltry ruby and emerald glow from her fo'c's'le sidelights showing only the horizontal slash of sleet and spray. Along her starboard side the wash foamed a sullen grey, sluicing the waist from time to time and making transit of the main deck a matter of increasing hazard.

When Munro turned out again for the first watch at eight o'clock in the evening, he was pleased that the ship was making such good progress.

'Twelve knots at one bell,' said Talham of the routine

heaving of the log-ship fifteen minutes before the end of the second dog-watch.

'Good,' said Munro, smacking the poop taffrail with his fist, a mark of his deep satisfaction. His judgement was vindicated, the wind had not increased and the ship sped on apace.

'Much weather helm?'

'No,' said Talham yawning, 'you had the spanker trimmed to a fiddle key. Haven't touched it at all.'

Munro felt a sudden surge of affection for the ship as Talham left him alone in the darkness. His watch huddled beneath the break of the poop, the occasional dull glow of a cigarette gleaming on dripping oilskins. Just astern of him, the face lit faintly from below and giving a mildly hellish cast to his features, the helmsman stood alone by the binnacle, hardly moving the big spoked wheel. *Erl King* was a sweet ship, well-mannered and sea-kindly.

By God, they could do it!

The shock of conviction thrilled through him: they could bloody well do it, he was certain of it . . .

He wedged himself by the weather mizen rigging, passing into that somnolent state which, like a submerged whale, allowed all his perceptive functions to work without undue demands on his strength. His mind split, half day-dreaming, yet half intent upon his business, as taut as the shrouds against which he leaned and doing his job with a similar appearance of inertia.

'All's well! Lights are bright!'

'Wheel's relieved, sir, course west b'south a half south.'

Lookout and helmsman were relieved on the hour and the double strokes of the bell slowly mounted, tolling the first watch of the night. At one bell, an intermediate stroke sounded to call the next watch. Munro went aft and watched the apprentices in his watch, Gordon and Stokes, heave the log. The old-fashioned knotted line ran out in the darkness. Munro watched the glass.

'Stop!' he called, and they nipped the line, jerked it to free the peg in the 'ship' and pulled its now unresistant length inboard again.

'Eleven and . . .'

'Call it a quarter.'

'Aye, aye, sir.'

Stokes would go and write the figure in the deck log. It was nothing like as accurate as the Walker's Patent that Hannah had lost, and it failed to give them the running total of their distance through the water, but Munro took a secret pride in working his traverse by the old methods. Ten minutes later he handed over to Talham.

'She's dropped a little to eleven or so; sea's had time to build up.'

'Yes,' Talham shouted back, 'there's more swell now than earlier.'

The port watch reported itself mustered and Munro turned the starbowlines below.

'Good-night,' he said, patting Talham's back.

'Good-night . . .'

Dog-tired, Munro stumbled below, tore off his sea-boots and oilskins, peeled off the outer layers of reefer jacket, trousers, muffler and guernsey, and threw himself across his bunk. In five minutes he was asleep.

Shortly after three bells in the middle watch, at half-past one in the morning, the wind veered. To hold their course Talham's watch turned-to, struggling in the darkness, one mast at a time, to haul the yards at a sharper angle to the bow. The weather braces belayed on pins along the port rails were eased, those to starboard hauled aft, while the tacks of the main and fore courses were hardened down, pulling the lower windward edges of the big sails further towards the bow. The loose sheets of these two huge sails were slackened. On the fo'c's'le they led the fore-tack to the capstan, via a block on the cathead, the little gang of able seamen rising and falling on the clipper's bow through thirty feet as the *Erl King* swooped to windward.

'Belay.'

They obeyed Sails's orders and trooped aft, in search of a pot of tea jammed on the galley stove. The Sailmaker took a look to windward. Occasional rents in the cloud showed a star or two, and the overcast was thinning enough to let the faint glow of a gibbous moon suggest its presence.

Above his head the hard flat triangles of the three headsails, the fore topmast staysail, the inner and the outer jibs, curved obliquely towards the bellying square-sails on the fore-mast. The Sailmaker studied them in the feeble light. Not given to

165

philosophising, something of the rightness of making useful things touched him and he went aft with what, for him, passed for cheerfulness.

'Yards all trimmed, Mister,' he reported to the figure of Talham.

'Very well . . . is there any tea in the galley?'

'Aye, the lads are mashing some this minute . . . I'll send some aft.'

'Thank you, Sails.'

Talham grinned into the darkness. Old Sails was a curmudgeonly devil. Not surprising, the young officer mused, that the petty officer refused to call him 'sir'. For one thing Talham was young enough to be his son, and for another Munro's idea of backing up his and Talham's lack of experience by putting the petty officers on watch was scarcely going to produce feelings of respect for rank!

Talham thought Munro ill-advised on that point. 'If he was advised at all,' he muttered to himself. Anyway, old Sails was a misanthrope. Not to be wondered at though. Poor old bugger spent most of his time working alone, sewing mile after mile of seam in thankless canvas. When anyone did call upon him, the occasion was rarely social.

'Hullo, Sails . . . could you knock me up a ditty bag? Say, Sails, have you a scrap of cotton duck for repairing my breeches . . . ?'

Offering to send aft some tea, Talham concluded, was really uncharacteristically decent of the fellow.

In the galley, beneath a light swinging wildly from the deckhead beams, Sails addressed the dripping members of his watch.

'One of you take a mug to Talham on the poop.'

'One sugar or two, dearie?' lisped a seaman.

A laugh rippled round them. 'You do it.' Sails pointed at an apprentice. The others laughed again.

'Wind's getting up,' remarked Sails, accepting a mug of tea with a nod.

'D'you tell him?' asked the man who had jested about the sugar, jerking his head in the direction of the poop.

'Let him find out for himself,' said another, 'he's paid enough.'

166

'Hang on, mate, I've five nicker riding on this hooker.'

'She'll stand it,' said the Sailmaker.

'Munro'll shorten down at eight bells.'

'Then he can do it wiv 'is bleedin' watch.'

'He'll want all bleedin' hands, an' *we'll* lose kip.'

'She'll *stand* it, I tell you,' repeated the Sailmaker, 'it's a breeze not a gale.'

At three o'clock the cold front passed over the *Erl King*, stripping the sky clear of its overcast, revealing the three-quarter moon and the Southern Cross. Only the isolated masses of towering cumulonimbus reared moonlit into the velvet sky. The shock of the cold air struck the deck of the ship with almost as much effect as a blast of spray. Three short days earlier, Talham thought as he ruminated on the sudden change that formed the vicissitudes of a sailor's life, they had been lolling majestically in the warm trades. Now he shuddered, turned and stumped aft.

'Still holding?'

'Aye, sir, she's holding west b'south a half south, sir.'

They were plunged into sudden darkness. The tall mass of the thunderhead loomed across the moon, its edges luminous, but the boiling rage of the thing was visible in this peripheral turbulence.

'Squall coming . . . watch her now . . .'

Talham scrambled forward again, meaning to shout down into the waist and alert the watch in case they were needed.

'Tea, sir?' He narrowly avoided cannoning into Apprentice Waller.

'Thanks; warn the men I may need to start the braces, squall coming . . .' He took the tea and bent over its scalding warmth, nodding to windward where the shadow of the cloud laid a dark patch on the silvered sea.

The boy turned, but he had not reached the galley when the squall hit. *Erl King* bucked and lay hard over with the lee rail driving down so that the wash boiled along the rail and jetted in round the wash-ports. Spray smoked off the waves and it seemed the very ropes protested at the weight they were compelled to support.

Bent over the tea, Talham staggered, slopped the scalding brew over his hand and swore. The moment's inattention, the staggering and disappearance behind the curved edge of the forward poop companionway, caused a second's hesitation by the helmsman. *Erl King*'s head fell off the wind, causing her to heel further as the wind came aft.

Talham slid across the deck, struck a ventilator and dropped the tea, fetching up against the taffrail, and striking his head on a rigging screw supporting a mizen shroud.

The helmsman put the helm down, fighting to bring the ship back on course, but she jibbed, the big courses driving her further downwind than the spanker could counteract. The slender rudder tore at the water boiling under the stern, dragging the ship rather than controlling her.

'Luff! Luff her!' The Sailmaker struggled aft, bumped into the dazed Talham and shoved him aside. He took one look at the spanker sheet, swung round and roared at his watch-mates: 'Let fly the fore-tack!'

There was no respite to the squall. The wind was steady now, already a gale. From below a crash of crockery told where Osman had left some washing-up undone in the pantry sink. Other noises were floating up from the accommodation below the poop. They heard Mai Lee scream, a thin, desperate note, and a bull-roar from Enright's ventilator. Then Munro was on deck, half-dopey with sleep, fighting his way into an oilskin that the wind was master of.

'Luff her, damn you!' he was bellowing at the helmsman, unable to see the Sailmaker at the break of the poop.

'She's not answering, sir,' shouted the struggling helmsman, 'they've gone forrard to start the fore-tack.' Munro managed to get the oilskin buttoned and went forward. He found the Sailmaker and Talham.

'What the hell's going on?'

'Squall, laid her down . . . not sure . . .' Talham mumbled.

'Third Mate took a tumble . . . watch going forrard to start the fore-tack . . .'

'Bloody hell!'

Erl King's starboard bow buried itself to the rail. Just abaft the starboard fo'c's'le ladder the sea poured aboard. The green glow of the sidelight shone ghoulishly on a wall of water and went out. The ship scythed through the sea, forcing her bow onwards, clear of the wave as her fore-foot, buried a moment

168

before, leapt clear. The water in the waist surged aft, clanging the freeing ports.

There had been a man on the starboard ladder. Munro was certain of that; a black shape struggling forward to carry out the Sailmaker's order. Men had gone up the windward side, hand-over-fist along the lifeline there, but one man, leaving the open door of the galley on the starboard side of the after deck house, had taken the short-cut up the lee side. Munro was sure he had seen the shape of him just before the ship had thrown her bow clear. Now the ladder was empty.

He half-turned, outboard and to starboard, his mouth suddenly, terribly dry.

'Is everything all right?' Hannah was there now, emerging from the forward companionway, reaching her hand out in the darkness as though she was playing blind-man's-bluff.

'Jesus Christ!'

Munro saw him, just for an instant, saw him level with them, no more than twenty feet away, a black shape against the seething white of the wash. Then he was gone, left far astern, and the stupid notion came to Munro in the numbness of his horror that had the log-line been trailing behind them, he might have had a chance.

'Is everything all right?' repeated Hannah. 'What's that making the ship shake?' Munro, turning forward again, felt her clinging to him.

'For Christ's sake, let go!' He pushed her roughly aside. As the sky cleared, he saw men on the fo'c's'le letting fly the fore-sail. No longer held down, its windward edge flew up, whipping sheet and tack in a murderous flailing of thimble, blocks and shackles.

'Fore clew garnets!' roared Munro, cupping his hands round his mouth.

'They know what to do, Mr Munro,' shouted the Sailmaker beside him, and from right aft, Munro heard the helmsman cry jubilantly:

'She's answering hellum, she's answering hellum!'

Relieved of the leverage of the forward course, *Erl King* came once more under control. Only the thought of the unknown seaman drowning alone in the vastness of the ocean astern of him, tempered Munro's own relief.

'Mr Talham,' he called harshly, 'call the roll!'

12

'HIS name wasn't Andrew Johnson,' said Hannah, looking up from the Articles with a startled face. Somehow the fact that, in death, a man assumed a new identity, shocked her.

'No.' Munro completed writing in the log-book and held out the pen. Their eyes met. Grief, anxiety, trauma and now responsibility had laid a curious beauty upon her. It had fined her features, etched character in her face and for all her mannish garb, Munro had never felt so strongly attracted. He thrust the irrelevant thought aside. He had let her down; he had let himself down. Most of all he had lost a man.

'You must sign the entry,' he urged, indicating the log-book. 'as the Master,' he added, in case in her shock, she failed to grasp the significance of her task. She pushed the Articles aside and he read: *Andreas Jansen, A.B., born Maasluis 1845, next-of-kin Mother, resident Schiedam. Allotment £2 per month payable to n.o.k.*

Hannah dipped the pen and drew the log-book towards her. Munro had written, *Andreas Jansen, Lost overboard in heavy weather . . .*

'Just sign it,' he prompted.

'That's all?' Munro grunted assent. 'He was only twenty-four,' Hannah said as she signed.

'Yes, he was a good man.'

'Not much of an epitaph. His poor mother . . . where's Schiedam?'

'Near Rotterdam.'

Munro bent to retrieve the log-book from Hannah's hands, but she suddenly gripped it, compelling him to look at her.

'Is this *my* fault?' she asked, assailed by momentary weakness. 'Did *I* cause the death of this man? Do you blame *me*?'

171

'For continuing the race?'

'Yes . . . and killing *him*,' she nodded at the name in the open book. 'I don't think I could stand it if you did,' she whispered.

Munro shook his head. 'No, it's my fault for letting you. I should have shortened down last night.' His voice was bitter with self-recrimination.

With a bewildering logic Hannah went on: 'Would my father have reduced sail?'

They were interrupted by a knock. Munro straightened up. 'Yes? What is it?'

The Carpenter's head poked round the cabin door. 'Beg pardon, Mr Munro . . . Ma'am, but she's sound aloft. No shakes or springs.'

It was a crumb of comfort, Munro thought, to know the *Erl King* could stand such driving. 'Thank you, Chippy.'

The Carpenter hesitated. 'We're all sorry, Ma'am, about Andy.' He attempted a smile. 'One of those things, like.'

'Thank you,' Hannah whispered. 'Would my father have reduced sail?' she repeated, the moment the Carpenter had gone.

'I don't know,' Munro said uncertainly, then, with mounting conviction, 'no, not at darkness; but he would have kept the deck all night and at the first sign of the squall he would have reacted.' He paused, then added in a firmer tone of voice, 'It was my fault, for relying on Talham.'

He felt her hand touch his wrist. 'It was my fault, Hannah,' he repeated, trying to convince her and rid her of guilt. 'And you mustn't allow the loss of Andreas to prey on your mind. Men go mad in such isolation of spirits; it is not uncommon for Masters in particular to fall victim to the mulligrubs. I've known of them . . . going overboard.' He managed an encouraging smile. 'Talking helps . . .'

She nodded, thinking of Mai Lee. 'Yes . . . yes, talking helps . . .'

Munro tore himself roughly away, stowing the log-book on its shelf, but his heart hammered at the sound of her sigh.

'James,' she began, using his Christian name for the first time, when the cabin door burst unceremoniously open after a peremptory knock, and Apprentice Stokes stood wide-eyed and dripping in the doorway.

'Sail, Mr Munro! Looks like *Seawitch*!' he announced, and as abruptly vanished with a clumping of sea-boots on the companionway ladder. Munro was after him in an instant.

'What d'you think it's like to drown? They say the whole of your life passes before you.'

'I don't know. Furthermore I don't much care. Andy was a good man, but your moping over the matter won't bring him back.' 'The Duke's' voice was languid with indifference.

'And fuck you too,' Gopher Stackpole replied truculently.

'Go to sleep, I want to read.'

The incipient row was ended with a crash. The companionway doors were flung open and a draft of cold air visible in a swirl of spray descended into the fo'c's'le.

'What the hell?' Gopher turned aside from his contemplation of 'the Duke's' inviting jaw-line.

'Come up, you lazy bastards! All hands! All hands!'

'What the hell for? We've only just snugged her down.' Legs swung out of bunks, groaning humps metamorphosed into grumbling men struggling into boots and oilskins.

'We've got the bloody *Seawitch* under the lee bow!'

Munro had given the order as soon as he had seen the distant ship. There was no doubt that it was the *Seawitch*, and the sudden jubilant realisation that they had made up something like three hundred miles on their rival drove all thoughts of mourning Andreas Jansen from his mind.

After the loss of the Dutchman Munro had belatedly reduced sail. Taking in the jibs, topgallants and the main course, he had driven the ship to windward under storm canvas. The wind had backed a point, freeing the ship; but an increase in velocity had produced a wild, tumbling sea, great rolling hummocks of spume-crested grey. The *Erl King* still ran her lee rail under as she rolled, but the reduction of canvas and the heaving of the sea seemed to have no effect upon her speed.

'If this wind holds,' he shouted to Talham, 'we'll fetch the Natal coast by tomorrow daylight.'

'But *how*?' asked Hannah, struggling up the heeled deck towards the two officers, '*how* have we caught him up?'

'Don't ask, Ma'am,' replied Talham, his handsome face grinning like an ape, 'just bless your good fortune.'

Sail after sail lifted over the horizon as they slowly over-hauled their rival. Richards had *Seawitch* snugged down, too, but about noon, as the two clippers raced hull-up from the deck, the observers aboard *Erl King* saw inner and outer jibs rise up their forestays, flog, then draw smooth, lifting *Seawitch's* bow and holding her lead.

'You don't think he's been waiting for us, do you?' Hannah asked Munro as she kept him company throughout the after-noon watch.

'Of course not,' laughed Munro, confidence surging through him at the sight of Richards and his ship so close.

All the same, Munro knew it was not his own expertise that had closed the gap between the two ships.

Out of a desire to immolate himself after the death of Jansen, Munro kept the deck, dozing in the hammock-chair, one eye cocked intermittently on the *Seawitch's* stern light. From time to time they opened the bearing sufficiently to catch a glimpse of her ruby-red port light, whose arc of visibility stretched to two points abaft her port beam. But always it closed again, winking derisively like a whore's eye.

At eight bells, as the watch changed and Munro spooned porridge and molasses into his mouth, the cry came from the lookout of 'Land ho!'

Africa lay athwart their hawse, a grey undulating line that, hazy at first, grew in substance as the morning wore on, reveal-ing the green-dun uplands of Natal Province. As the sun climbed and warmed the distant *veldt* it drew in the sea-breeze, backing the wind and causing the vigilant Richards to hoist topgallants. Gradually, as they drew in to the shore, it moder-ated to become a strong and spanking breeze. By noon both ships were covered in canvas to the royals. Flying jibs rose at the extremity of the long jib-booms and studding sails were spread on fore and mainmasts. Munro devoted his anxious attention to his own ship, to the tension in every sail, the angle of every yard; but he kept a close watch on the progress of *Seawitch*.

She was a beautiful ship, slightly larger than *Erl King* in terms of tonnage, with finer lines and six feet more on her waterline, a wooden vessel of proven strength and endurance, commanded by one of the finest seamen in a trade renowned for the quality of its commanders. Slightly fuller in form, *Erl King* conceded slimness for less displacement, an advantage gained from her composite construction. In the varied conditions of the China run the delicate matter of compromise aimed at by their designers gave one a tiny advantage over the other in given circumstances, which was lost in others. Both ships possessed long lower masts and deep false keels, making them well-known for their weatherliness and their ability to hold a course with the minimum of helm. Munro was acutely conscious that their main difference lay in the men who commanded them.

For all the skill and experience Richards was master of, Munro knew that there were other ingredients that contributed to the success of one ship when pitched against another. Setting aside the vagaries of wind and weather, there was luck. Luck was an enigma; unproveable, insubstantial, chimerical, it nevertheless existed, as any seaman could testify. But one did not pluck it out of the air, nor was it conferred on one by some agent of providence. Men, it was said, made their own luck, a mixture of seized opportunity, confidence and fate. As he watched *Seawitch* that forenoon, Munro prayed for that supernatural interference that was, he felt, missing from his own situation.

Here, with his rival running under his lee, was an opportunity; and the erosion of *Seawitch*'s lead had given him confidence, howsoever it had occurred. All that was needed was some trick, some wrinkle, as Hannah had called it, to pit against Richards.

Richards was a man who made his own luck. Richards had made his own luck in the Shanghai drinking den, and Munro still flushed at the memory of his own humiliation and Hannah's discomfiture; Richards had made his own luck in Foochow, in Cha's studio behind the British Consulate above Cushan Creek; and Richards had made his own luck off the coast of Cochin, gaining almost two days on the *Erl King* at Anjer. Munro could almost grind his teeth with the nature of his recollections. And yet . . .

Here they were, racing neck and neck for the Cape, setting southwards in the Agulhas current, edging round the salient of Africa for the northward funnel of the Atlantic! The thought

175

made his heart pound and turned his attention once more to his own ship.

'A trifle more in on the lee main-brace, Mr Harris, if you please, then you may let fall the cro'jack!'

The mizen course, or cross jack, often blanketed the main-sail, actually slowing the ship, but the wind was now exactly right for carrying it.

'Gordon! Stokes! Lay aft and prepare to stream the log!'

Coming aft from the midships pinrails, the watch mounted the poop rail and leapt, laughing, into the mizen rigging. Munro stood beside the helmsman and watched as they spread out along the yard, casting off the gaskets.

'Let fall!'

The sail fell in its buntlines, filling and flogging until the buntlines and clew-garnets were let to run, when its clews were drawn down to the rail and adjusted by the sheets and tacks. As soon as the sail was drawing, Munro turned.

'Give her a moment to feel the benefit,' he called to the two apprentices. Five minutes later, pegging the 'ship', Gordon trailed it astern while Stokes held the reel. Bouncing in their wake, setting up a feather of white, the log-ship attracted the attention of an albatross. On motionless wings the huge bird glided sideways, its tuberous yellow beak questing the lure. Gordon took the glass from the chartroom.

'Let run.' Stokes let the line free, the log-ship dug in the water and then tore the line off the reel.

'Turn!' They watched the glass as the knotted line trailed astern, drawing off fathom after fathom until the glass was nearly empty.

'Stand-by . . . stop!' Munro nipped the line himself, jagged it to free the peg, and handed the now jerking line to Gordon. 'Pull it in and count 'em again.'

Panting up a few minutes later, Gordon reported 'Seventeen, sir.' His eyes were glowing with excitement.

'Seventeen . . . that's very good. Now go forrard and tell the men that they can hang their shirts in the rigging and let's see if we can make it eighteen.'

The loss of Andreas Jansen was dislodged from the forefront of Munro's mind.

The sight of *Seawitch* had unsettled Hannah. Actual knowledge of Captain Richards's whereabouts reminded her of the genesis of the race and of the consequences of its loss. She wanted to study the contending clipper through the large watch-glass, but the thought of focusing upon the grey-coated figure of Captain Richards sent apprehension shivering down her spine. Instead she went below, to sit with Mai Lee alongside the emaciated body of Lenqua.

The old Chinaman lay upon his bunk like the effigy of a knight she had once seen in a country church. His thin moustaches drooped alongside bloodless lips and his skin was parchment-thin over the skull. In the greenish light that washed into the cabin, his skin acquired a translucent quality that possessed a kind of strange beauty, as though it showed the glow of the soul within.

The paradox confused Hannah. How could she reconcile this sad, yet dignified figure with the man whose imaginative demands had occupied the best years of Mai Lee's life and provided her with a rich fund of anecdote? There was nothing goatish about the head or the hands that lay across the thin chest as it rose and fell beneath the silk robe. The shallow respiration augured badly. From time to time she smiled encouragingly at Mai Lee.

Hannah felt real affection for the little Chinese woman with her oiled hair and her painted face, looking her best for the man whom she called 'master'. Though Hannah did not understand it, there was something almost noble in Mai Lee's devotion. Hannah leaned forward and touched Mai Lee's hand.

'You go topside, Mai Lee, catchee fresh air. Make more-better. You too-long wait here. Bimeby come back.'

Left alone Hannah sat without moving, but the flogging of the cro'jack roused her from her reverie and she was aware of the stiffness in her limbs. She stood and stretched herself, then tried to see *Seawitch* through the porthole which seemed to spend most of its time under water. Periodically *Erl King* lifted her long counter and the cabin was transformed from being bathed in aquatically green light, to a flood of daylight. In such a heave Hannah caught sight of *Seawitch*. With a sudden urgent sense of excitement she leaned across the bunk, stretched over Lenqua's inert body and waited for *Erl King* to lift again.

A large swell building over the shallowing water off the coast held *Erl King* and raised her stern. With a little gasp, Hannah saw that they had gained on Richards, that she could actually see the man on his own poop! Then he was gone. A dark green gloom engulfed the cabin with a slopping thump against the ship's side, then she could see him again. She was sure it was Richards: a solitary figure standing at the port quarter of his ship, staring over the interval of water surging between the two clippers. They were on converging courses now, running ever closer together. Should she go on deck?

No, there was something thrilling about spying on the man as *her* ship overtook his. She would go up presently, but not yet. For the moment she could enjoy the spectacle in private, seeing, but not being seen.

Her heart was pounding. The sight of his black whiskers was inexpressibly overpowering. She felt a flutter of desire such as Munro had stirred in Shanghai and the images of the coital act had awakened in Foochow. Again the sea slopped up to shut off the view for a brief moment, and she closed her eyes as a sweetly tactile sensation spread through her being.

Daylight streamed back into the cabin; she looked down. The ascetic, thin hands of Lenqua caressed her breasts. *Erl King* lurched to leeward and Hannah was unable to draw back. Her arousal was overwhelmingly intense and she hung over the old man, allowing him to spread his long-nailed fingers across her bosom.

Lenqua was no threat and she had forgotten about Enright, until, that is, the sense of pleasure flooded through her, and she remembered his words: 'You will enjoy it.' Lenqua's dark, hooded eyes stared unblinkingly upwards, his hands remained upon her breasts and she saw his lips move.

'You are very beautiful . . . all my life I am curious about English woman . . .'

Tears of shame filled Hannah's eyes. Daylight again filled the cabin and she recoiled with an indraught of breath. Lenqua clung on as she backed away, the ship staggering and sending her crashing across the cabin against the far bulkhead. Lenqua was turned towards her, his face lifted above the bunk, his ancient hands still outstretched. Trembling violently she reached out behind her and found the

178

door-handle. As the *Erl King* buried her stern, Hannah fled.

On deck, Munro lifted the megaphone and smiled at Mai Lee. The frail Chinawoman clung to the mizen topmast backstay, her yellow silk robe fluttering like a prayer flag in the wind.

'How is Lenqua, Mai Lee?'

'He more sick, Mr Munro . . . no get better, bimeby die now.'

'I'm sorry.' Munro turned aside impatiently. He could see the poop of the *Seawitch* quite clearly, for Richards had edged up to windward and was trying to cut across *Erl King*'s bow.

'That's Richards, right aft with the glass trained on us,' said Talham from the side of his mouth, staring through a telescope.

'Yes,' Munro raised his voice. 'Captain Richards, do you hear me?'

They saw Richards lower the glass and his hand went out in an imperious gesture. Someone ran aft with a megaphone.

'Yes, I hear you.'

'We heard at Anjer you were ahead.'

'What kept you in the China Sea?'

'What shall I say?' Munro asked Talham, unable to think of a quick, facetious reply. But Richards gave him no time.

'I don't see Captain Kemball on the poop. Is he unwell? Is that what delayed you?'

Munro took a deep breath. 'Captain Kemball is dead . . . we were boarded by pirates . . .'

'Tell him I'm in command.' Munro looked round. Hannah stood by the companionway, one hand supporting herself. Her father's serge trousers were tucked into over-large sea-boots, but her hair was tousled in the wind and she wore no jacket.

'Who's in command?' shouted Richards.

'Tell him!' Hannah's order was peremptory. Astonished, Munro raised the megaphone again.

'Miss Kemball's in command . . .'

'*What?*' Richards roared, dispensing with the speaking trumpet so that they heard the legendary bull-roar. 'What's the matter with the Mate?'

Hannah shoved herself up the heeling deck from the companionway and took the megaphone from Munro.

'Can you hear me, Captain Richards?'

'Aye, Ma'am . . . my condolences . . .'

179

Hannah brushed the insincere formalities aside. 'I command, Captain Richards, and the terms remain the same.'

'You intend to continue the race?' Richards bellowed incredulously.

'What does it look like? We are about to steal your wind!'

A cheer rose across the heaving sea that ran like a mill-race between the two ships. The *Erl King*'s company lined the lee rail and waved their hats and hands, hung the ends of ropes over the side as though trailing tow-lines, and called a variety of suggestively insolent remarks at their rivals.

'We shall see, Miss Kemball, we shall see . . .' Richards turned and addressed some remarks to his officers.

'Captain Richards,' Hannah cried again, suddenly bold. 'The high stakes remain!'

'Hannah!' Munro's protest was sharp behind her.

Richards turned back to her. 'I'll see you in London, Ma'am,' he roared at her.

'That will fuel his vanity,' she said, handing the megaphone to Munro. He was wearing that wounded look again. Exasperated she asked, 'Well, Mr Munro, what does he mean "we'll see"?'

'We're running neck-and-neck . . . Ma'am,' Munro replied with frigid formality. 'He'll close the angle with our bow, then haul his wind when he's right ahead of us.'

'Why?'

Munro shrugged. 'To intimidate us, I suppose.'

'But surely, if he can sail a point closer to the wind, so can we . . . run parallel to him . . . that way we might yet steal his wind. We did it before.'

Munro blew out his cheeks. 'Yes . . .'

'Very well; then see to it, Mr Munro, a point closer if you please.'

Munro hesitated and stared down at Hannah. What the hell had got into the girl? Her shirt was open at the neck and . . .

'Mr Munro!'

He had never seen her look so determined. Was it that bastard Richards? Jealousy had uncoiled itself in Munro's belly, worming out of the repose in which it had slumbered since Foochow. 'You look cold, Ma'am,' he said, and turned forward. 'Braces there, steer sou' west a half west!'

180

Hannah made for the after companionway and the chart-room. She met Mai Lee coming up from the saloon. She seemed excited.

'Missee Hannah!'

'What is it, Mai Lee? What is the matter?'

'Mr Lenqua . . . he more better . . .'

'Better?' Hannah frowned.

Mai Lee nodded, her eyes bright. 'After you come topside I go below . . . Lenqua belong very happy. He say thank you . . . I say thank you . . .'

'Mai Lee, I don't understand.' The shameful episode of arousal at the hands of the old man could surely have had nothing to do with whatever Mai Lee was referring to.

'Lenqua tell me, Missee Hannah,' she lowered her eyes shyly, 'I savee . . . Lenqua more better now.'

Hannah stared in astonishment at the little woman. Her face was radiant, in stark contrast to the cloudy jealousy of Munro. Whatever the effect of the incident upon herself, its therapeutic value was incontrovertible as far as Mai Lee and Lenqua were concerned. She felt an overwhelming and preposterous desire to laugh and was joined by the shrill tinkling of Mai Lee. When she had calmed herself she asked, 'Mai Lee, what was the matter with Lenqua?'

Mai Lee wiped the tears of relief from her face. She beckoned Hannah nearer and whispered, 'Lenqua smoke opium . . . opium all finish long-time . . . Lenqua very sick . . . no can . . .'

Hannah frowned. 'No can what?'

'Jig-jig, but all better now.'

Hannah straightened up. So Lenqua had been prostrated by withdrawal symptoms, not cancer, and she had sat sympathetically with a drug-addict while another, beyond the width of the alleyway, lay confined from the same cause. And irony mounted upon irony, for something of what she had denied Enright, she had not withheld from Lenqua. For a moment she felt again the embarrassment of pleasure, but this was disarmed by Mai Lee's happiness. The sight of Mai Lee's smile dispelled Hannah's guilt and she was suddenly aware of the power she possessed, conferred by her own sensuality.

'We've altered our course, Miss Kemball.' Munro's head was shoved in the companionway above the two women. He stared pointedly down. Hannah felt the exposure of her open-necked shirt.

'Thank you, Mr Munro.' She brazened it out; he dipped his head and disappeared. Then Hannah knew, recalling Munro's words on the Bund in Shanghai, his own feelings as clearly expressed as possible, even while he sought to explain the general attitude of the Chinese: 'As for your overall dimensions,' Munro had said, 'they are elephantine!'

'Oh, Missee Hannah, I forget . . . Lenqua promise you one hundred pound you come Londonside number one.'

Hannah smiled ruefully. 'Please thank Lenqua. You were right, Mai Lee, Lenqua belong proper gentleman.'

It was that, of course, that made the difference.

Enright heard something of the encounter with *Seawitch* and learned more of the details from Osman. His mind was lucid now, his wound healing slowly. The enforced confinement of the strait-jacket compelled him to think, rather than act in response to his disturbed moods. His mind circled endlessly, from considerations of his victimisation to dark thoughts of revenge. At first these vengeful humours had sparked off violently tortured paroxysms of impotent rage. He had tossed shouting in his bunk, sweating and biting his tongue until pained and exhausted. But gradually the extreme nature of his illness diminished. His damaged mind began to repair itself.

The strait-jacket wound this cyclic thought spring-tight. With victimisation at its centre it spiralled outwards now, to terminate in the delicious contemplation of revenge, inventing scenarios by the score, dramatic dénouements in which Enright resurgent triumphed.

And always he had the girl.

'What d'you think, eh?' Dando Douglas asked the fo'c's'le as the starboard watch peeled off oilskins, kicked off boots and shook up the straw in its palliasses. 'And which of you bastards has stolen my baccy?'

'Which question d'you want answered first?' enquired 'the Duke'.

'I ain't fussy,' Dando said with a grunt, wrenching his left boot off and wriggling his toes.

'D'you mind if I ask a question first?' said 'the Duke'.
'What?'
'When did you last wash your feet?'
'Bugger off. Where's my baccy?'
'You're probably sitting on it.'
'Funny . . .' Dando located the pouch, rolled a cigarette and cocked an eye at his watch-mates. They were mainly character-ised by disappearing backsides clothed in flannel diving under blankets. 'Well, what d'you think?'
'What about, Dando?' said Gopher wearily.
'Why the frigging *Seawitch*, what d'you think?'
'Look, as long as that bastard Richards can flaunt his arse at us he's ahead, we're astern and he's winning. All right?'
'Yes, but . . .'
'Go to sleep,' snapped Gopher and was supported by grunts of agreement.
'What do *you* think, Duke?' asked Dando, leaning forward. They were the last men up, sharing the bench and table and the single lantern, the one smoking ruminatively, the other trying to read.
'I'm not thinking, Dando, I'm reading,' 'Duke' replied in a low voice, turning a page.
'Yeah, but what *do* you think?'
With a sigh 'the Duke' closed his book and laid it down. 'I'm not paid to think, Dando, merely to pull and haul, to hand, reef and steer. Of all other things *liberavi animum meum* . . .'
'What?'
'I have cleared my mind.' 'The Duke' turned to his book.
'No you fucking haven't!' Dando's face stuck pugnaciously forward. 'I know you're an educated cove and I'm pig ignorant, but you can't gull me with that French or Latin. You think all right, you think all the time. If you didn't think you wouldn't read.'
'The Duke' smiled and abandoned his book. 'Well done, Dando.'
Dando grew almost coy. 'I read a book once, and quite a good book,' he added hurriedly. 'What I remember most was, it made me think . . . so don't give me none of that crap. Now, what do you think?'
'The Duke' conceded defeat. 'All right, Dando, you win.

We've a chance, that's what I think. No more than that, and an outside chance because you can't pit determination against experience. Richards has got a full crew of officers, we've got a girl who's beginning to find her feet and a Second Mate who's a good seaman, but whose experience is limited. We got away with it the other night at the expense of Andy Jansen.'

'We got Talham,' put in Dando.

'The Duke' raised a dissenting eyebrow. 'He's got no drive, Dando, no vigour.'

'No guts, you mean?'

'The Duke' nodded, then reached across the table for Dando's tobacco pouch.

'My consulting fee is one roll.'

Dando shrugged companionably. 'Help yourself.'

'Now,' 'the Duke' said, lighting his cigarette from the chimney of the lamp, 'you tell me what *you* think.'

Dando rubbed his jaw and sniffed. He looked round at the inert hummocks in the bunks, then leaned forward confidentially. 'I'll tell you, an' it's kind of what d'you call it . . . when you think something you're not supposed to . . . like you was burned at the stake for?' Dando groped for the word.

'Heresy?'

'Yes, heresy, that's it . . . most of 'em,' he gestured at the sleeping shapes, 'most of 'em think it's unlucky having a woman in charge. Kind of unnatural. But I reckon . . . I reckon it ain't. I reckon that Miss Kemball's got something of her old man in her . . . some of his luck . . .'

'It'll need a bit of help,' said 'the Duke' drily.

'*Exactly!*' Dando leaned forward and tapped 'the Duke's' forearm. 'Bit of help, mate, that's exactly what it'll need.'

'The Duke' frowned. 'I don't quite follow . . .'

'You said it yourself. "Richards's got a full crew of officers" and we ain't, have we, eh?'

'The Duke' stirred uneasily, shaking his head.

'We could do with another one, eh?'

'The Duke' fixed his eyes on Dando. 'No.'

'You've got a bleedin' ticket . . .'

'No, I haven't!' 'the Duke' snapped, taking a final draw on his cigarette and pinching it out. 'And I don't much care who wins this race.'

184

He made to rise, but Dando's hand tightened its grip on his arm.

'But *we* do, Duke,' Dando gestured round at the somnolent forms, '*we* care 'cause it's all we've got to care about; a few bob extra, a present for the wife, a pair of shoes for the nippers on Sundays . . . *we* care. Reckon you owe us something.'

'*Owe?*'

'You're not one of us, Duke. You *fell* to our level to hide. You know it, an' I know it. I don't know what it is, but we took you in, and we ain't asking a lot . . . when it's over you can come back 'ere an' welcome, but I reckon you owe us for our 'ospitality.'

'The Duke' expelled his breath in a long sigh. Dando pushed his tobacco pouch across the table.

'I didn't know you resented me,' he began, picking out a twist of tobacco and laying it in the paper.

'We don't resent you, mate. We need your help, an' you can give it us. Look, Munro asked the Bosun and Chippy and that miserable sod of a Sailmaker to bear an extra hand, right?'

'The Duke' nodded, blowing a cloud of smoke.

'But they're only good at their own jobs, they ain't makee-learn officers like the 'prentice boys. That old bugger told Munro to hold on to canvas 'cause he *made* the bloody muslin, see; clouded 'is judgement. But you . . .' Dando terminated the sentence with a drag at his own cigarette.

'You're an astute bugger, Dando . . . what d'you want me to do, run aft and submit my *curriculum vitae* to Munro?'

'If I knew what a curry veetai was I'd probably tell you to stick it up your arse,' grinned Dando triumphantly, 'no, let me get a word with Mr Munro . . . or even Miss Kemball . . . p'raps she'd be better.'

'The Duke' shook his head. 'You know, I thought you were a fornicating little runt . . . never thought of you as a husband and father.'

Dando rose, stubbed his cigarette and turned to his bunk. 'You can't tell a sailor by his skin, Duke . . . you should know that.'

And long after Dando was snoring, 'the Duke' sat alone, smoking the tobacco Dando had shrewdly left on the table.

13

'IT'S A bloody headwind, damn it!'
Munro came aft, clutching his sou'wester, dripping and gaunt with fatigue. Hannah stood in the imperfect shelter of the after companionway, staring the length of the wildly pitching ship, watching *Seawitch* to windward of them now, though no more than two miles ahead. It was still neck-and-neck as the two ships ran down the coast of Cape Province over the Agulhas Bank. Closer inshore, taking advantage of the fierce counter-current, the smudge of an east-bound steamer's smoke disfigured the clarity of the horizon.

Offshore, where the clippers beat to windward, carrying sail to their double-reefed topgallants, the westward-setting Agulhas Current carried them inexorably to windward. With wind opposed to the set of the ocean, monstrous seas flung the two ships about like corks in a mill-stream, flicking the tall masts until they whipped and strained the stays to breaking point.

'You look tired,' Hannah said, as Munro came and stood beside her, anxiety plain on his drawn face.

'I'm all right,' he replied, his eyes searching for the weak point in *Erl King*'s top-hamper that he knew to be lurking somewhere in the miles of rigging; some splice waiting to draw under the strain; some shackle pin or hook abraded with wear; some chafed rope stranded from constant use. But all held, and Munro, despite himself, half-hoped something would part and give substance to his apprehension. He stared to starboard, under the taut curve of the courses; the steamer smoked eastwards on the quarter, beyond lay the loom of the coast.

'We must tack soon, or get caught in the counter-current,' he muttered.

'There goes *Seawitch*,' said Hannah.

Munro ducked across the deck, transferring his attention to *Seawitch* just as Captain Richards ordered her helm down. 'Ready about!' he roared, aware that *Erl King* was fully a quarter mile inshore of *Seawitch* and consequently that much farther from the strength of the favourable current. The watch went to their stations, those amidships at the lee pinrails up to their waists in water, black shapes whose flapping oilskins made them look like crows.

'Keep her full now,' Munro growled at Dando Douglas, the helmsman; then he raised his voice. 'Rise tacks and sheets!'

With a rattle and a mighty flogging the mainsail's hard curve bellied, cracked like a gun, then rose in its gear, tack and sheet rattling in their blocks.

Munro cast a quick look along the deck to see that all was ready.

'Lee-oh!' and to the helmsman, 'Down helm!'

Dando pulled the spokes down towards the wind. Hannah was on the grating beside him, bearing a hand. She could feel the bite of the rudder kicking the stern towards the coast, saw the long jib-boom scrape the sky with an upward pitch and swing away towards the Southern Ocean. On the fo'c's'le the headsail sheets were a-shiver and beside her the Sailmaker was drawing the spanker to windward, helping the rudder in driving the ship's head through the wind. For a long, hesitant moment it seemed as if the vibrating ship would shake herself to pieces as aloft the sails were flung back against the masts.

'Mains'l haul!' Munro bellowed. The main and mizen braces were cast off and their respective yards hauled round for the starboard tack while the ship passed her head through the eye of the wind and the after masts were blanketed by the foremast.

'Ooh! Look at *Seawitch*!' Hannah's voice was jubilant at Richards's misfortune. Munro's high-strung concentration wavered; he stole a look at his rival, glimpsed the cockbilled yard and erratically billowing topgallant that told of a parted lift and wildly flexing yard; then saw, like a mote of dust caught for an instant in a shaft of sunlight, the black speck of a falling man. He heard Hannah gasp as she observed the luckless seaman plunge into the sea.

'She's aback, sir . . .'

Munro recalled his own situation with the dullness of fatigue. A head sea had arrested the ship's turn and her backed foresails sent her skittishly astern in his momentary distraction.

'She's making a stern-board, sir,' Dando called desperately as Munro stared stupidly about him. 'Put the hellum over t'other way, Miss,' snapped Dando Douglas, tugging furiously at the spokes. 'Sails!'

Stimulated by Dando's initiative the Sailmaker let fly the spanker as Munro came to himself. 'Forrard there! Back the heads'l sheets!'

The faint cry of acknowledgement carried aft as the headsail sheets were pulled back to port. Going astern now, *Erl King*'s jib-boom drew a curve against the sky back towards the Cape coast, falling all the while to leeward amid the curses of her crew. Hannah was aware of the smooth crescent of water fanning out to windward of the ship's retreating hull as she drove in reverse. As the angle opened off the wind, the main and mizen sails now filled with wind while aback; at the same time those on the foreyard were once more drawing. *Erl King* slowed to a stop, neatly hove-to and making leeway. To windward, the crescent of smooth water had become a wide swathe.

'Jesus bloody Christ . . .' The Sailmaker muttered and Munro swore too, red with the indictment of incompetence that the struggling crew hurled in stage whispers at his lonely figure.

Embarrassed and confused, Hannah looked again at *Seawitch*. The hull of the rival ship was hidden by a wave, dead to windward of them, the shaking sail already under control, the distance between them increasing rapidly. Then she saw the man, quite close to her in the smooth water made by *Erl King*'s drifting bulk. A wave rolled under him and flung him up, hands waving, against the sky.

'James! A line . . . merciful God, Richards left him to his fate! A line, quick . . .'

It was Gordon who answered her excited cry. The apprentice snatched a heaving line from the pin-rail, coiled it swiftly and flung it at the figure. Hannah gasped as the line fell far short and *Erl King*, making greater leeway than the half-drowned man, drew out the distance. But they were shouting now, and perceiving rescue, the stunned man struck out with a final desperation. Gordon's third throw landed within a fathom of

189

him and he seized it. A ladder was thrown over the side with 'the Duke' at the bottom of it, one arm outstretched to assist. A few minutes later they drew the sodden wretch on deck. Voiding himself of copious sea-water, he gasped his thanks.

'I didn't . . . expect . . . you . . . to heave-to for me.'

'Neither did we,' replied Munro acidly, preparing to get the ship under way again.

'Thank God we did,' said Hannah.

'Amen to that, Ma'am,' said the newcomer, 'amen to that.'

It was a million-to-one chance, thought Hannah triumphantly, that their momentary misfortune had saved Jackson's life. In some primitive way it seemed to even the score after the loss of Jansen, and the odd similarity of names struck her with particular force. As she sat alone in her cabin, the now familiar logbook in front of her, waiting for the inked name of the new able seaman to dry, there came to her the strange sea-madness that persuaded lonely commanders that they communed with God.

'Jansen . . . Jackson . . . the Lord giveth,' she whispered, her eyes huge with awe, 'and the Lord taketh away . . .'

It seemed to her that the *Erl King* had indeed felt the touch of a providential hand. She closed the log and sat staring into space. There was more than that untimely missing of stays that had cast the ship astern and into the path of the drowning Jackson, for after they had hauled the yards, gathered way and tacked the ship successfully, Dando Douglas on the wheel had made a suggestion, a suggestion which had borne useful fruit.

''Scuse me, Miss,' he had said, staring first aloft, and then at the compass card swinging in the binnacle, 'it's none of my business, but I hear'd you saying Mr Munro was tired like an' I doubt we'd have missed stays if,' he had shrugged, 'well, you know . . .'

'He's doing his best,' Hannah recalled saying, following Dando's tugging on the opposite spokes and feeling a sudden surge of defensive loyalty towards poor Munro.

'No doubt, Ma'am, no doubt,' Dando had countered swiftly, shooting a sideways look at the girl, 'but he could do with some help, like.'

'Are you trying to say something?'

'Suggest, more like, Miss . . .'

190

'Go on.'

'Well, Ma'am, you've got a man with a ticket in the fo'c's'le . . .'

Dando had left the remark hanging, and its import dawned slowly upon Hannah.

'You mean a certificate of competency?'

'Well, it ain't issued by the Board of Trade, Ma'am . . .'

'I don't understand . . .'

'It's an Admiralty commission!' Dando Douglas had produced his ace.

'I still don't understand,' Hannah frowned, 'you mean someone aboard here is a naval officer?'

'*Was*, Ma'am. Court-martialled . . . conduct unbecoming, or some such thing . . . dishonourable discharge.'

'You mean . . . he could come aft . . .'

'And stand a watch, yes, Ma'am.'

And although 'the Duke' refused to leave his berth in the fo'c's'le, or to answer to any other name than 'Duke', he now worked watch-and-watch with Talham, while Munro took over the active command, free of the regular demands of a watch. Even now Munro lay exhausted in his bunk, fast asleep.

Hannah felt a surge of affection for him. Dear James, he had said nothing recriminating to her, though she knew it was her own cry of jubilation at Richards's loss of a topgallant lift that had precipitated their own misfortune. But had she held her tongue, had they not missed stays, Jackson would be drowned now, leaving a widow and three orphans! Hannah was light-headedly happy, feeling none of the professional disappointment and self-disgust that infected Munro and his crew. The fact that *Seawitch* was hull down to windward of the *Erl King* meant less to Hannah than to them. They had snatched a lost chick from certain death, cheated the ocean and besides, they had caught up with the Welshman before, and, *ergo*, could do it again.

Hannah put the log-book back on its shelf, helped herself to a nip of cognac from her father's tantalus and raised the glass to her eye in unspoken damnation of Captain Richards who had left a man to drown. Tossing off the cognac she left the cabin and went forward, an impish mood upon her. Osman was busy in his pantry and the accommodation was empty. She paused

191

outside Enright's door. No noise came from within. Beyond the panels of Lenqua and Mai Lee's cabin came the chatter, slap and bang of a *mahjong* game. She turned the handle of Munro's cabin door and slipped inside. He lay on his back, his belt loosened, his boots kicked off.

Hannah stood beside him, recalling the incident with Lenqua, almost willing Munro to wake and touch her where Lenqua's dessicated fingers had stirred her. But the exhausted Munro slept on in blissful ignorance of his missed opportunity.

'Missee . . . Missee . . .'

Hannah woke in the late afternoon, guiltily aware that she too had fallen asleep in her clothes. 'What is it, Mai Lee?'

'Mr Munro speak you come topside.'

Hannah nodded, feeling her mouth dry and her head aching. 'I come bimeby.'

'Mr Munro speak you come quick.'

'What is it?'

'I no savvy . . . Mr Munro say you savvy when topside.'

Feeling awful, Hannah dragged herself out of her bunk, drew on her pilot jacket and made for the after companionway. Munro met her in the chartroom. His eyes were alight with excitement. He grabbed her by both arms and she stared dully back at him.

'Hannah! We've doubled the Cape.' She could feel him shaking her slightly, communicating his high spirits, 'And Richards is no more than three miles ahead . . . I don't know how and I don't care, I think he must have damaged that fore topgallant when the lift parted and Jackson fell. We've eased the helm and the ship's going like a racehorse.'

Hannah, properly awake now, could feel the change in *Erl King*'s motion. The ship still heeled over, but her pitching was easier, a longer frequency with less jerk in it. No wonder that she had slept like a child!

'Our luck's changed, Hannah . . . *your* luck's changed.'

'I knew it,' she said, catching Munro's mood, 'the minute we picked up Jackson!'

He was still holding her by the shoulders. Impulsively she reached up as, simultaneously, Munro bent towards her. They kissed, unmoving until the sibilant wonder of an appreciative whistle came from the man at the wheel. In the square of daylight framed by the doorway, Dando Douglas grinned at them from the eminence of the helmsman's grating. Embarrassed, Munro turned to the chart, Hannah leaning beside him laughing at his discomfiture.

'I knew we could do it,' she said, covering his confusion, 'the minute Richards left that poor man to drown. He flew in the face of fate.'

'You sound like your father,' said Munro, looking at her again.

'Are you surprised?' she asked.

'No . . . and you are a darned sight better-looking.' They smiled at each other, ignoring Douglas.

'Thirteen knots, sir,' reported Gordon, having heaved the log and blocking the daylight in the doorway.

Munro turned. 'Very well.'

'You did well to save that man,' Hannah said, smiling at the apprentice.

'Thank you, Ma'am . . .' Gordon smiled. 'We're overhauling *Seawitch* fast,' he said, nodding at the horizon ahead.

'Let's have a look.' Hannah pushed past the apprentice and stood in the tearing wind. Almost with the habit of instinct, her glance took in the compass course: north-west, legging up for St Helena and the blue wastes of the South Atlantic. They had succeeded in doubling Africa and now laid a course for the equator.

'Be so kind as to pass me the long-glass.' She held out her hand as Gordon fetched the telescope.

The image danced in the lens, an intervening sea, grey-blue and streaked with spume, its crest breaking in a riot of foam, subsided to reveal her rival. Something was wrong aboard *Seawitch*. She had no idea why, but it was clear Richards had taken in sail and there was no doubt that she was losing her lead and *Erl King* was coming up hand-over-fist.

'Ease that weather topgallant brace there . . . on the main . . .'

The voice was unfamiliar; Hannah had forgotten 'Mr Duke'. His face turned towards her with a smile. 'Ma'am,' he acknowledged her presence. 'Fine tuning, Ma'am, like a violin. One has to tune for perfect pitch, *feel* the ship . . .' He was coolly urbane, almost unsurprised at his sudden promotion, and clearly enjoying the experience. 'One makes one's own luck in these matters, Ma'am.'

'I heard you were rather down on yours,' replied Hannah, disturbed by the man's easy familiarity and confident manner. She had expected a measure of diffidence, gratitude even, that she had rescued him from the obscurity of disgrace. In the euphoria of the morning she had even thought it a further manifestation of providence, that she had been able to offer him a second chance. Her reply, though not intentionally withering, was delivered to arrest his assumption of equality.

'The Duke' stared at her, his eyes suddenly icy, though the smile remained fixed. 'You should not always believe what you hear, Ma'am.'

'Nevertheless, I am intrigued . . .' Hannah's own effrontery amazed her. A new-found confidence surged through her as she stood her ground.

'Curiosity killed the cat.'

'Not if the cat provided a reference at the end of the voyage, surely?'

'The Duke' opened his mouth, thought better of it and snapped it shut. Some of the ice melted.

'All things in due season, Ma'am. For the nonce I'll practise fiddling.' He turned forward again, one hand half-raised to his cap in perfunctory salute, so that Hannah thought the gesture prompted by some long dormant instinct.

They were abeam of *Seawitch* by nightfall, to leeward of her, but too far off for her to steal their wind. The sunset was a watery reddening of rent clouds that denied them the satisfaction of an explanation as to *Seawitch*'s plight. Dawn found them almost alone, the tiniest fragment of white dotting the horizon astern, where *Seawitch* caught the morning sun – and disappeared.

It proved to be the best day's run noon-to-noon, nearly three hundred and twenty miles of hard sailing in a steady, quartering wind and a fine, tumbling sea. It seemed to Hannah's fanciful imagination that somewhere off the Cape of Good Hope, *Erl King*'s people had paid their debts to fate and were acquitted of further misfortune. It did not matter as another night settled over the ship that the rising wind forced them to reduce sail.

194

They had a lead on their rival and the lumpy seas that rolled up on the port quarter were too heavy to argue with. Hannah was radiantly happy as she left the deck to Munro and 'Mr Duke' who were bawling orders for the mustered watches to race aloft and stow the clewed-up canvas of the mainsail and topgallants.

Below in the saloon, the warm yellow glow of the lamp swung, casting shadows that danced with a wildness matching Hannah's mood, and threw a spot of light hither and thither across the polished wood of the table and bulkheads. She smiled at Mai Lee who sat on the settee with her malformed feet curled beneath her and the pack of cards ready in her hands.

'You play, Missee?'

'Yes . . . you like small-piece brandy, Mai Lee?'

Mai Lee nodded, her eyes sparkling. 'Lenqua sleep after he take tea. He very happy. Now Mai Lee drink small-piece of brandy, make Mai Lee very happy.'

Enright was delighted. The first part of his plan had worked perfectly. He was in no hurry. There was to be no botched assault this time. His prolonged isolation had taught him the pleasure of anticipation. Haste, he knew now, was the secret agent of disappointment. To attain that sublimity of achievement he sought, he had to assume complete mastery. The situation had to be manipulated in its entirety; there must be no margin for individual assertion that could throw his calculations awry. *That* had happened the last time. How could he have possibly foreseen the girl would have had a gun? And yet he ought to have known; he was no fool, he knew Kemball had had a gun in his cabin and he ought to have guessed Hannah would have secured it, for he was certain he had not misread her. The thought brought a warm glow to his entrails. No, he understood her all right: she was ripe and ready, panting for it, he was sure! He had read the desire plain in her eyes and if the silly bitch had not been squeezing a trigger when she felt the prompting of old Eve . . .

Still, Enright consoled himself, there was no point in crying over spilt milk. He had been shot for his pains and the thought made him relish the prospect of consummation all the more. Revenge was unutterably sweet.

He moved to the door of his cabin and pressed his ear to it.

Osman had freed him from the strait-jacket a week earlier. A little bribery mixed with some intimidation had secured the steward's loyalty. They had been together a long time. Osman was not going to be gulled by a self-seeking bastard like Munro, or impressed by the voluptuous Hannah. Osman felt nothing towards women and Enright had made it his business long ago to gain influence over the unfortunate man's peccadilloes. The threat of denouncement, the promise of continued employment, meant more to Osman than Munro or Miss Kemball could imagine. Besides, Enright, feeding on delicious dreams of vengeance, had not touched a drop of liquor, nor made any attempt to leave his cabin, once again lulling the pathetically gullible Osman into a compliance with which, stealthily, Enright had initiated his plan. Now, head bent to the locked door, he could hear the laughter of the two women in the saloon. Beyond the alleyway Lenqua lay in his bunk. Enright knew from Osman's gossip that the ancient Chinaman had run out of opium, and that from deprivation, he had become ill. Now weak and debilitated, the old man was making a slow recovery, tended by Mai Lee.

One bell sounded on the poop overhead. Half past eight o'clock in the evening. In a minute Osman would come with Munro or Talham to clear away his supper tray. Enright climbed back into his bunk, drew up his knees and lay groaning. When Osman came in Enright groaned again.

'What's the matter?' It was Talham in the doorway.

'My stomach, Talham, I've appalling gut-ache . . .'

'I'll get Osman to give you some Kaolin and Morph . . . I'll get you the keys, Osman.' Talham withdrew as the steward bent for the tray. Enright reached out and grabbed the thin figure by the throat, drawing the skull-like head towards him. 'Bring me laudanum, Osman,' Enright hissed into Osman's ear.

'Daren't,' spluttered Osman, 'daren't!'

Enright released him. 'In your own time,' he whispered, 'it's not for me.'

At two bells that evening, as Hannah and Mai Lee played cards and Enright suborned Osman, as Talham turned in and Munro wrote up the deck-log after shortening down, Able Seaman Molloy stood at the wheel.

196

He had stood thus countless times before, his glance alternating between the mizen topsail and the glow of the compass bowl, his shoulders hunched in his oilskins, his leathery palms passing a spoke or two of the smooth, worn steering-wheel back and forth as the ship dived and lifted to the scend of the sea. He had stood, times without number, at the wheels of other ships; barquentines, a brig, topsail schooners, barques. He had voyaged into the Pacific for sperm whales and through the Bering Strait for seals, he had fished the Grand Banks in a Blue-nose schooner when he married a Nantucket widow to whom he supposed, in the rare moments when he considered the matter, he was still bound. And he had steered *Erl King* since her maiden voyage when a cocky young Mate named Kemball had been recruiting a crew in Mother Vinney's knocking-shop off the Ratcliffe Highway.

Mother Vinney had tried throwing Kemball out, shouting that she dealt in girls not seamen, and he should try the shipping master for men. But Kemball had stood at the foot of the rickety stairs that were emblazoned with the crudely lettered legend 'The stairway to paradise', and bawled that Mother Vinney was too modest, that only men who knew how to use marline spikes came to her house, and after her girls had tested them, he would find them a berth, aye, and pay half their expenses!

The suckers had come out of the woodwork like worms at the news, and Kemball had signed them on. Now he was the last one left of the original crew. She was a fast ship, by damn, a real flyer! So good was she, that she forgave fools! Munro would get the hang of her and be one hell of a driver one day, and the ship knew it; so she had forgiven him his momentary lapse of attention off the Cape. It was a hard way to teach a man a lesson, but Munro would never make the same mistake again. All young men thought they were heroes, but the truth was they needed their sleep. It was old men that could stand for hours without relief. They had a lot more to think about . . .

'Easy girl,' Molloy muttered, feeling *Erl King* swoop sideways and down into the hollow of a following sea. Her fine after run made her difficult to steer in these conditions, as she sank her quarters into the bosom of the onrushing sea. Molloy felt the diminution of wind as, somewhere astern of them, the

197

oncoming wavecrest sheltered them. Then the ship lifted; with a mighty hiss the sea foamed almost to the rail, lending a ghostly lambency to the dark of the night. The wind tore at Molloy's oilskin coat-tails and drummed the flaps of his sou'wester. He palmed two, three, four spokes, felt the rudder bite deeply into the weight of water, and then turn easily, too easily, as the wave rolled away. Unsupported, the stern hung, then fell, fell into an ominously windless silence. Instinct caused Molloy to turn. The towering sea was monstrous. He could see the moving filigree of its tumbling crest against the dark blue of the sky. *Erl King*'s descent was arrested. She began to lift, but the concavity of her after body, that slender convergence of her shape that made her so swift, possessed too little buoyancy to respond quickly enough to the mass of water that rose about her. Molloy could not take his eyes from the majesty of the thing; he knew, an instant before it broke, that Cracker Jack was in the black heart of the wave, and that his own hour had come.

The breaking sea caught the lip of the deck, swept across *Erl King*'s poop in a torrent of green water. Molloy was torn from the wheel, flung full-length, and thrust forward. 'The Duke' turned and clung to the rail while in the waist the duty-watch seized the grablines as they sensed danger. Washed into a heap, soaked to the skin, they struggled to their feet cursing.

In the chartroom Munro felt the lack of wind and turned in time to see Molloy washed from the helm and hear his body flung against the wooden companionway. Deluged with water, Munro fought his way on deck and grabbed the wheel.

Water squirted into the saloon. Flung across the settee, Mai Lee found herself clinging to Hannah.

Relieved at the wheel, with the ship once more under command, Munro bent over the inert body of Molloy with the chartroom lantern. The old seaman's face was deathly white, almost blue beneath the thinning hair. There was no sign of bleeding.

'He's concussed,' said 'the Duke', holding a knife blade to Molloy's nostrils. The faintest misting told where the man still breathed. 'Better get him to his bunk.'

'Put him on the saloon settee,' said Munro to the men gathering round.

Hannah was calming Mai Lee when the clump of boots and swish of oilskins ushered in the stretcher party. Placing the old man on the settee the men trooped gloomily back on deck, leaving Munro with Hannah. Mai Lee sobbed in a corner. Munro sighed. 'He's pretty bad . . .'

Hannah felt for the pulse. It was fast and feeble, no more than a flutter of life.

'What can we do?' she asked.

Munro shrugged. 'I think his skull's cracked. He needs a surgeon . . .'

'The Cape?'

'There'll be a naval doctor on one of the warships at Simonstown.' Hannah could sense Munro's reluctance to put about for the Cape, for it meant defeat, loss of profit, the abandonment of all they had achieved.

'We've no choice, have we?' said Hannah, stating a fact.

'No . . .' Munro turned away, his hands out to grasp the rails of the companion ladder, 'I'll attend to it.'

'Yes . . . please do.'

Hannah squatted down beside the old man. His shallow breathing was light as a child's. How long would it take them to reach Simonstown? Would Molloy live long enough?

She heard the bellowed orders, felt the motion of the ship change as Munro swung *Erl King*'s head round towards the south-east.

'Race finish?' asked Mai Lee, tearfully.

'Yes,' Hannah replied. Now they were engaged in a grimmer contest, a race against death itself.

14

IT WOULD never have occurred to Hannah in the circumscribed world of her Islington upbringing to have resented
performing an act of humanity. But in the hours that followed
the pooping and Molloy's injury, she was honest enough to
admit harbouring such uncharitable thoughts. It was almost
more than she could bear to know that it was her own decision
that had reversed the course of the clipper. Nor could she derive
much satisfaction from the attitude of the men. With the perversity of their profession she had, perforce, to accept that in
their eyes she had acted wrongly; Molloy was obviously a
goner; Cracker Jack would never have put about, anymore
than Dandy Dickie Richards had done when Jackson had fallen
from the fore topgallant yard of the *Seawitch*.

Hannah had no way of knowing that had she made no
attempt to save Molloy she would have been tarred with the
same brush, but she was perceptive enough to sense that some
of the ill-grace with which the men moved about their duties
was in contempt of her female sentimentality.

'If', grumbled the Carpenter, 'we didn't have a woman back
aft there, none of this would have happened.'

'Cracker Jack wouldn't have turned back, I will say that
much,' concurred the Sailmaker, 'though I mind him getting
pooped one night when we ran down to the east of Formosa.'

'You'd think different if it was you lying there half-way 'twixt
heaven and t'other place,' said Bosun Harris, coming to
Hannah's defence, his oilskins dripping as he came to call the
watch. 'What else can she do? The problem is that old Jack
Molloy don't know when to kick the bucket.'

'He's stood his last trick anyway,' added the Sailmaker.

'And lost me half my bloody pay-off,' whined the Carpenter

resentfully, pulling on his sea-boots as he prepared to turn out on deck.

The *Erl King* ran south-eastwards until dawn. Mai Lee and Hannah took it in turns to nurse Molloy. Twice the old man came near to consciousness, murmuring a few disjointed words before relapsing into silence. As the saloon filled with the first grey light of the following dawn, Molloy slipped his last moorings.

'Old man makee die, Missee,' Mai Lee said quietly, shaking Hannah as she dozed in a chair. Wearily, Hannah came through to the saloon. For a moment she stood looking down at the frail shell, then she turned for the companionway.

'"Mr Duke"?' she called up to the poop.

'Ma'am?'

'Put the ship about. Molloy's dead!'

Heading north again *Erl King* ran her best distance noon-to-noon, a staggering three hundred and thirty-eight miles.

'That's a whisker over fourteen knots,' reported Munro as he and Hannah bent over the chart table and looked at the latest tiny cross that bore the legend of the date, the ship's noon position for that day. 'We *must* have made up what we lost.' He paused, looking at Hannah.

'We don't *know*, though, do we?' she said, 'And we have to bury Molloy.'

'I'll read the service . . .'

'It isn't that . . .' Hannah sighed shamefacedly.

'You mean you don't want to stop?'

Hannah looked at him, her expression candid. 'No, though I'm ashamed to say it . . . Please don't laugh at me.'

Munro was grinning. 'Molloy would have understood, you know,' he said. 'You are no longer among the dour plumes and black-horsed hearses of home, Hannah. You must see by now that seamen hang upon a thread of life of less substance than a skys'l halliard. We must check the way on the ship out of respect for the dead, but it need take no more than a moment . . . now you are laughing at me.' Munro frowned; Hannah's hand had flown up to her mouth. Unable to think what had caused her mirth, he asked, 'What have I said?'

'"Black-horsed hearses of home, Hannah"' she spluttered,

and they giggled ridiculously together, subsiding at last to a sober contemplation of the chart.

'D'you think he's ahead of us?' Hannah asked after a pause.

Munro shrugged. 'I doubt it, but one can never be sure.' A thought struck him. 'Wait a minute.' He ran up on deck and returned a moment later with Jackson. The seaman took off his sou'wester and nodded respectfully at Hannah.

'We were just wondering, Jackson, how you came to fall from the fore t'gallant yard of the *Seawitch*. I had meant to ask you earlier, but,' Munro shrugged again, implying other matters had intervened, 'is all well aboard her?'

Jackson studied the growing pool of water spreading from his dripping figure. 'Well enough, sir,' he mumbled.

'We were trying to judge, Jackson,' probed Hannah, 'why, after you passed Anjer ahead of us, we were able to overhaul you by the Cape; trying to guess how well *Seawitch* is sailing. Have you any idea how we caught you up in the trade wind passage?'

Munro could scarcely conceal his admiration for Hannah's handling of the matter. She was undeniably persuasive, melting any residual loyalty Jackson might have felt for the man who had left him to drown. 'If you've money on *Seawitch*, rest assured I understand, but I feel you owe us a little . . . mm?'

Jackson looked up. 'Aye, Ma'am,' he said. ''Tisn't easy, Ma'am . . . you see I've been with Captain Richards these past eight years . . .'

'But you fell from the yard,' Hannah reminded him softly, 'and he left you to your fate . . .'

'Aye, Ma'am, and you stopped for me . . .'

It amused Munro that none of the *Erl King*'s crew had disabused Jackson of his misapprehension. His own mismanagement shamed them all and they would have closed ranks, kept Jackson aware of his status as an alien, tolerated, but not quite welcome, for all that Hannah had signed him on the articles and made him work his passage. That, thought Munro, was the way of things on board ship.

Jackson could not fail to be aware of this slight hostility, nor fail to acknowledge that Hannah was now offering him a chance to prove his gratitude.

'Ma'am, I hope I knows my place, but, since the wager got to be common knowledge, Ma'am, begging your pardon, but

Captain Richards . . . well he was always a driver, Ma'am. Reckon 'tis my opinion that he were a better sailorman than your father, rest him, Ma'am, and no disrespect to Captain Kemball intended.'

'Go on,' coaxed Hannah, to whom the respective merits of sailorising were arcane enough and of far less interest than something she scented and wanted confirmed; something intuitive that she had known in the bizarre moment when she had contemplated Richard Richards from the secrecy of Lenqua's cabin, and the lecherous old man had touched her.

'Well, Ma'am, like I was saying, he was always a hell-driver, made his ship carry sail like, when other men thought it weren't prudent, but this trip . . . this trip he was like the devil himself, Ma'am, begging your pardon . . . like a man with a demon on his shoulder . . . we had a couple of accidents . . .'

'That slowed you down?' asked Hannah impatiently.

'Aye,' Jackson nodded, 'he padlocked the sheets and halliards, Ma'am, wouldn't let the Mates take sail off of her unless he was on deck.'

Beside Hannah, Munro whistled. She frowned quizzingly at him.

'Chain sheets on the courses,' explained Munro, 'you padlock 'em and pocket the key. It makes reducing sail a trifle difficult to do in a hurry. Chain snotters on the halliards . . . very dangerous practice.' Munro turned to Jackson. 'That's how the topgallant lift parted and threw you into the sea then?'

'Aye, sir.'

'And how did he explain this behaviour?' pursued Hannah.

'Explain, Ma'am? Why Cap'n Richards didn't ever explain nothing.'

'Very well, Jackson, thank you,' Munro said, and as the man turned away he added, 'Jackson . . . you wouldn't do anything to prejudice our chances would you?'

'I don't understand, sir.'

'Do anything to slow us down . . . deliberately.'

Jackson was affronted. 'No, I would not!'

'That's all right, Jackson,' soothed Hannah, 'I trust you implicitly.' She nodded dismissal.

'Now we know', said Munro, 'that Richards is running scared.'

204

'Yes,' said Hannah, smiling to herself, but Richards was not scared of Munro, Richards was scared of losing. And he was driven by something whose potency Hannah was only just beginning fully to understand. The attraction at Shanghai had been mutual and had nothing to do with the acquisition of Hannah's shares in her ship. Richards was spurred by desire.

They had passed the meridian of the Cape of Good Hope forty-four days after leaving the Min River. Eleven days later they passed St Helena, the conical summit of the island truncated by a layer of orographic cloud. Like the Cape, the land was too far distant to communicate by signal flags, so *Erl King* swept on, passing almost unchecked from the westerlies to the trades, through the high pressure of the horse latitudes. A steam frigate off St Helena made no attempt to speak with them and though they dipped their ensign as a mark of respect to the puissant might of Her Majesty's Royal Navy, the black-hulled ship with her low, antediluvian rig, wallowed blindly past them. In lighter winds three days later off Ascension they spoke to a German barque eight days out of Conakry bound for Rio de Janiero. Not surprisingly, she had seen nothing of the *Seawitch*.

As they edged northwards, the southerly latitudes that Hannah was now regularly observing by meridian altitude decreased in their value with each successive noon. They passed the equator without ceremony, carrying the south-east trades with every stitch of sail set until, eleven degrees north of the line, the winds became light, then variable and finally died into a doldrum calm.

Since the morning they had paused in the headlong homeward run to bury Molloy, the calm of routine had settled on the ship. Their misfortune off the Cape, the loss of Molloy and the leaked news that Richards was driving his ship with the sheets padlocked to the pinrails, had served to weld them into that mysterious sea-synthesis, a ship's company. How this process had worked no one knew precisely. It had something to do with Hannah and her swift, intelligent acquisition of sea-lore; it had something to do, too, with a natural authority she possessed, and this in turn might never have emerged had Mai Lee's counselling after her assault not proved timely. And Munro had played his part well. Awareness of his own inexperience

205

had tempered his handling of Hannah, helped by his innate respect for order and ownership. Shouldering the true burden of responsibility, yet deferring to Hannah as an equal in love, Munro fulfilled the promise spotted earlier by Cracker Jack.

But there were other factors, minor circumstances in addition to Mai Lee's fortuitous presence. The promotion of 'the Duke', which eased the strain on Munro, relieved some of the tension his acerbic presence had produced in the fo'c's'le; while Jackson, accepted at last, confided the eagerly swallowed secrets of the *Seawitch* that so delighted his watch-mates. These things produced a mood which, with the steady wind and romping progress of the ship, inspirited the morale of *Erl King*'s company.

Even Enright, after seven weeks of incarceration, was not governed with so much harshness. In Hannah's absence, he was occasionally allowed on deck, to speak of 'a cure' and 'past mistakes' and roll soulful eyes that fooled nobody in their insincerity, except that they eased the regimen of his confinement. Within such a corporate euphoria Enright's aggrieved soul machinated. Osman, by stealth and subservient weakness, obtained for him the laudanum from the medicine chest and, while Mai Lee and Hannah laughingly played their cards, a few crucial minutes of liberty. The glass of best *pekoe* that Lenqua took nightly stood in the fiddle fitted by his bunk. The old man sipped contentedly and, with the flavour of the Bohea leaf, imbibed the alcoholic tincture of opium. Enright ensured that the dose increased daily, reducing Lenqua to a state of somnolence. Mai Lee was deceived by its regularity, thinking it was due to age and exhaustion.

'Lenqua belong very old man,' explained Mai Lee, her eyes dark with tears, 'maybe no come Londonside.'

'Why he want to come Londonside, Mai Lee?' Hannah asked, as for the third evening Mai Lee reported Lenqua sunk early in sleep.

'I no savee,' Mai Lee had replied simply.

Eleven degrees nineteen minutes north of the equator, the full-rigged ship *Erl King*, bound from Foochow to London with 14,000 chests of *pekoe* and *kaisow* tea, was becalmed. She lay almost motionless, her sails slatting, the weary watch tending

206

the braces to every puff and catspaw that Talham or 'the Duke' felt, or imagined they felt. By such patient and remorseless effort they sought to work her through the doldrums, beyond which lay the fresh sailing breeze of the north-east trade winds. Only a keen observer would have noticed the fine ripples that drew out from her bow, and the imperceptible, turgid swirl round her rudder that accompanied the exaggerated movement of her bored helmsmen.

Munro, too, kept the deck, refreshed after the plain-sailing of the last weeks, but frustrated as their daily runs shrank from an impressive three hundred miles to a hundred score, then a single century and finally to a miserly dozen miles, a bare half-knot of speed.

But the lack of surface wind belied the torment in the atmosphere above them. The movement of the air here became vertical; surface wind metamorphosed into updraughts, rising to replace the displaced air of the trade-wind belts. Vast thunderheads reared into the sky, illuminated internally by flashes of lightning that lit up the deck and deluged them in torrents of heavy rain. The men brought out their clothes and stripped to their waists, washed and scrubbed so that the rain and soap-suds gurgled in the scuppers. They stretched spare sails and funnelled fresh water into the ship's tanks, and fought the endless war against chafe amid the slack bunts of the all but idle sails.

In this charged and humid atmosphere Enright moved to consummate his plan. Daily administration of laudanum to Lenqua had reduced the old Chinaman to a compliant state, while the regularity of Mai Lee's routine had prepared her unwittingly for sacrifice. Osman came as arranged, and slipped the lock while Mai Lee and Hannah played at chequers on the motionless saloon table. Enright, with the patience of a vulture, waited in excited anticipation. When he heard Mai Lee retire, he remained alert but unmoving. When he knew her to be disrobing herself, Enright left his unlocked cabin, crossed the intervening alleyway with a stride and was inside the opposite door.

Already aroused, his heart thundered with the power he possessed and the extremity of his desire. At a glance he took in the light breathing of the old man who lay like an ivory image, dismissing Lenqua as no impediment to his lust. The woman

207

stood before him, slender as a reed, not young but vulnerably desirable, teetering on her ridiculously disfigured feet. She had paused, her brocaded robe drawn half off, masking her head. Enright smiled, stirred still further by Mai Lee's uncertainty. She would have sensed the door being opened, but he did not move. He wanted to measure his sense of omnipotence against her reaction. He watched the flat muscles of her belly contract in fear as she half turned away, hiding the dark triangular prize he sought. Mai Lee pulled the robe from her head and stared at him. He allowed her a split-second of recognition, standing against the door.

He stepped forward and forced an arm around her waist. His free hand slapped over her mouth, drawing with it the silk cravat he wore ashore. Forced back against the high bunk Mai Lee covered herself, disgusted by the stink of him. Grinning, Enright fixed the gag in a second, his practised seaman's fingers working the reef knot in the nape of her slim neck. Then his hands ran down over her, seeking his long contemplated satisfaction, a satisfaction that was to be but the prelude to a far greater delight.

In his calculations Enright knew Mai Lee for a whore, a woman to be purchased, cajoled and made an ally of; a concubine who would shortly be in need of a new master by the look of the supine Lenqua; a Chink slut who would, when she came round to his way of thinking, lend her expertise and knowledge of the Thousand Delights to the ultimate, delicious humbling of Hannah Kemball. Enright grinned again, probing her, drawing aside her obstructing hands.

Mai Lee twisted her hands free. Her left hand trailed down over his belly in a gesture of acceptance; her right moved upwards, its palm flat as a board. As her left hand fondled him, her right swept across his mouth, smashing into his nose as the old Shanghai brothel-keeper had taught her long ago. Enright's nasal bone splintered as Mai Lee's blow drove the shards like lances into his brain.

Without a sound he arched back and fell dead at her feet.

15

'MISSEE . . . Missee, please!' Mai Lee hissed urgently outside the after cabin. Hannah opened the door with her hair already down and stripped to her shift.

'What's the matter?'

'Come, please come.' Mai Lee, wrapped in a chemise, backed round the saloon table, beckoning Hannah to follow. Her agitation was clear and at first Hannah assumed that Lenqua was suffering a relapse. Mai Lee led Hannah into the cabin where the old Chinaman slept obliviously. Hannah's foot stumbled on Enright's corpse and she drew back with a gasp. It was obvious he was stone-dead.

His body was half-draped by his dressing gown, his eyes dark-staring with the shock of the death blow. 'What happened?'

'He come here . . . like this . . .' Mai Lee gestured disgustedly at Enright's nakedness.

'He tried to . . . to . . . ?' Hannah could not bring herself to utter the word.

Mai Lee nodded. 'He try jig me!'

'Did you kill him?'

Mai Lee held her hand blade-flat and chopped upwards. 'Old lady Shanghai-side tell me long-time . . . Ay-ah, now we take cabin-side, chop-chop . . .'

'How did he get out?' asked Hannah as, holding one leg each, they dragged Enright, head bumping, across the alleyway and into his own cabin. With a shudder they left him there, spread-eagled upon the worn square of carpet. Hannah flicked the opened padlock hanging from the staple. She frowned. 'You come my cabin, Mai Lee, have small-piece drink, make more better.'

After the shaken Chinese woman had calmed herself Hannah sat alone. It was odd how little conscience she felt at having been an accessory after the fact. Enright had been murdered, or at least killed in self-defence; but, apart from the shock of handling his body, Hannah could not find it in her heart to feel anything other than unbounded relief. Enright's death was infinitely more justified than that of Jansen. She wondered who had set him free, then dismissed the thought, helped herself to another brandy and, undisturbed at her lack of remorse, turned in to enjoy a dreamless sleep.

Osman found him the next morning. White as a sheet the trembling steward, riddled with guilt at his collaboration with Enright, unsure of how much his weak compliance implicated him in a course of events of which he was largely ignorant, reported the matter to Munro. Obligingly, his sense of guilt prompted him to supply a cause of death.

'Must have fallen, sir. Struck his head, or something . . .'

Munro was no pathologist. Taking a superficial look at the body, he concurred. He was tempted to ask Osman if the steward had resumed the supply of liquor to the persuasive Mate, but he forebore. He went aft to Hannah and the log-book. His anxiety for want of a wind was greater than that to establish the cause of Enright's death.

Found deceased in his cabin, was all he wrote, pushing pen and log towards Hannah. 'Well, at least his burial will scarcely delay us under the circumstances,' he remarked, standing over her while she signed.

'No,' said Hannah, her hand trembling a little, touched at last by the finality of her act.

'Dead men tell no tales,' said Munro in an almost piratical vein. 'You are well rid of him, my dear,' he added sententiously so that Hannah, who had changed so much in the last weeks, felt again that prickling resentment at his patronisation.

'Someone unlocked his door, Mr Munro,' she said formally, 'so someone could tell a tale.'

The sea-gods seemed mollified by the death of Enright; the disposal of his corpse appeared to Hannah's imagination to pluck out the offending part of the body corporate, and release the *Erl King* from those contrary spirits that held the ship in the

210

doldrums. Hardly had Enright's body settled on the deep ooze of the ocean floor, than a breeze, capricious at first, but steadily filling the sails with stronger gusts, built itself slowly during the forenoon into a wind. By nightfall the ship was free of the doldrums and making nine knots. By the following dawn she was bowling along, taut on a bowline, her weather tacks hauled forward, her lee sheets aft, yards braced sharp up and driving through the north-east trades.

Twelve days later she passed the Cape Verde islands and signalled two ships. The next day she was in contact with a barque out of London bound for Yokohama. *Erl King* was the first ship they had hailed from China and the news ran through the clipper like fire. The outward ship hoisted further strings of bunting, but the *Erl King* was upwind, unable to read the flag hoists, and in a hurry.

'We can't be sure,' Munro said, jumping down from the saloon top, 'but I've a feeling in my bones . . .' he stared astern, as if seeking a sight of the *Seawitch*. 'She cannot possibly have overtaken us.'

Dolphins lifted under their bows, the last of the flying fish fanned from their speeding shadow as the undulations of the sea caused it to run out ahead of them as if impetuously drawing them onwards. The sabre-winged fulmars cruised back and forth across the wake that lay like green marble astern of them. Wildly screaming herring gulls and the lesser black-backs of temperate latitudes fought for the galley scraps, and in the troughs the tiny, dark petrels dabbled their feet in search of their minute prey.

Excitement mounted as they reeled off the miles. An increasing number of sails were seen. The dark smudges of steamers' smoke sullied the hard edge of the horizon; the sight of other ships became commonplace and was no longer the rare news-hungry encounter of ocean wanderers. In the prevailing tension Hannah was unable to stay below. Leaning on the rail she marvelled at how much she had changed since, outward bound, they had traversed the same seas. Dragged by her father's avarice from comfortable obscurity, she had become mistress of her own fate, God and the spirits of the sea willing.

'You have the Channels, Hannah,' Munro said, joining her as she leaned upon the after rail and stared astern.

211

'The *what*?'

'The Channels – a nervous excitement relying heavily on anticipation and expectation, epidemic among seamen entering soundings in the Channel . . . you have an early attack, that's all.'

'You are an impertinent fellow, Mister Mate,' she replied laughing. 'Will you ship out with me again?'

'Will you have me?'

'Of course!'

'Very well, then . . . subject to a few conditions,' Munro added seriously.

'Conditions, sir, you dare to speak to me of conditions,' she said with mock haughtiness.

'Oh, yes, Hannah, because the gentlemen of the Board of Trade will not permit a repeat of this irregularity and it would make life less complicated if . . . we were, er, better mated than by our present arrangement.'

Hannah straightened up from the rail and turned to face Munro. 'Is that a tarpaulin proposal, Mr Munro, or a mildly offensive pun?'

'I'm serious, Hannah . . . I have hopes . . . expectations . . .'

'Yes, I know.' She turned again to contemplate the wake and lowered her voice, shedding her bantering tone. 'Let us wait and see, James. No promises yet on either part . . . Captain Richards also has . . . expectations.'

She left Munro by the taffrail and went below. The Scotsman stared gloomily astern, watching a tiny storm petrel quartering their wake; a tiny bird that rode the wind and seemed unafraid of the roil of the sea. It made him think of Hannah. She had looked so vulnerable when he had caught her donating the log-line to the beggar-woman in Shanghai. Yet he found the revelation of her hidden strength did not diminish his fondness for her. He too must have changed, changed by association with the deceptively adaptable stormbird. But what did she mean by Captain Richards having expectations? Surely she had no intention of standing by her father's bet?

The early northern autumn morning found them to the west of Finisterre. In thick, damp weather with a heavy sea they ran before a south-westerly gale. The plummeting barometer warned them to batten down, and once again they rigged life-lines and fisted the upper canvas. The sea seethed alongside, a hissing accompaniment to their impetuous progress.

Munro waited patiently for hours, his sextant crooked in his arm, hoping for a glimpse of the sun as they stormed along, racing into a bottleneck crowded with the commerce of Europe. Bounded to the north by the rocks of the Scilly Isles and the rampart of Cornwall, and to the south by the reefs of Ushant and the salient of Brittany, the chops of the Channel lay ahead.

'We want to make our landfall on the French coast, if we can,' he explained to Hannah, 'but to approach too close without a good fix could be hazardous.'

Munro was frustrated. The sun set unseen. He remained on deck all night, keeping the lookouts vigilant as they ran in among other ships making anxiously eastwards for their ports of destination, or debouching west, into the vast Atlantic. Munro bowed under the weight of responsibility he bore. Though Talham and 'the Duke' had proved able subordinates, the one unexceptionally, the other with a grating flamboyance, the 'leisure' of command bore heavily upon him. So much depended upon him: the success of the voyage, the well-being of the crew, to say nothing of his personal future. But Munro was a man of true rectitude, setting personal ambitions aside and accepting the burden of his post. He commanded, and for him alone was the choice between daring and caution. Eventually caution won. The unflinching steadiness of the glass persuaded him they would carry the thick, misty weather right into the Channel. He bore up a point, keeping off the dangers to leeward, hoping for a glimpse of a dawn star or the morning sun. But overcast draped the heavens, denying him a fix and leaching a grey dawn so that, when Talham came on deck at eight o'clock, a frustrated Munro dozed fitfully in the salt-stained hammock-chair.

Hannah was on deck a few moments later. A sleeting rain fell upon her tanned face bedewing the lock of hair that escaped rebelliously to leeward. She barely noticed the chill of the rain as she waited for the apprentices to complete the ritual heaving of the log.

'Twelve, Ma'am, and a half if you wish?'

'A half for prudence, I think, 'tis better to be ahead in our reckoning in this weather.'

The boys exchanged winks. They had taken to calling Hannah 'the Old Woman', as much for the airing she gave her newly acquired knowledge as for her ownership of the clipper. They knew, too, that their future careers depended upon her, and were careful to keep the nickname to themselves. Sniggering, they coiled the log-line, looking up as Hannah shouted: 'Mr Talham! Look!'

Hannah pointed out on the port bow. Emerging from the mist the low black hull of another full-rigged ship ran parallel with them, her hull in a smother of foam. Tier above tier of sails took substance as the rain passed ahead and the mist evaporated. Munro was suddenly awake and on his feet.

'Watch for the change of wind,' he shouted, staring anxiously to windward where the grey scud was rent, peeling back to reveal patches of blue as the cold front swept down upon them from the north-west with its promise of a veering wind.

'It's them!'

Hannah's shrill cry cut the air as she stared at the strange ship through the hurriedly snatched up watch-glass. She recognised the solitary grey figure on the poop, saw the movements of his arm command men aloft to shake out the royals.

'It can't be!' shouted Munro dismissively, knowing full well their rival could not possibly have caught them. Silently Hannah held out the telescope.

Munro seized it, twisted the brass barrel into focus and swore with unashamed vehemence. 'Bloody hell!'

There was no denying the gold letters curved across the other ship's counter: *Seawitch, London.*

'Call all hands and set the royals, Mr Munro!' snapped Hannah, taking station beside the helmsman, 'and if *you* lose a knot through inattention,' she hissed at the startled Gopher Stackpole, 'you'll wish you'd never been born.'

An overwhelming feeling of anger and, at the same time, exhilaration filled her. She knew this to be a moment to be seized. Hannah was unconcerned that Richards had stolen a march on them. Her mind was untrammelled by frustrating calculations, of reassessments of decisions that she had never had to make. She appreciated Munro's professional aggrievement, just as she appreciated his professional caution. He had been more than an asset throughout the voyage, but his

214

anxieties had worn his nerves thin. Poor Munro was exhausted; he had done all that she could expect him to do and she sensed his humiliation as keenly now as she had in the Shanghai grog-shop. Richards's dominating presence was almost tangible. The technical miracle of arriving in the Channel ahead of them smacked of his reputed wizardry, and such was the power of so potent a reputation that it had the men open-mouthed with shock, their shoulders drooping in defeat as they stared at the *Seawitch*. Munro was stunned, paralysed by indecision, alternately staring aloft and then across at *Seawitch*. He had not yet acted on her order.

Hannah jumped up upon the saloon top. 'Royals, Mr Munro!' she repeated sharply, 'And all hands!'

Another glance at the *Seawitch* revealed a flutter of white blooming from her foretop. A few seconds later, set with the precision of rigid discipline and superb training, *Seawitch* stretched her lee foretopmast studding sail.

Hannah stood and observed as the watch below turned out. Alarm that they had been called for some dire emergency caused by the thick weather prevailing at the time of their going below, changed swiftly to eagerness as they saw the blue sky and sunshine – and then the *Seawitch*. Munro's despair was not endemic, she noted, and the duty men's despondency, understandable though it was, was swept aside on this wave of corporate enthusiasm.

'Royals, boys!' she shouted, seizing this initiative, and the men sprang aloft.

'Then we'll give her the stuns'ls, Mister!' she cried, slipping below and leaving Munro to recover from his shock. She gathered a few things from the cabin, wound a silk scarf about her neck and made for the after companionway. Mai Lee met her in the saloon.

'Missee . . .'

'Not now, Mai Lee . . . ship race Captain Richards, bimeby Londonside soon. You tell Lenqua.'

Back on deck Apprentice Waller bumped into her. 'Portland Bill, Ma'am.' He pointed to port and she could see the red and white banded tower of the lighthouse set beneath the dark grey hummock of the Verne. She looked at the *Seawitch*. There was no doubt her relative bearing was drawing ahead: *Seawitch* had

215

the legs of them. Peering aloft she saw the studding sails unset.

'Mr Munro!' Her voice cracked with harshness. Munro's face turned towards her.

'What?'

'Get the stuns'ls set, lee main and foretopmast first, then give her the lee t'gallants, if Richards gains another yard . . .'

'Don't talk like a fool, Hannah,' Munro was beside her with a bound, grabbing her wrist in his urgency. 'This wind will freshen and is squall-bearing . . .'

'I don't care,' she snapped, out-staring him. 'All right, I take responsibility . . . I'm sorry it's come to this, but I own the ship. Look, I appreciate your caution, admire your skills and I am relying on you now not to make a mess of it, but when Richards hoists his weather kites, out go ours as well, d'you understand me?'

Munro havered, tired and angry that she might cheat him of his nearly realised ambition to bring home the *Erl King* from China in one piece. What did it matter now if Richards pipped them at the post? Their time and performance were creditable, they had killed one man and could claim a moral triumph in saving another whom Richards had left to die. And now this chit of a girl, lovely and desirable though she was, was snatching the real command from him, usurping his rightful position on the basis of ownership and a stupid, overweening pride. He knew she was at liberty to tell Richards to go to hell if the Welsh goat came demanding her hand in marriage, for he had been a silent and embarrassed witness when the wager had been made. Besides, surely fifteen thousand miles had cooled the ardour of a drunken bet?

And yet to win outright . . .

'Do I have to make it an order, James,' she hissed, 'or can we do this together?'

Her eyes were alight with an impetuous madness; her breath was sweet on his face and he caught the youthful infection of audacity from her.

'You're mad, Hannah, and foolish, and that's my professional opinion; but I admire you and love you, and if you've a mind to give that Welshman a bloody nose I'm not averse to it. He who pays the piper calls the tune, eh?'

216

'Good,' Hannah nodded, 'now set those weather stuns'ls, then call all hands aft.'

She stood at the break of the poop as they trooped aft, the silk scarf bright at her throat, the only feminine concession in her garb, dressed as she still was in her father's cast-offs. Tearing off the small-crowned hat she shook her hair free in the wind and watched their mouths open and their eyes fasten upon her.

'It's Paddy's watches, boys,' she called, 'go-on and stop-on until we're in the London River with that ship there', she stabbed a finger dramatically to port, 'astern of us.'

The Carpenter led the cheers. 'Half my bloody pay-off's on her bowsprit over our arse-end, Miss,' he yelled.

'And mine's on *my* bowsprit being anywhere but aboard this hooker next time *I* doss down,' muttered another, staring up at Hannah.

'Bloody Channel fever,' warned the Sailmaker loudly.

'Will your sails hold?' countered Hannah sharply.

'Aye, they'll hold, don't you worry . . .'

They cheered and Hannah drew two bottles of her father's brandy from her pockets. 'Here,' she said, tossing them down, 'one for each watch, another when the pilot boards and a third when we dock.'

She turned away, smiling triumphantly and ignoring Munro's ruefully shaking head.

'Miss, Miss?' She swung round to see Jackson half-way up the poop ladder.

'Yes, what is it, Jackson?'

'Mind him, Miss. Keep an offing, he may attempt to run in close an' put you off.'

'He wouldn't dare,' she called, self-confidently tossing her head again.

But he did.

By noon they were off St Catherine's with the Isle of Wight already fading astern. Three cruisers under power exercising off the Owers crossed in impeccable line-astern a mile ahead of them. Munro ordered the ensign dipped and then their numbers hoisted below it.

'Signal your requirement for a tow,' said 'the Duke'.

217

'Don't be facetious,' snapped Hannah, watching the closing distance between the two ships.

'Append the geographical tag for Dover and you might be luckier than you think. The Royal Navy use long-range semaphore and might be in an obliging vein,' went on 'the Duke' unabashed by Hannah's tartness and her misinterpretation of his meaning.

Munro nodded. 'Good idea,' he said, and Gordon, Waller and Stokes busied themselves with bunting and flag halliards.

'Well, they've acknowledged; perhaps they'll pass it on.' Munro scooped the flags off the deck and helped the boys to fold them.

'They'll pass it on . . . it's good practice, just the sort of thing they enjoy,' 'the Duke' remarked bitterly.

Erl King was neck-and-neck with the *Seawitch* by the time the two ships passed Beachy Head. Here the tide came foul, chopping up a nasty head sea that pitched the ships, whipping the upper spars and causing the lighter sails to spill wind.

'Take in the kites, Hannah,' cautioned Munro, staring up at the straining gear.

'No!'

'You'll carry something away if you don't,' he warned.

She was staring at the *Seawitch*'s poop. 'I want to pass him,' Hannah muttered intensely, watching at Richards through the glass.

Munro stared at her. He wanted to say they had done their best, that she was being childish, but something stopped him. He turned away exasperated, angry with himself for chancing these last vital miles to . . . to what? *Her* expertise? Hunching his shoulders, his hands in his pockets, he went aft to growl at the helmsman for being three degrees off course.

There was a sudden crack from aloft followed by a thundering flogging. For a few seconds the tatters of the main skysail streamed from their bolt-ropes, then shredded away to leeward. Almost alongside them the *Seawitch*'s crew were leaping into the rigging, and they could hear the orders bellowed by Captain Richards from his poop.

'Aloft and cut that mess away,' shouted Hannah as Munro ran forward.

'Hannah, get the stuns'ls off her for heaven's sake!'

218

'No, not until *he* does.' She nodded at the *Seawitch*.

'He *is*, Hannah, can't you see the men going aloft now?'

'It's a ruse! He's trying to frighten us into following his lead before he reduces sail!'

Munro stared at Richards. Was she right? It was quite possible. *Seawitch's* crew were spread out along the yards and stationed in the tops, but not a sheet had been started yet.

Inch by inch *Erl King* gained a lead. Her mizen mast drew level with *Seawitch's* main. Hannah turned triumphantly to Munro. 'We've done it . . .'

'Not yet, you haven't! By God, watch him!'

'Water, damn you!'

Richards's stentorian bellow carried over a rapidly narrowing gap above the slop and hiss of the sea running confused between the two ships.

'Water!'

Hannah turned to Munro. 'What does he mean?'

'We are the overtaking vessel and obliged to keep clear.'

'But he's edging over deliberately,' Hannah cried indignantly, 'look, you can see what he's up to!' She pointed to Richards standing coolly beside the wheel of his ship, steadying the nerve of his helmsman. 'Water!' he claimed again. Both had forgotten employing a similar ruse in the China Sea.

'Isn't he obliged to hold a steady course, or something?' Hannah asked desperately as, from aloft, there came the unmistakable sound of more splitting canvas.

'Weather foretopmast stuns'l's parting company with its boltropes, Ma'am, shall I douse the kites?'

'No!' Hannah rounded on Bosun Harris as the men moved instinctively towards the halliards coiled on their pins. 'Leave those ropes alone!'

She drew the heavy revolver from her waistband and raised it. 'Hold your course, Captain Richards!' she cried.

'Keep off, Ma'am, you're crowding me dangerously!'

The gun cracked, leaping in Hannah's hand, then cracked again.

'Hannah, for God's sake,' began Munro, but the voice of protest was drowned in the noise of catcalls and whistles as the tiny holes joined each other in a rent, and *Seawitch's* huge lee foretopmast studding sail split from head to foot. A moment later, after Richards had run forward to the break of the poop and his mate had shouted the extent of the damage, the *Erl King* was clear ahead of her rival. In the gathering darkness to the eastward, the loom and then the light of Dungeness winked on the horizon.

'All's fair in love and war, I believe,' Hannah called laughingly astern.

They held the lead as the wind veered with nightfall, coming off the land and cutting down the sea, to give them a broad reach for the South Foreland with the turn of the flood tide.

'We'll prepare the night signal for a pilot,' said Munro, 'the cutter will be cruising just beyond the ness.'

'Very well . . .' Hannah said, preoccupied. The germ of an idea was teasing her brain. She watched as, in the dusk, the men prepared the tow-rope for the tug and the flares for the pilot.

'Will we get a tug?' she asked Munro as he came aft, satisfied that all was ready.

'I hope so. If "Mr Duke's" traverse works, someone will have got wind of us. The two of us will be expected by now, especially if we're the first of the China fleet . . .'

'I hope we are!' said Hannah vehemently.

'Yes, yes,' soothed Munro, 'I'm sure we are. We are bound to have been reported from Portland or St Catherine's, even if the Navy's let us down, and with this in mind the tug-masters in Dover will be out touting for business.'

Hannah bent her head, lost in thought.

'Now, for God's sake get the upper stuns'ls off her,' Munro looked astern. The red flush of sunset spread across the western sky. Puff-balls of cumulus were ink-dark against the after-glow and the silhouetted *Seawitch* trailed *Erl King* by a mile.

'Very well,' Hannah agreed, 'and then I want you to gather up the ship's papers and prepare to get ashore.'

'*What?*'

'I'll tell you why when you've shortened down.'

Munro stood in the darkness amidships, glad of its cover to conceal the awkwardness he always felt in shore-going clothes. He was loathe to leave, loathe to be party to a subterfuge that reeked of sharp practice. But he knew now that Hannah was not to be crossed, that Cracker Jack's daughter was a woman of spirit, and he was too good a seaman not to take advantage of any fair wind. If she had denied him a final answer to his proposal, there had been nothing equivocal in her offer of command of the *Erl King*, and he doubted there was a Board of Trade Examiner that would fail him his master's certificate if he brought home the first of the season's tea from China!

'Good luck, Mr Munro,' said Bosun Harris as they secured the ladder over the rail and Gopher Stackpole hung a lantern next to it. They were suddenly lit by an iridescent flare and then the tiny pilot boat surged out of the blackness, the well-scuffed hull rubbed their topsides and the ladder jerked tight. A few minutes later the pilot stood on deck, to be conducted aft by Apprentice Gordon and to express his surprise at being met by Hannah Kemball.

'Damn it, Ma'am, but I expected John Kemball. Though I heard his daughter was aboard,' he added hurriedly.

Hannah crossed to the side. She was just in time to catch sight of Munro in the deckhouse doorway of the steam pilot cutter as it turned away after recovering its boat.

'Is your father . . . ?' The pilot made a gesture, clear enough in the dark, to indicate a bottle being swigged.

'My father's dead, Pilot,' Hannah said tartly, 'have we a tug?'

'Aye, Dover Steam Towage have had the *Impellor* flashed up since tiffin-time and she should be off the Foreland about now . . . I'm sorry about your father.'

Hannah ignored the artificial condolence. 'Then let's square away, I've a mind not to lose the lead through gossip.'

'By all means,' said the Pilot, giving Talham the order and steadying the helm as they gathered way, making up into the crowded Strait of Dover. A steam packet crossed their bow ablaze with deck-lights. Further offshore the lights of larger vessels, the green eyes of outward sailing ships and the white masthead lights of steamers, criss-crossed the water. On the port bow the glow of Dover loomed beneath the white welcoming wink of the South Foreland lighthouse. Far to starboard the flash of Cap Gris Nez echoed the greeting.

'Steamer coming up astern,' remarked the pilot conversationally, as he set a match to his pipe and joined Hannah at the poop rail. 'I wonder if . . .' he began, but Hannah cut him short.

221

'You're sure there'll be a tug?' she asked.

'Sure as one is of anything at sea, Ma'am.'

'And we are the first ship home . . . from China, I mean?'

'Means a lot to you, does it?'

'Of course it does!'

'Pardon my curiosity, but did *you* bring the ship all the way from China?'

Hannah smiled in the darkness. 'Yes. I had a first-class Chief Mate, he's away with the ship's papers in your boat. And I have the first-class crew my father left me.'

'And you beat Dickie Richards in *Seawitch*?'

'Yes.'

'Then I hope, young woman, you've a guinea or two riding on the outcome, for as far as I know, no other ship has arrived from China though they've been expected . . .'

But Hannah was no longer listening. There was more than a guinea or two riding on the outcome, and she had promised both watches another tot when the pilot was aboard.

'Excuse me a moment.' She slipped below to get the cognac, returning to the deck to find some confusion reigning.

'But I thought . . .' Talham's voice was raised in anger.

'That damned steamer's got in the way . . . ' the Pilot countered, and Hannah was aware of the black shape two cables to windward of them. The white flurry of water under her stern showed where her screw thrust the overtaking steam-kettle past the clipper, and then they were engulfed in sulphureous clouds of noxious smoke that nearly choked them. The men swore, as much with frustration as from the suffocating effects of the funnel gases.

Just beyond the stern of the passing steamship, the low lights of a tug emerged, heading, amid a thrashing of paddles, for the flares burning on the deck of the *Seawitch*.

'That's *our* tug,' said Hannah in disbelief, 'and it's going to the *Seawitch* . . . Pilot, I thought you said . . .'

'It might not be our tug, Miss Kemball . . .'

'Of course it's our tug!' snapped Hannah, and her voice cracked with intense, infuriating disappointment. An uncontrollable lump rose in her throat and tears welled in her eyes. Only the merciful darkness hid the extent of her bitterness.

A second tug, the *Sultan* found them half an hour later, but it

222

was with *Seawitch*'s stern light winking ahead of them, that they passed inside the South Goodwin light-vessel and turned north for the Gull Stream and the estuary of the River Thames.

16

HANNAH'S disappointment at missing the tug was intense and was compounded by her loss of Munro's support. She began to repent of the subterfuge on which she had dispatched him. Could she deny Richards the victory he had earned? It galled her that *Seawitch* had left Foochow after *Erl King* and would have made the faster passage even had they held their lead. Yet the thought of being beaten, of not meeting Richards as an equal in London, made her even more determined that she must yet steal a march on him. Disappointment began to change to a determination that, even now, she must find a way to deprive him of victory. In this turmoil, she was unable either to be sociable to the Pilot or to take herself below.

With the tide, *Erl King* towed past the Gull Stream light-vessel and round the North Foreland, astern of the thrashing *Sultan*. Dawn found them off Sheppey, butting a backed wind, a short sea and an ebb tide. On the port bow the red hull of the Nore light bobbed amid a crowd of shipping waiting for the flood. Swim-head barges, inbound stackies and big sprit-sail coasters waited among the barques and brigs from the Baltic and the steamers from the Mediterranean. To the south, over the Kentish Flats, oyster-dredgers from Whitstable and smacks from Brightlingsea worked the fishing grounds, while closer, off the Yantlet and the Maplins, Leigh bawleys trawled industriously.

Seawitch was two clear miles away, in the charge of the *Impellor*, a faster tug than the *Sultan*. To Hannah's jaundiced eye an investment of one hundred pounds for the tow was one more spur to her desire to get even with Captain Richard Richards. And then she thought of the expense of Munro's train fare from Folkestone or Dover and her ineptitude struck her again, and again she missed Munro.

The Pilot had made consoling noises on Hannah's behalf, but they only served to increase her irritation, reminding her that she was coming home, home to a world where a decorous demeanour would be expected of her. Even, she reflected with horror, a subservience, should she marry. After her ocean freedom the thought infuriated her: it was intolerable! Nor could she expect to be allowed to continue in her present life. The gentlemen at the Board of Trade, as Munro put it, would not permit it. Nor would any other 'gentlemen'. And although she had a good man to command her ship in James Munro, she did not feel inclined to devote her life to playing the passive role of Master's wife!

As they struggled past the Nore the Pilot turned and said for the umpteenth time, 'Don't take it too hard, m'dear . . . you were first ship to the pilot station. You did your best, and no one can do more.' She might have taken some comfort from him if he had not added, nodding at her inappropriate and salt-stained clothes, 'Perhaps you'd like to change? Don't worry about the ship, she's safe in my hands.'

In the end she had gone below, but only to cry the bitterness out of herself.

Mai Lee, entering the cabin without knocking, put a commiserating arm about Hannah. She, too, was in tears.

'Mai Lee,' Hannah said, raising her head and sniffing indecorously, 'what is it? What is the matter?'

'Lenqua,' sobbed Mai Lee, 'Lenqua belong dead, Missee Hannah . . .'

'Oh, Mai Lee, I'm so sorry . . .'

Hannah took the tiny, fragile figure into her arms, and smoothed the oiled hair. Shamefully she remembered how she had brushed the tiny Chinese woman aside the day before.

A knock came at the cabin door. 'Who is it?' Hannah disengaged herself.

'Gordon, Ma'am. Mr Talham says to tell you we're abeam of the Chapman lighthouse.'

Something stirred in Hannah's memory. 'Gordon!' She called the boy back.

'Ma'am?'

'How many days are we out of Foochow?'

'Ninety-two, Ma'am,' the boy answered unhesitatingly, from beyond the door. The exact number of days on passage had been the talk of the ship for a week. Gordon could gleefully reveal 'the Old Woman' had lost count!

'Thank you,' she called. Ninety-two days was what O'Halloran had bet Willis they would do it in. It was an irrelevant thought, but it stirred Hannah. 'Come, Mai Lee, we must put on a bold show . . .' She opened the cabin door. 'Osman!' she cried, 'Hot water, and jump to it!'

'Aye, aye, Ma'am,' answered the startled steward.

'What belong "bold show", Missee Hannah?' asked Mai Lee.

'Bold show, Mai Lee, means do things proper-fashion. Just now we come Londonside. We come Londonside proper-fashion. You savvee?'

Mai Lee nodded and dried her eyes. 'I savee.'

Talham, 'Mr Duke' and Bosun Harris, the misanthropic Sailmaker and the spendthrift Carpenter; Gopher Stackpole, Bill Bailey and Dando Douglas; Apprentices Gordon, Waller and Stokes, the Cook and Jackson the castaway had all done things proper-fashion too. When the two women came on deck *Erl King* was rounding the Ovens and heading up Gravesend Reach. Every yard was squared, every sail punched into a finger-thin harbour stow. The oiled brass was wiped clean and bulled up with brick-dust, a new red duster snapped from the peak of the spanker gaff and at the lofty main truck, just below the gold circlet, John Kemball's house-flag, a dark blue pendant with a white Maltese cross, streamed in the breeze. The *Erl King's* decks were snow-white, washed off with the fresh water that was now no longer so precious.

'Thank you very much,' said Hannah appreciatively to the two Mates.

'Our pleasure, Ma'am,' mocked 'Mr Duke', doffing his hat and footing an elaborate bow. In the dark green silk dress that she had packed in ignorant expectation of some great social occasion, Hannah stood beside the helmsman as the ship glided past Tilbury Fort and the collier hailing station. The signalman came out on to the balcony to wave at them and a small crowd shouted from the landing stage.

'What were they calling?' Hannah asked.

'Something about it being a shame,' said Talham.

'Because we're beat into second place, I suppose,' added 'Mr Duke'.

They made slow, time-wasting progress stemming the ebb in Long Reach. Beyond the embankments the marshland spread out. A distant harrier lazily quartered the beds of reed and sedge. Along the tideline piebald avocets and orange-billed oystercatchers foraged amid a crowd of smaller waders. Sheldducks paddled in the shallows and a heron lifted and flapped lugubriously across the river.

Off Erith the barges on the moorings were swung to the flood tide and a pair of billy-boys ran past. Mai Lee joined Hannah on the poop. She too wore her finery, a magnificent yellow silk robe that bore heavy and elaborate brocaded embroidery. Her black hair shone in the sunshine that was breaking through the clouds as she stared about her.

'This belong London?' she asked, gesturing at the salt-marsh.

They passed into the environs of the great city as under a cloud. Almost imperceptibly the air thickened with smoke and the wharves, intermittent at first, became continuous. The river-traffic grew denser, with tugs and lighters, sailing barges and coasters, and a paddle-steamer with the mails for Rotterdam. Off Woolwich a steam-sloop lay at a buoy, her boats at the booms and the flaunting jack and ensign of naval might at stem and stern.

'Like a bloody herring-box,' said Gopher on the wheel, meeting the starboard helm the Pilot had just ordered, and steadying the swing as Bow Creek opened to the north. Here, as they crossed the Greenwich meridian, they passed the gleaming black hull of the Trinity House yacht *Galatea* at her moorings off Blackwall.

'We've an hour before there's water over the cill, Ma'am,' the Pilot explained, referring to the locks giving entry into the West India Docks, 'I don't know if your competitor has any clever ideas, but it would be best just to stem the tide again, letting the tug hold her. If we anchor . . .'

'No, no, please do as you think fit, Pilot, and thank you.' Hannah managed to smile at the man, and he exchanged his pipe for a whistle, emitting a series of blasts answered on the tug's siren by echoing whoops.

'Hard a-port!' snapped the Pilot.

'Hard a-port, sir!' replied Gopher, tugging on the wheel. 'Wheel's hard a-port!'

Seawitch had already turned head downstream, the *Impellor* holding her against the tide just off the lock-heads.

Now, in response to the Pilot's command, *Erl King* followed suit, both ships lying almost alongside one another. A curious armistice existed between them, as though there was some tacit understanding, the one not to gloat, the other not to insult. Each crew took no notice of the other as they busied about their respective decks, preparing the mooring ropes and knocking the wedges out of the hatches.

Hannah looked across the gap. She resisted an infuriatingly adolescent impulse to cry tears of impotent frustration. Richards was clearly visible, a supremely self-confident figure arrogantly ignoring her and her ship as though the whole enterprise was, and had been, a foregone conclusion from the beginning. In his grey top hat and tailcoat he was shouting at a brass-bound officer on the jetty who in turn looked at a large watch and shook his head. If only there was something she could do . . .

Beside her the Pilot chuckled. 'Dickie Richards'll be trying to browbeat the Dock-Master into opening the lock gates early. Mind you it's probably too late.' He paused, took his pipe out of his mouth and cocked a ruminative eye at Hannah. 'The dress suits you, Ma'am, if you don't mind my saying so.'

'You mean you prefer me out of breeches?' Hannah asked sharply. The man's attitude had changed now she was wearing conventional female clothing. Coupled with the sight of Richards this patronising was insufferable!

'I mean I prefer you in a dress,' he rattled on, 'your temper's better, if you'll forgive my saying so. I've a daughter of your age myself, m'dear, and I'd not like to see *her* gallivanting about the world.'

She was damned if she was going to forgive him. 'You'd like to see her settle down in harmonious matrimony producing a string of grandchildren, would you?'

He removed his pipe to chide her for the indelicacy of her remark until he saw the expression on her face. Anger, inherited authority and new-found confidence confronted him and he recalled who, or perhaps, what she was, and rammed the briar back into his mouth. He clamped his teeth on the stem and it broke under the strain. The bowl dropped on to the deck, spilling hot ash on the immaculate teak.

'You know, Mister Pilot, that's nearly as criminal an act as my wearing breeches . . .'

'Damn it, Ma'am, your father had a tongue like a rope's end; no wonder you damn near whipped the hide off Dickie Richards.' The Pilot spluttered with embarrassment, bending to retrieve the wreck of his pipe.

'Not near enough . . .' she said, as he touched the true source of her anger.

'Your Second Mate told me there was a wager between you,' the Pilot said in an attempt to regain his lost dignity. 'What are the stakes?'

'My father's hat,' Hannah replied coolly, 'and a hundred guineas. Captain Richards put up a similar stake.' She was damned if she was going to admit more.

The Pilot whistled. 'And what exactly decides the winner?'

'The first of us to break bulk and land tea in our berth. The Chief Mate should have entered the ship at the Custom House by now . . .'

'So you still have a chance . . . I mean the race is between you two, isn't it? Even if another ship *had* delivered the first China cargo?'

Hannah nodded. 'Yes, but there's no possibility of that now, despite entering the ship at the Custom House.' She was thinking of Richards's private side-bet and found the thought of confronting him made her tremble.

'You never know,' said the Pilot, 'Dickie Richards has a reputation for driving his ship hard, padlocking the sheets and so forth. Perhaps he's got salt-water below and spoiled the cargo.'

She looked at him sharply. He was getting his own back, twisting the knife of false expectation in her disappointed woman's flesh. She knew well enough that a man of Richards's professional skill would not spoil his cargo.

'I hardly think that's likely,' she replied coldly, angry at being taken for a dupe.

The whoop of first the *Impellor*'s siren and then that of the

Sultan interrupted them and indicated the opening of the lock-gates. *Impellor* was already under way, nudging *Seawitch* in against the wooden staithing so that she could warp round into the lock. Docilely, the *Erl King* waited her turn and they could hear the bull-roar of Richards trumpeting victory.

'Ninety-one days from the Min River to London, fourteen thousand and sixty-two miles run! The *Seawitch* is cock o'London, my bully boys! Cock o'London and the Seven Seas, by heavens! First with the season's tea!'

The braggart! She thought of Richards, his padlocked sheets and Jackson left floundering astern of *Seawitch*. The thought made her ask for Jackson. There was perhaps one humiliation she could inflict upon Richards when he came aboard! The able seaman came aft.

'Would you oblige me by keeping below, out of sight of Captain Richards if you please,' she ordered.

He caught something of her meaning, for he smiled and went below.

'Our turn. Trim those yards there, Mr Mate,' said the Pilot, as with another toot *Sultan* trembled into life again, drawing them closer to the quay. With a creak of fenders inserted by the dockers, *Erl King* bumped gently and her warps snaked out on the end of the heaving lines. Slowly she was hauled round into the lock, sharing it with her rival. In enforced intimacy the two ships lay side by side, their yards braced sharp up and cock-billed. Behind them the gates were swung shut and the sluices opened. The malodorous water in the lock began to rise. The Pilot crossed the deck and leaned over the rail to exchange some remarks with the men on the quay. Hannah, lost amid these technicalities, cast a look for Richards, half fearful that he would lean on his own rail and exchange some remarks with her. But he continued to ignore her and, like the Pilot, leaned over on his side of the lock, deep in conversation with the Dock-Master. There was something potent in his indifference, for she was woman enough to know it was feigned, and pregnant with intent.

Amidships she noted a degree of fraternisation then Mai Lee claimed her attention and she was drawn into concern for the landing of Lenqua's body and Mai Lee's future.

'What happen Mai Lee, Missee Hannah? Have got no

money go back Shanghai. No can. Mai Lee too old work for jig-a-jig, Londonside.'

Hannah was appalled. 'No . . . no, you must come with me. I have a house and no family, all same you, Mai Lee. We stay together. You no go back to, to *that* kind of work.'

Mai Lee's face was radiant with happiness.

She looked up as the Dock-Master blew his whistle. The men at the ropes wore gloomy expressions. They were the faces of losers. Both clippers rode high above the lock-sides and Richards was glaring at her from his poop. The whistle-blast signalled the opening of the far gates, then the Pilot was beside her.

'Ladies first!' roared Richards, his black beard stiff above his grey coat. His eyes glittered, but Hannah, discomfited by this sudden attention, was unable to tell whether lust, anger or arrogance prompted this bizarre act of chivalry. 'Ladies first!' he repeated, raising a small derisory cheer among his crew.

With her hatches open and the smell of tea in the air, *Erl King* towed slowly out of the lock ahead of her rival. Hannah was so embarrassed at this final humiliation, this public affront to her sex, that she failed to realise this thin cheer was not the triumphant acknowledgement of victor for vanquished.

'I don't believe it! I *won't* believe it! It's not possible!' Hannah banged her fist on the saloon table until it hurt. 'No! No! No!'

'It's true,' said Munro flatly.

'I feared it possible, my dear,' said the Pilot, waiting patiently for Hannah's signature on his chit and despairing of the customary glass for his services.

'I guess that Yokohama-bound barque we spoke to was trying to tell us something about it when we didn't read his last signal,' said Munro.

'But if that barque knew about it why didn't *you* tell us?' she rounded angrily on the Pilot, tears welling in her eyes.

'You *were* the first tea ships *I* knew of, said the Pilot, absolving himself and pushing his chit forward, his duty done now that they were secured in a berth. Hannah signed it and Munro poured a glass of cognac for each of them.

Hannah noted this small presumption and it fed her ire. She swallowed the cognac and swung on Munro. 'You said we couldn't go *through* Africa,' she said, her voice thick with contempt.

'How the hell was I supposed to know?' replied Munro with a matching anger that caused him to lean forward on the saloon table. He had spent a night in a hotel bed and found the experience of clean, unmoving linen had left him more exhausted than rested.

'Obliged, Ma'am, I'll be off then,' said the Pilot, taking his leave as the mood in the saloon deteriorated.

'You've had your pound of flesh, and more, out of me, Hannah,' said Munro the minute the Pilot had gone. He poured another brandy for himself. 'I'm as disappointed as you are, but not even your expert father thought the French could dig a bloody canal through Egypt! Perhaps if he'd kept himself and us better informed, we'd not have lost the premium . . .'

Hannah said nothing. Munro had a perfect right to be angry and she realised now that the Pilot had hinted at the possibility of their being beaten by more than just *Seawitch*. It was clear that he was unaware of the fact, but he knew of the possibility of an earlier arrival because news of this canal must have reached England weeks ago. It was also obvious that Richards had clearly learned the news in the locks and his sarcastically chivalrous gesture had stemmed from his own furious disappointment. How could he have imagined she remained in ignorance of the fact?

Her own preoccupation at that moment with Mai Lee had prevented it, she realised, for the Pilot had probably known from the man on the lock-side. The fact that he had then kept it from her for fear of some womanish outburst, or out of spite at her treatment of him, only made her more and more wretched.

'A canal . . . through Africa,' she whispered, half to herself, sitting down to digest the fact while Munro still towered over her angrily. '*Through* Africa,' she repeated, amazed.

Munro expelled his pent-up breath and sat opposite, his tired head in his hands. 'Through the isthmus of Suez and it cuts three thousand miles off the distance from China.'

'Then the season's tea has already arrived?' she said in a low voice.

'Yes, Hannah,' Munro said, gently now, 'via the Suez canal in a steamship in fifty-one days.'

233

'That's half the time we took.'

'Yes.'

'We've had our day then,' she said, looking up with tears in her eyes, '*Erl King* and *Seawitch* and *Actaeon* and the rest.'

'I wouldn't say that,' temporised Munro, unwilling to face the unpalatable truth on the verge of securing a command. He put out his hand across the table.

'Don't humour me, James,' she said, standing up and ignoring his outstretched hand, 'what was this steamship called?'

'The *Glencarron*, I believe . . .'

'We saw her,' said Hannah frowning, 'the day we left the Min River, and laughed that she'd taken fifty-four days from the Cape!'

'So we did,' replied Munro wearily, 'she had the last laugh then, didn't she?'

'Not quite . . .' The recollection had stirred more than the single memory of the sighting of the *Glencarron*. There was something else gnawing at her memory, something linking the period of their departure and her father's death with something said that day. She frowned.

'What d'you mean?'

'I'm not sure what I mean at the moment, except that there's still a race between us and Richards!' she said with mounting excitement, turning for her father's bookshelf. 'Whose tea was ashore first?'

'The *Seawitch* beat us, Hannah,' said Munro with finality. 'Beat us in days, beat us to the locks, and beat us to the berth because Richards had obtained one closer to the locks than our own.'

'But you entered this ship at the Custom House *before* the *Seawitch* and our cargo will be cleared first on to the market.'

'A technicality, Hannah . . . what does it matter? The first tea of the season was landed by the *Glencarron*, the steamer gets the premium; Richards landed fifty chests of tea within five minutes of running his lines to the berth. Richards wins the wager made with your father. If the other matter bothers you, all you have to do is tell him to go to the devil . . . your father's death removes all that nonsense about you from the bet. Besides,' he smiled, 'I can always knock his block off for you!'

His attempt at levity fell on deaf ears; Hannah was turning

234

the pages of her father's journal with an expression of extreme urgency on her face.

'Hannah . . .?'

Munro sighed. He had known she would take losing badly the moment she had taken the ship over from him in the Channel. Like those ridiculous pistol shots, this was a manifestation of silly desperation. 'We'll make arrangements to pay the hands off tomorrow at noon . . .' He paused, then added, 'D'you want me to keep Richards off the ship? Hannah . . . ?'

She looked up with a sudden smile and closed the journal. 'Not quite, James, get Gordon or one of the boys to run to the *Seawitch* with a message. I'll receive Captain Richards tomorrow morning at ten sharp, but not before. I'll sign the crew off as you suggest. And tell Bosun Harris that I want a word with him . . . then I want a funeral arranged, Lenqua died while we were in the Channel . . . just do it, James,' she said, shooing him out of the saloon, 'and I promise you will not be disappointed with me.'

Munro rose reluctantly to his feet. 'Very well,' he said, 'I hope you know what you're doing.'

'Oh yes, James, I do now.'

She waited until he was gone and then turned to her father's journal. With a beating heart she read again what she had found, confirming the matter. Then, smiling, she poked her head into the alleyway and called Mai Lee.

17

THE hackney carriage Hannah ordered was at the foot of the gangway an hour later. She spent the interim period with Mai Lee and Harris, the Bosun. With Mai Lee she had concluded a few details relative to Lenqua, with Harris she had taken a different line.

'A glass of cognac?' she had offered, motioning the Bosun to a seat and putting him at his ease.

'Obliged, Ma'am.' Harris had relaxed, preening himself as Hannah doused him with preliminary compliments. 'I wanted to thank you for working so hard on the homeward run.'

'Thank you, Ma'am, though it's a pity it's done us no good.'

'I'm not entirely sure that it hasn't, Mr Harris,' Hannah had said enigmatically. The Bosun had frowned, falling under the spell of her eyes as she regarded him over the rim of her glass. 'How long would it take you to organise the discharge of fourteen thousand chests of tea if I give you some silver to spread around, plus a bonus for seeing to the matter?'

The light of avarice had kindled in Harris's eyes. 'Well now, I *might* stop the hands from going ashore tonight,' he had begun doubtfully, 'once they're paid off you won't see 'em for dust . . .'

'How long, Mr Harris?' Hannah had quizzed, never taking her eyes off him.

Harris had shrugged. 'The *Fiery Cross* did it in thirty hours once, in sixty-four I think.'

'Could you match that?' Hannah's voice had rasped.

Harris had nodded with sudden resolution: 'I could try.'

Now, as she paused at the head of the gangway, with Munro fussing beside her, she could see Harris was living up to his promise.

Snatched from her 'tween decks and holds by the stay-ropes

237

and swung out on to the quay by those run through yardarm blocks, the netted chests of *Erl King*'s thousand tons of tea was being discharged. Though she did not fully appreciate it herself, it was a measure of respect at her final effort, that the crew forebore the pleasures of the shore that night to toil alongside the greased palms of the dockers.

'I knew she were a chip off the old block,' Harris had said as he had divided out Hannah's small stock of silver among the half-drunk denizens of the fo'c's'le.

'That's the trouble with women,' Gopher Stackpole had said, heaving himself wearily out of his bunk, 'they never know when to let up on a man.'

'D'you want the money?'

'Aye, of course I do.'

'Stow your gab then, and turn-to.'

And turn-to they had, hoisting out the chests almost faster than the dockers could roll them through the warehouse to the drays.

'You have lights for the night-time?' Hannah asked Munro.

'Aye, of course, I'll see Talham . . .'

'You see to it, James. You're not coming with me.'

'But . . .'

'I shall need you later. Goodbye.'

And she descended the gangway to the appreciative whistles of her crew and the dock labourers who sweated over *Erl King*'s scented cargo. Grinning, Gordon opened the door of the hackney carriage. As she stepped up she cast a look along the quay. In the berth astern *Seawitch* was frantically discharging her own cargo. She half-hoped, half-feared to see Captain Richards, but he was likely closeted in his cabin as bitterly disappointed as herself. The thought made her smile. He did not yet know the worst!

'Mincing Lane!' she commanded the driver, and Gordon shut the door as the hackney lurched forward.

As her last act of devotion to her master, Mai Lee had laid out Lenqua's body in almost mandarin splendour. It was sad that his bones would not lie on a south-facing hillside in his native province, as he had desired, but Mai Lee knew the old man had wanted to come to London before he died, and, in her

238

ignorance, thought that the *fan kwei* would allow him a space in their own burial grounds, where the sun might warm Lenqua's mortal remains and mollify his spirit.

Her own spirit was a child of fortune. Sold into the gutter, Lenqua's wealth had raised her to the status of a rich man's concubine. Now she had found Missee Hannah, a woman who, so much younger than herself, would see that her last days were not those of an outcast. Thinking these thoughts, Mai Lee tidied the cabin and awaited the men from the undertakers that Munro had dispatched an apprentice to summon.

Carefully she folded Lenqua's remaining clothes. Opening his lacquered chest she stored them away, smoothing the heavily brocaded silk of his gowns and laying on top his spare peacock's feathers. Then, as she completed her task, she recalled the key she had found on the chain about his neck. She had never seen it before, but since Lenqua never removed all his garments when they made love, the discovery did not surprise her. She knew the box it fitted, a heavy black steel chest of Western make. She pulled it out and sat hunkered down on her haunches, regarding it for a long time. She supposed that it was hers now. Lenqua had many sons, but they were far away, while she was in London, and in London, Hannah had explained, a man could leave money to his wife or daughter. The thought overcame her inhibitions. Mai Lee had been wife to Lenqua. She inserted the key and turned the lock. Lifting the heavy lid she peered inside.

'Ay-ah,' she murmured in awe, as the dim light in the cabin was reflected from the hoard of silver.

The offices of Pettilow, Deever and Speare were almost as active as the quayside. The first carts had just arrived from the West India Docks with the sample chests and Hannah caught sight of the tiger marks of *Erl King*'s consignment among the dragons of *Seawitch*'s lading. A neat stack of chests stood against the far wall of the warehouse as Hannah descended from the carriage. They bore an unfamiliar mark, a pagoda, and they had clearly been there for some time.

A sober-clad clerk enquired her business.

'I am Miss Kemball, daughter of Captain John Kemball, late Master of the ship *Erl King*.'

'Of course, Miss Kemball, Mr Pettilow was expressing a keen desire to make your acquaintance and was saying that he considered it his duty to call upon you . . .'

They passed through a glass door into a vestibule. The still, heavy air was thick with the odour of China tea. Ascending a staircase Hannah was shown into a dark panelled office on the first floor. Late afternoon sunshine filtered through grimy windows, but oil lamps burned to throw a rosy glow on pictures decorating the walls. There were three depictions of clippers, elderly ships, Hannah now knew, by their single, deep topsails. Beside the ships hung a botanical representation of a *pekoe* sprig, and a large Chinese-executed painting of the Bohea hills. Hannah wondered if it had been done by Mr Cha.

'Miss Kemball . . .' the clerk announced her.

There were three men in the room, two of whom rose at her entry. The third, somewhat younger, remained seated. He flashed her a swift, dour look, though whether this was due to Hannah's presence, deducible from his want of courtesy, or from some business then under discussion, she could not say.

'*Miss* Kemball, our congratulations, a most magnificent effort. In other circumstances equity would have dictated a draw,' said the taller of the two men who stood. 'And you must forgive our manners; had not urgent business with Captain McAllister here not detained us, *we* would have called upon *you*.'

'Please forgive my partner's loquacity, Miss Kemball,' said the older, 'pray take a seat. I am Pettilow and this is Mr Deever.' The two bowed, their black frock coats giving the appearance of dark land-birds, Hannah thought irrelevantly. 'Would you care for tea or sherry?'

'A glass of sherry would be most acceptable, Mr Pettilow.' She sat in the chair drawn forward for her by Mr Deever.

'This is Captain Matthew McAllister, Miss Kemball,' said Deever.

Hannah inclined her head at the Captain, wondering where she had heard his name before.

'Of what ship, sir?' she asked, accepting the sherry from Pettilow.

'The *Glencarron*, Ma'am,' said the Captain frostily.

'We were so very sorry to learn of the sad loss of Captain

240

Kemball, m'dear,' said Pettilow, casting a quick look at McAllister, 'but as far as we are concerned, Miss Kemball, as consignees and charter party it makes no difference.'

'I should think not, sir,' said Hannah, sensing patronisation again. Her bristling seemed to prompt a response from Captain McAllister.

'You speak your condolences for yourselves. As for me I do not share the sentiments of these estimable gentlemen, Miss Kemball,' said McAllister in a strong Scots brogue, turning towards her.

'Oh dear,' muttered Mr Deever, wringing his hands.

'Sir?'

'Ah'd cheerfully see your father in hell!'

'Captain, please . . .' Pettilow restrained.

Comprehension struck Hannah. 'You . . . are you the man who designed the *Erl King?*'

'Aye, and the same man your father ruined, Ma'am!' McAllister stood and scowled down at her. 'And it looks as though his daughter, or his ghost, is going to do it a second time, by God!'

McAllister picked up his hat.

'Oh dear, oh dear, I'm so sorry, Captain McAllister, and after so fine a run too . . .'

'I don't understand,' began Hannah.

'Your father, Miss Kemball, ruined me years ago with a detestable piece of trickery and sharp-practice! Did you know he cheated me over the building of that ship of yours? Eh? Now I find the devil has had the last laugh in death.'

'But you are landing the first of the season's tea, sir . . .'

'I overtook you the night before last, Ma'am, off Dover. I had every expectation of landing the first cargo of China tea; but these . . . these *gentlemen* who deal in the confounded stuff tell me that the condensation of the passage through the desert has tainted the tea, that despite the lead foil, the iron hull of my *steam*-ship has wrecked the cargo! That, Ma'am, is nonsense; prejudiced, unscientific nonsense! But I am tied by charter hand and foot, mortgaged with little redress from my lien. The best price these vultures will give me will scarce cover my expenses! The palm of victory, Ma'am, lies with you or Captain Richards, it seems! I wish you joy of it! Good-night!'

'Oh dear, oh dear, oh dear,' repeated Mr Deever after McAllister had departed.

'Might I have another glass of sherry?' Hannah asked disingenuously.

'Of course, Miss Kemball, and I apologise for the Captain's unfortunate outburst. Such a shock for you,' said Pettilow, producing the decanter.

'Unfortunately, Miss Kemball, you will appreciate we are obliged to maintain our standards,' explained Deever, 'the public has come to expect a high quality product from the house of Pettilow, Deever and Speare.'

'Oh, quite, Mr Deever. Being a woman I *do* understand these things,' she replied ironically. Her anger at this continuous patronisation melted in favour of a more pragmatic purpose. 'And you insist on these standards at all times?'

'At all times, Miss Kemball,' reassured Deever, 'absolutely without exception.'

'Gentlemen,' she said coyly, lowering her voice and her eye-lashes so that they instinctively drew closer, 'I would not have you deceived; *entre nous* I suggest you sample the chests now below from *Seawitch* . . .'

Pettilow and Deever exchanged looks. 'I'll see to it,' said Deever with a sudden access of resolution. He left the room and Hannah could hear his footsteps hurrying on the stairs.

'You'll not find I'm mistaken, Mr Pettilow, and now, if you would be so kind, would you call me a hackney?'

Hannah rose smiling in a whisper of green silk and followed Mr Pettilow.

18

'HE WAS here last night, breathing fire and damnation over us.'

'Was he sober?'

'Oh yes,' replied Munro, watching Hannah's face with dismay, 'but he was angry at your not being aboard, and not too pleased about waiting until ten this morning.'

'You didn't tell him where I was?' asked Hannah in sudden alarm.

'How could I? I didn't know.' Munro replied bitterly. 'Will you now tell me? Or shouldn't I ask?'

Deaf to subtlety, Hannah's mind was busy weighing the success of her scheme against the possibility of it now going awry and she failed to notice the wounded intimacy in Munro's voice.

'I . . . I was with Messrs Pettilow, Deever and Speare.' Her reply was abstracted.

'The consignees?'

Hannah nodded. 'Yes, and now let us get down to these final accounts.' She indicated the crew's wages sheet that spread before them amid a pile of papers through which she and Munro had been working since Osman had cleared breakfast from the table. Munro gave her a last, despairing look, and then bent sadly over the columns of figures.

Hannah's stomach fluttered nervously. She had staked a great deal upon her last gamble, and although she had found the ace in her sleeve largely through her late father's devious foresight, both it and the fact that she had played it now made her apprehensive. The last exhilarating hours of the race had raised her to such a pitch of expectation that it was difficult to descend among the mundane preoccupations of commerce; her

243

soul still yearned for a victory she felt to be morally hers. But all those high-flying emotions belonged to yesterday; today she must face the consequences of her actions concentrated in the person of Captain Richard Richards.

During a sleepless night she had rehearsed a hundred times the scene shortly to be played here, aboard *Erl King*. Now she wanted the confrontation to occur, wanted to try the temper of her nerve, a mettle that had been tested with deadly effect upon the hapless Munro. She looked affectionately at his bent head as he diligently worked his way down the earnings and disbursements of each member of *Erl King's* crew. Munro's dutiful compliance reminded her that she must not overplay her hand with him, not out of weakness of purpose or pusillanimous apprehension at the force of Richards's opposition.

Hannah swept aside the intimidating thought in a sudden access of self-confidence. *Of course she could do it!*

Under her elbow lay a torn envelope, brought down from Mincing Lane by an agent's runner late the previous evening. It was from Pettilow, Deever and Speare. *Erl King's* chests had proved immeasurably superior to those from the *Seawitch*. Mr Deever had personally confided that he and his partner were eternally grateful for her vigilance, and further, expressed their concern that so trusted a party as Captain Richards should have attempted to palm off on them an inferior *souchong*. They were abject in their certainty that they could do business again, steamships, they assured, notwithstanding. Picking up the note, Hannah contemplatively tapped it against her pursed lips. *Erl King's* cargo would be first on the London market after all.

'Well,' said Munro, thrusting the wages sheet aside, adding the grand total to a separate list and carrying out a swift calculation, 'with expenses at Foochow and the sixpence a ton import duty here in London, and the deductions for wages, pilotage, port and light dues to set against the freight rate of six pounds seven shillings and threepence, the voyage will yield you some two thousand four hundred and thirty-two pounds net profit.' Munro looked up, a wan smile on his face. 'I congratulate you.'

'I think we might celebrate that,' said Hannah brightly, unlocking the tantalus. Though she knew little about such things, a survey of her father's voyage abstracts revealed it a handsomely competitive sum.

'Why not,' remarked Munro ironically, watching her pour from the decanter, 'the early hour need not bar a *small* celebration.'

They clinked glasses chummily. Munro felt a revival of hope. 'Hannah . . . I . . .'

'Not now, James, please . . .'

'For God's sake, Hannah, you blow hot and cold – I don't know where I am. You are not thinking of accepting that Welsh goat are you?' he asked, suddenly alarmed by her erratic unpredictability.

'James,' said Hannah coolly, ignoring Munro's outburst, 'I want you to have command of *Erl King* on the next voyage. It was my father's intention to make you Chief Mate – I think he knew Enright's time was running out. Will you accept?'

'Do you offer me command or . . . or a partnership?'

Munro stood, his intent unambiguous in his own mind, but complicated in Hannah's by her other preoccupations. She was not yet ready to discuss Munro's future in detail. She nodded, looked down at the columns of figures and the double underlined total of net profit. Some of it was indisputably Munro's . . .

'Much of this is due entirely to your own skill, James,' she said matter-of-factly.

'That wasn't what I meant . . .'

'Missee, Missee, black-devil come!'

Mai Lee burst into the saloon as fast as her diminutive, bound feet could carry her. Hannah stared, her heart thumping painfully. Snatching up Munro's pen, she began to scribble on a piece of paper. At the same time she rapped out instructions to Munro. 'Have one of the boys deliver this to Captain McAllister of the *Glencarron*.' Hurriedly she sealed the note and held it out to Munro. 'At once, James.'

Munro took the note and stood hesitantly. Mai Lee plucked at his sleeve. 'Please go.'

A bull-roar of anger accompanied the heavy tread of shod boots on the deck above.

'*Cythral!* Out of my way, man! Stand aside or by God you'll feel my cane about your ears!'

Munro stood his ground, disappointed in his offer of a partnership for life, yet unwilling to appear the junior in the recently offered commercial union.

'James! Go!'

'But you can't . . .'

'Of course I can. I know why he's angry.'

'Is this some kind of game, Hannah? Because if it is, I wouldn't play games with Richard Richards.' Munro frowned with confusion.

'No, it's not a game. It's deadly serious. But I made the rules.'

'Mister Munro . . . more better go now.' Mai Lee pulled insistently at Munro's sleeve, drawing him towards the after companionway. The clumping of feet on the forward stairs marked the approach of nemesis.

'It's the last order I shall give you, James. I promise!' Hannah hissed urgently, 'Now *please* go on deck!'

Mai Lee pushed Munro bodily upwards, turning to give Hannah a quick, complicit smile. 'You no forget. If trouble . . .' The tiny Chinese woman took one fist from the small of Munro's disappearing back and chopped her flat hand obliquely upwards. 'If no trouble, everything more better bimeby.'

'*Miss Kemball!*'

The forward saloon door was flung open and Hannah rose slowly, disguising under a spurious dignity her thundering heart and knocking knees. She held her back ramrod straight and clasped her hands at her waist in a primly decorous attitude that concealed their shaking. This rigid self-control conferred upon the rustle of the green silk dress a discreet, feminine mockery of the heavy breathing of Captain Richard Richards.

He leaned on his cane in the doorway, one hand on the brass door handle, immaculate in his grey suit and top-hat. He was flushed with anger and exertion, the pearl cravat-pin twinkling opaquely as he caught his breath. But despite his flushed appearance, his black beard gave his face a powerful authority, and his black eyes glittered with an implacable vengeance.

'Captain Richards,' Hannah said, her voice cool with amusement, 'have you *run* all the way from Mincing Lane? How very ardent of you.'

'*Diawl*,' growled Richards breathlessly, his eyes upon the wide curve of her smiling mouth. He stepped into the saloon and turned to close the door. Hannah's heart pounded out of sheer exhilaration; that turning away was the gesture of a discomfited man! She knew, with a surge of confidence, she could match him as she had dreamed. He turned back towards her scowling.

'Don't be impudent, my girl.'

'Don't patronise me,' she snapped, her voice steely with sudden, flaring anger, 'or call me "girl".'

'Patronise you?' Richards said, frowning, '*Patronise* you? If you were a man I'd *whip* you, or knock your damned head off . . .'

'But as I'm a woman what do you intend?'

'As you're a woman . . .'

Richards paused. Hannah was no longer standing upright. She was leaning forward on her hands, thrusting her face towards him, her red mouth and large eyes laughing at him. 'As you are a woman,' Richards repeated, his voice suddenly husky as he stepped forward and laid his hat and cane on the table between them, 'I should . . .'

He stopped again, and she raised one arched eyebrow that was both brake and spur to his imagination. She straightened up and crossed her arms amid a rustling of silk and the subtle movement of soft flesh. Richards drew in his breath. Hannah guessed instinctively, and confirmed from the wisdom conferred by Mai Lee, that she had him physically entrapped. But Richards was not utterly lost to her charms, only aware of them; powerfully aware, to be sure, but they had not yet expunged the passion of his grievance.

'You have dishonoured me, slandered me, defamed me!' Richards's voice boomed and in a crescendo of mounting anger he picked up the heavy, jade-headed malacca and banged it down on the table with a crack of emphasis at the catalogue of infamy which Hannah had perpetrated. 'You have attempted what no *man* would have dared! Where you could not win – you cheated!'

His heavy, handsome features were flushed again, suffused with blood and now his whole head vibrated with suppressed fury. Hannah put her hand to her mouth.

'God damn it, Ma'am . . . you . . . shall . . . not . . . laugh!' Richards spat the words, staccato commands that he rammed home with a matching tattoo of the cane.

'Have a care, sir, for my table!' Hannah gurgled, spluttering with almost as much abandon as her rival.

'Damn your blasted table! What about my foretopmast stuns'l, eh? What kind of braggart stupidity was that!'

'Captain Richards,' Hannah gasped, one hand supporting herself on the table, the other at her throat, 'of what specifically do you accuse me?'

'Accuse you? Why . . . why . . . you told those damned tea-brokers my samples were old *souchong* . . .'

'And weren't they?'

'Why . . . why, yes, but . . .' Richards perceived the trap too late.

'How then can you accuse me of slander if I told the truth?'

Richards blew out his cheeks and exhaled in a long breath. Hannah poured two thimbles of cognac and pushed one across the table. Richards's gloved hand seized her wrist in a powerful grip. 'But how did you know, *Cariad*, eh?'

'You're hurting me, sir,' Hannah felt a sudden loss of the initiative. Her magnanimous offer of brandy had been neatly turned by Richards to his own advantage. Hannah's discomfiture was brief and discarded with the contemptuous realisation that in his extremity Richards had played the card of male strength.

'How did you know?' he repeated, the intensity of his grip revealing the extent of his own disappointment at losing the race into which every ounce of skill and tenacity he possessed had been invested.

'*How?*' He drew her closer, so that she leaned across the table again.

His breath fanned her face and she felt again that inner melting, that irresistible weakening that was at once pleasurable and alarming. They faced each other for a long intimate moment, a consummation of intent laid plain between them. Richards thrust aside her wrist, picked up the glass and drained it at a gulp. Then he arrogantly held it out for refilling.

'*How?* Hannah Kemball, that is what troubles my soul.'

His voice thrilled her, and she refilled the glass secure in the knowledge that, whatever else, they talked now as equals.

'I did not know it until, after my father's death, I examined his papers. In his journal were several references that, at the time, were only partly comprehensible to me. As time passed and I became more knowledgeable about matters, I realised

248

what he had done. He had taken out a form of insurance, to spoil your win if, and he never for a moment thought you would, but if you succeeded. You see he did not care about me very much, only about the shares I possessed falling into the hands of my husband.'

'*Du*, I never . . .'

'Bear with me . . . He bribed the *chaa-tzes* through Lenqua to top off your cargo with old *souchong* – the last tier of your cargo, the last chop alongside at Foochow was deliberately certified by the Chinese tasters as good *bohea*. He knew that after his own departure, you would be in too much of a hurry to check it . . . you see?' Richards nodded as he understood the trick Cracker Jack had played upon him. Hannah smiled and added: 'Forgive him.'

'Forgive him?' Richards replied, his voice low and vibrantly thrilling, 'Your father was a rogue, a braggart and a palpable cheat . . .'

'Yes, yes,' she agreed, 'and he was wicked, devious and disloyal, as I have good cause to know, but you demanded his soul and since that was with the ship herself . . .'

'No. I demanded *something* of his soul, for I knew his black heart lay as deep in this ship as her mast-steps.' Richards paused, looking about at the bird's eye maple panelling as if seeking a remnant ghost of Cracker Jack. Hannah watched him, fascinated. He was sleekly handsome, yet without a trace of foppishness, for no mere fop could drive a China clipper home in ninety-one days. His vanity she now forgave him, as though she suddenly understood the strange, direct *honesty* of the man. He had absolutely no time for anything but the business in hand, proceeding through his life with the remorselessness of an uncoiling spring. This quality of latent energy triggered an irresistible response in her own heart.

'What are you thinking, *Cariad*?'

He was looking at her now, and it was she who dropped her eyes to hide her inner feelings. He did not wait for an answer. 'But why did you have to *tell* those merchants? Eh? Why was it necessary to have me ridiculed?'

His vehement Welsh accent attenuated the syllables so that they struck her independently, rousing her for one last effort.

'Because I wished to teach you a lesson!' she snapped,

249

appallingly aware that tears were in danger of unaccountably welling in her eyes.

'But why? What had you against me?'

'Why, sir, the arrogance of your presumption in the wine-shop in Shanghai! The need to revenge myself for the humiliation you subjected me to! And to remind you, sir, that you stood on and left a man to drown off the Cape!'

'Ah, then that *was* Jackson I saw on your deck . . .'

'Didn't you care?'

'About Jackson? Yes, but I had little chance of picking him up in that sea . . .'

'No! About me!'

'You?' Richards frowned. For the first time she saw perplexity cross his face. '*Diawl*, the truth is . . .' He stopped and looked at her, abandoning personal excuse for the sudden intimate connection that now existed between them. 'Did I offend you that much in Shanghai?'

'Yes,' replied Hannah simply. She longed to say more, yet could find no words apt enough. Instead she added, 'And took advantage of poor Munro's subordinate rank.'

'Your father was as guilty of that as I . . .'

'I credited you with more sensitivity than my father.'

'You thought something of me, then,' he said, a rueful expression that possessed a disturbing charm crossing his face.

'You made an impression, yes,' she replied softly.

'Ahhh,' he smiled with satisfaction, 'and what of "poor Munro" now?' Richards lifted his eyes to the skylight above.

'He will not need to be so humiliated again. I have made him Master of the *Erl King*.'

Richards nodded approval. 'He's a good man, but does he expect more?'

'More . . . ?' The question invited a direct comparison between Richards and Munro, leading the conversation inexorably to the matter upon which Richards had set his heart months earlier in Shanghai.

Hannah had spent those months in the company of Munro and there was no denying the fact that they had contained moments of delightful intimacy, moments that she recalled with a wistful pleasure. But she knew that she had forsaken Munro in the Channel, when she had assumed sole responsibility for

250

the ship, and that the pistol shots fired as the *Seawitch*'s sails had a greater significance than mere 'braggart stupidity'.

The desire to meet Captain Richards as an equal at the end of the voyage had driven her to such a wild expedient. Nor, with him standing opposite her, did she now regret her conduct.

'No. Poor Munro can expect no more,' she said quietly, 'he has his just reward.'

'And I . . . ?'

'Here is my father's hat.' She turned, and picked up the battered hat and a leather purse, 'And your guineas . . .'

'I don't want them, Hannah.' He moved round the end of the table so that as she held them out to him he took them from her and laid them beside his cane and gloves.

'Are you still intent upon revenge?' she asked, her heart thumping, aware that he had taken hold of her right hand.

Their voices had dropped to a husky concupiscence and both knew they had come to the crux of the interview. He shook his head. 'No, *Cariad*.'

Then very slowly he dropped on to one knee.

Hannah smiled. 'Please,' she said, 'there's no need for that now.'

19

M R MUNRO stood on the poop. Chest after chest was gathered up in the net slings and swung out over the ship's side, on to the flat carts drawn by patient and spavined nags. The quay was covered with a faint dusting of tea, a dark aromatic detritus, that rose in swirls as the wind teased it out from between the cobbles. They might yet salvage a little honour and beat *Seawitch* in the complete discharge of their cargo, for their rival had been held up until the matter of her lading's quality had been settled. The irony of Cracker Jack's trick cut both ways, so that the *Erl King*'s hands sniggered at their quondam skipper's shrewdness, and the *Seawitch*'s people at the fact that it profited him nothing.

"Bout another two hours, sir,' reported Harris, climbing over the coaming of the main hatch and removing his hat to wipe a hand across his brow. 'Should just about equal the old *Fiery Cross.*'

'You've done damn well. We'll pay off the moment the last sling goes over the wall.'

'They'll be thirsty men by then, sir.'

'I've sent "Mr Duke" to The Gun for a barrel . . .'

'I'll tell 'em then, it'll spur 'em like nothing else.' Harris turned away and Munro grinned. Talham would be back by then from the bank with the money to pay off the crew, and when that was done Munro was going to have a drink himself, not a thimble of brandy, but a long, slow swallow of India Pale Ale chased by the best whisky he could find in Sassenach London!

He wanted a woman too; wanted Hannah, if she would have him, though what game she was playing with that Welsh goat only she knew. He did not like the sound of it, but proximity to

253

other game and Hannah's cooling had had a reciprocal effect on Munro. They would always be friends, of course, but shipboard romances were often founded on sand. Sadly, Munro was coming to the conclusion that that was going to be the fate of his relationship with Hannah Kemball. Besides, he was a pragmatist; he wanted a ship. A woman could give him pleasure, but a ship could give him wealth! He patted the teak rail of the *Erl King* possessively. Well, he had her now, or as good as, unless steamships were to prove the thing.

He shook his head. Perhaps they were, but they needed less nerve in their commanders and he was still too young to resist a challenge. If the China run was closed to ships like *Erl King*, there was always the Australian wool trade, which though it might not generate premiums, would still match ship against ship. Steamships could wait.

But steamships could not wait. Munro was jerked from his reverie by the appearance of a raw-boned gentleman in the brass-bound reefer of a Master in the Mercantile Marine. The stranger stood in the waist, at the head of the gangway. His eyes scanned the ship with every appearance of interest. Alarmed, Munro stepped forward, his expression truculent.

'Are ye the Chief Mate o' this ship?' the newcomer asked brusquely.

'Aye,' Munro replied cautiously, 'and what might your business be?'

But the newcomer ignored him. He continued to peer, pale-faced, round the deck, his eyes falling upon the gleaming brass and the painted panels depicting the Erl King's enchanted wood. Munro heard him mutter: 'Well I'll be damned! The branky bastard!'

Munro was about to ask the meaning of this outburst when Osman appeared at his elbow.

'Miss Kemball's compliments, Mr Munro, and when Captain McAllister arrives, will you bring him down to the saloon please.'

'Well, ah've arrived,' said the stranger curtly.

Convinced that he was about to be replaced, that the fickle, unpredictable Hannah had now changed her mind about his own appointment to command *Erl King*, Munro angrily led the way below.

Hannah and Richards sat on opposite sides of the table. Both nursed glasses of cognac and it was clear to the jaundiced Munro that strong words had passed between them. Richards sat staring intently at Hannah. Hannah had clearly given as good as she had got, for stray hair had tumbled from her head, her face was flushed and Munro had heard shouting and banging from the saloon before first Mai Lee shooed him away and then the foreman stevedore distracted him.

'This is . . .' he began morosely, scowling at both Hannah and Richards.

'Captain McAllister, please sit down.' Hannah was at her most charming as well as her most beautiful, Munro thought peevishly. And the jade knew this Scots skipper! It was almost certain, then, that her promises were as worthless as her heart! Fuming, he turned to go back on deck.

'Join us, James. Captain McAllister, this is Captain James Munro . . .'

Munro stared at Hannah, his face scarlet with confusion and bad conscience. He shook hands with McAllister, his own awkwardness preventing him from taking notice of the hostility in the other's eyes.

'James, would you help Captain McAllister and yourself to drinks.' She smiled at him, a devastatingly sweet smile.

'Would you tell me why you've sent for me, Ma'am? Ah've business to attend to and no overmuch time to do it in,' McAllister said shortly. 'Your note implied a certain urgency.'

'Of course, Captain,' Hannah said soothingly, 'Captain Richards and I have agreed to form a company. You are, I understand, trading on your own account and at your own risk. I know, by your own admission, your voyage has not been a success . . .'

'That's my own business . . .'

'We would like to make it ours,' Hannah went on, unruffled at McAllister's roughly aggressive tone. 'Knowing that you have much to offer we are asking you to join us in a partnership . . .'

'Ha! So that's your game!' McAllister dismissed the idea, 'You'd double-cross me like your damned father!'

'I think not, sir,' put in Richards authoritatively. 'Like yourself, though possibly with less cause, I had no love for Captain Kemball. Your association with him was somewhat

255

sentimental. I guarantee you'll not be crossed. You see, McAllister, Miss Kemball and I are pragmatists enough to recognise the age of the steamship is here, though at the moment, it's our two ships that have made the profit.'

'You mean you want my expertise as an exponent o' steam . . .'

'And we'll take over your debts.'

'They amount to nine hundred an' forty-two pounds seven shillings an' eleven pence.'

'Then the matter's concluded, sir,' said Hannah picking up her pen, 'and here's a bill of exchange for one thousand sterling with which to bury the hatchet between us.'

McAllister looked round the saloon at each of their faces. Then he picked up the untouched glass before him and tossed it off with a wince.

'Ach! That's no the water o' life,' he paused, cocking his head sideways, 'but it'll do. What becomes o' my tea, inferior though it is said to be?'

'That's for your own pocket, Captain,' Hannah said slyly, and Munro was compelled to admire the way she had handled the affair.

'Very well, I agree!' McAllister nodded.

'James,' said Hannah happily as they shook hands, 'would you do the honours?'

'No, no, new Captain no-can-do. More-better I fix.' Mai Lee appeared from the pantry with Osman in tow. He bore a tray of coffee and she bobbed between them, pouring more cognac.

'To the "United Shipping Company",' Hannah proposed.

'Aye!' agreed McAllister, mollified.

'*Da iawn*,' said Richards, and Munro was perplexed by his manner. What on earth had transpired between him and Hannah?

Munro sipped his cognac, watching Hannah cagily. The spirit warmed his belly and helped lessen his disappointment. He could, after all, reflect on his own achievement with satisfaction. He had brought *Erl King* safe home from China in damned near record time. He had his own command and if he had failed to secure Hannah's heart, she would not deny him her friendship or her goodwill. Perhaps, in the long run, it was for the best; there were other women, and his new status as Captain offered new possibilities.

256

He relaxed and smiled at Hannah over the rim of his glass. 'Aye,' he said, 'the United Shipping Company.'

It no longer hurt him so much that she seemed to have eyes only for Richard Richards.

The men had come aft to be paid off. All that remained of the *Erl King's* fourteen thousand chests of *bohea* tea was a fine dust over the shingle ballast and a fragrant scent that filled the cavernous hold of the ship. Apart from Osman, only 'the Duke' had been retained, a man with no ties and nowhere to go, kept on board to carry out the duties of nightwatchman. Talham, the apprentices and the rest had gone; Bosun Harris and the Sailmaker to their homes, the Carpenter to get drunk and ease the pain of losing half his pay-off, and Gopher Stackpole to size up the whores in Mother Vinney's knocking-shop. In Wapping police station the first of what would be several fights between the rival crews was already the subject of a report made by an arresting constable. Dando Douglas was hurrying to see his children and Apprentice Gordon had his mother and his younger brother spellbound by his account of the two clippers off the Cape. The hero of this yarn, Able Seaman Jackson, a little maudlin, was offering thanks for his life, kneeling among the tombstones of St Anne's, Limehouse.

In the Master's cabin of the steamship *Glencarron*, Captain Matthew McAllister closed his account book with a sigh. He had a bottle of fine malt whisky before him and he mused on the irony of fate. Secure from ruin, he poured a peg of the water-of-life and downed it with a brief, rapturous shudder.

Aboard *Seawitch* Captain Richards was restless. He alternated between lying prone upon his settee, his mind dallying on the delights of the morning, of the soft, yielding body, and of the sudden passion that had matched his own, only to find that the recollection goaded him to his feet. Back and forth he paced, tormented by a mounting frustration that fed on the knowledge that Hannah was but a ship's length away, until the sensuous recollection flung him down on the settee again, and his thoughts came full circle.

From *Erl King's* pantry came the chink of crockery as the ever-faithful Osman prepared supper. On the saloon settee Hannah

257

and Mai Lee sat side by side. The little Chinese woman was shrewdly aware of what had passed between Hannah and the Black Devil.

'You no want?' And she chopped upwards with her flattened hand.

Hannah, occupied with her own thoughts, shook her head and smiled contentedly. 'No, Mai Lee. No want that . . .'

'I sorry for Mr Munro; he want belong Captain *and* have Missee.'

Hannah laid her hand on Mai Lee's. 'Mr Munro happy. And Captain Richards belong proper gentleman.'

Her contemplation of the morning, pleasurable though it was, was tempered by grotesque comparisons. Enright, bending over her, his lust frighteningly apparent, and Enright dead and shrivelled. And then Richard Richards . . .

Beside her, Mai Lee bent her head over her hand. Hannah reproached herself for her own selfishness, suddenly recalling Mai Lee's bereavement and the removal of Lenqua's body.

'Oh, Mai Lee, I'm so sorry, how thoughtless of me . . .'

Mai Lee caught Hannah's outstretched hand and stared at her through swimming eyes. 'Everything all right, Missee Hannah . . .'

'Yes, yes, of course,' soothed Hannah, remembering her promise and Mai Lee's insecurity, and regretting her allusion to gentlemen which had clearly upset Mai Lee by reminding her of her master.

'You will come and live with me and help me with our new shipping company.'

Mai Lee was suddenly smiling and nodding vigorously. 'Yes, yes, I help proper fashion. I help like Lenqua.'

Hannah frowned; Mai Lee had been laughing, not crying!

'I help proper fashion . . . become partner . . .'

'Well I don't know about that . . .'

'Yes, yes,' nodded Mai Lee, still smiling. 'Lenqua come Londonside with plenty money. He have box very full topside with cash. Lenqua always say "Mai Lee, cash make everything more-better." He come Londonside to save cash from Imperial taxes. I think your father tell him Londonside bank make no questions. Lenqua come Londonside live like Prince of Wales.'

The full import of what Mai Lee was saying dawned on

Hannah. The irony of having another woman with a major interest in her new company struck her. 'That's wonderful, Mai Lee. You are very welcome as a partner.'

They were both laughing now, Mai Lee clapping her hands with unfeigned delight at Hannah's enthusiastic acceptance of her.

'Mai Lee very happy,' she said simply.

'I'm so pleased . . .'

'Missee Hannah . . . ?'

'Yes?'

'What belong "Prince of Wales"?'

As the sun set 'the Duke' sat alone in the warmth of the galley. He had laid aside his book and held a mouth organ. Alongside, a tug thrashed at the filthy dock water, dragging a large outward-bound barque towards the locks. The tug's seething paddle-wash set the lightened clipper to a gentle rocking, so that the shadows moved eerily across her deck.

'I thought I heard the Old Man say,' 'the Duke' sang in a low voice, 'leave her Johnny, leave her; you may go ashore and draw your pay, for it's time for us to leave her . . .'

Hannah stood listening in the shelter of the after companion-way, staring astern where, beyond the gaunt outline of *Erl King*'s wheel, lay the *Seawitch*. She was smiling to herself, thinking of Richard Richards and tomorrow, and all the successive tomorrows. Turning, she went below.

In the galley 'the Duke' took up the air on the harmonica. The quavering tune echoed round the dusty decks where only the ghosts heard his imperfect music: Enright lying drunk in the scuppers, Lenqua soporifically mystified at the vastness of the ocean wherein the hapless Jansen drowned. On the poop Cracker Jack strutted back and forth, seen only by 'the Duke' who was used to the company of ghosts.

The tug's churning paddles left a line of scum along the *Erl King*'s waterline. Above the curve of her bow, tucked below the long tapering jib-boom, the gaudily painted figurehead bobbed. Unsleeping, the bright, painted eyes of the Erl King regarded the fates of all his captive children.